THE NIMBLE ELEPHANT

Agile Delivery of Data Models using a Pattern-based Approach

first edition

JOHN GILES

Technics Publications

Published by:

Technics Publications, LLC

966 Woodmere Drive
Westfield, NJ 07090 U.S.A.
www.technicspub.com

Edited by Carol Lehn
Cover design by Mark Brye

ISBN, print ed.   978-1-9355042-5-2

First Printing 2012
Library of Congress Control Number: 2012933844

ATTENTION SCHOOLS AND BUSINESSES: Technics Publications books are available at quantity discounts with bulk purchase for educational, business, or sales promotional use. For information, please email Steve Hoberman, President of Technics Publications, at me@stevehoberman.com.

Praise for *The Nimble Elephant*

I'm delighted to see that John has put his extensive experience and broad knowledge of data modeling into print! I've worked with John on a variety of projects over many years, and his solutions to company problems are as creative and innovative as they are pragmatic, practical and highly focused. John's ability to simplify the complex, and to share his knowledge and enthusiasm – and humor – with colleagues, comes through in this very useful and readable book. I recommend it to anyone working with data.

Monika Remenyi, Senior Data Architect, Telstra

I have worked with John off and on for 15 years now and John is the best and quickest developer of powerful and practical data models that I know, and it is because of his extensive use and deep understanding of data modeling patterns. I have been in the data game for 25 years but I still found John's book new and refreshing and I believe the top-down pattern-based approach John proposes is the only way to get agile with data modeling that produces robust sustainable solutions.

Mark Kortink, Chief Architect, Telstra

Those new to the dark arts of modeling will find easy access to great stories full of practical insights, tips and techniques - all reinforced by copious reference to other leading authors in the field. A great resource for old and new hands who find themselves at the sharp end under relentless pressure to deliver quality design solutions at speed across a range of contexts.

Damien McAree, Independent Consultant

I enjoyed this book immensely. It was chatty, cheerful and cheeky. Sometimes, in the heat and pressure of delivering a large IT project, it is easy to forget the impact that John's ideas and his clarity of vision had on us. Reading this book brings this clarity to mind once again. His book provides fresh and compelling means of analyzing and resolving not only the issues faced in delivering any IT project, but lessons for use in unraveling any complex problem.

John Barry, Former Deputy Registrar of Titles and Chief Legal Officer, Victoria Land Titles Office

John's real world scenarios and entertaining analogies help the reader in the understanding of a complex subject. I found that in reading the book I was able to put my context into the subject and found a greater depth of understanding. Consolidating each chapter helped me digest the information provided in a succinct manner.

Larry Reed, Information Technology Manager, Salvation Army

John Giles has written a compelling and engaging book about the importance of data modeling patterns in the world of agile computing. His book is clearly and simply written, and it is full of excellent examples drawn from his extensive experience as a practitioner. You will see the enthusiasm and passion that John clearly has for his work in data modeling. As a reader, I am certain you will find yourself drawn into the excitement John has for his work. John is a world-class practitioner of data modeling. In the past I have had the pleasure and privilege of working with him. He is highly experienced, highly knowledgeable, and ever-thoughtful and reflective about the work he undertakes. And you will see in his book that any interchange with John will always have its fair share of good humor and wisdom!

Professor Ron Weber, Dean, Faculty of IT, Monash University

If you're thinking a patterned based solution won't work for your business because it's different to every other business, think again. John's approach will show how to develop a quality database design for your solution without needing to compromise on the speed of delivery, especially when you're working in an agile environment. Having used John's approach, not doing so would be like taking a knife to a gunfight. This book will show you how you can plan for success by identifying areas that are open to a common platform and therefore allowing you to spend more time on any genuine areas of uniqueness. This book will help navigate the building blocks of pattern based data architecture. After reading it you will know the type of thinking required to build a successful data model / architecture or entice you to explore the fundamental models that John refers to both in this book and in his day-to-day work.

Doug Cameron, Systems Manager, John Holland

Contents at a Glance

Contents

"A majority of projects driven by agility … lack a big-picture focus and often strive to deliver small slices of functionality within tight timeframes, at times redoing and revamping prior work. If we can initially create at least a high-level, broad enterprise view or reference an existing industry data model, then we can confidently deliver small pieces of functionality knowing each piece fits with other pieces …"[1]

---

[1] (Hoberman, 2010)

Acknowledgments

This book would not exist if not for the "pattern" works by those such as Dave Hay and Len Silverston (with Paul Agnew making a later appearance alongside Len). Their willingness to share with the world their accumulated experiences has enriched my working life, and that of so many others. They, and a number of others from the object-oriented world, have created entire libraries of assembly patterns. We all owe them much.

My own foundations in the data modeling world were challenged and extended when I was privileged to join Graeme Simsion and his team. They were heady days, and I am sure every one of Graeme's team came away better for the experience. I hesitate to name any of them as they all gave so much to me, but the patience and insight of Bill Haebich and Don Watson in helping me, an old-school data modeler, to "get" what object-orientation was about, is noteworthy.

This book is based solidly on real-life stories. I've worked on great projects with great people. Again I hesitate to name any of my clients for fear of missing out on others who are worthy of mention, but I do want to give credit to two outstanding visionaries. They both led by example, and both were willing to be more than a little unconventional where necessary. And both were a challenge to work with – when either of them called me for assistance, I knew ahead of time I would be stretched! Andrew Matthews and John Barry – thanks for the pleasure of working with you both.

Then there were the clients who not only let me loose on their enterprise models, but generously provided feedback and allowed me to print their comments in this book. In all cases I am grateful for their trust and friendship. Special thanks go to Doug Cameron, Damien McAree, Larry Reed, and Ron Weber.

My most recent major consultancy has been with one of Australia's best known companies. The chief data architect, Mark Kortink, himself a leading practitioner, has shown real leadership in "playing to the strengths" of his team, and trusting us to do the job. Terry Bell mentored me an embarrassing number of decades ago, and continues to politely but directly suggest improvements to my models. Wayne Sigley has a hunger to keep at the cutting edge, and has often been my "go to" person. Sam Kiokakis is another who, like Terry and Wayne, keeps me on my toes, and whose opinion I deeply respect. Further, Monika Remenyi and Wayne Sigley kindly reviewed an earlier draft of this book – you are both true data professionals, and your feedback has been very welcome. It has improved the final result (my incessant fiddling with the words may have undone some of your good work – sorry).

My earlier experiences were solidly based in the "data" world; more recently I have enjoyed playing on the edges of the "agile" world. It is not a coincidence that Scott Ambler was invited to write the foreword – he has lived in both worlds for many years, and has generously reached out to me, encouraged me, and offered constructive advice. Hopefully this book is a worthy jigsaw-puzzle piece to be added to the already extensive published works of Scott and other agile practitioners.

I have often seen other authors express appreciation to their publisher. I now know why. Thanks are due to Steve Hoberman and his team, especially his editor.

There are so many, many more I could and should thank, but I will close with just one more – my wife. Her support for me at a time in her life where she, herself, was under enormous pressure has been astounding. A heartfelt "thank you".

By now, early 2012, it is spectacularly clear that agile software development is not only here to stay it has become the dominant development paradigm worldwide. Organizations have discovered that the claimed benefits of agile – improved quality, improved business value delivered, improved return on investment (ROI), and improved time to delivery – are observably and measurably real. It is also spectacularly clear that data is here to stay too, that data has been important for decades and will continue to be important regardless of development paradigm or even underlying implementation technology. Because these two industry trends are spectacularly clear (yes, I love the term "spectacularly clear") a wealth of books have been written about how you can marry agile and data together. Ummmmm…

The challenge is that these two trends aren't spectacularly clear to everyone. Data professionals have long been leery of new development paradigms and development professionals have long been weary of onerous data strategies. As a result, until just recently data professionals really haven't been clamoring for books describing agile data skills to their detriment. Agile professionals have also underestimated the need for agile data skills and have forgone opportunities for even greater productivity and quality.

The focus of this book is on agile data modeling, one of several key skills required for data professionals to effectively support agile software delivery teams. It does so by arguing for a nimbler approach to data modeling, one that promotes some initial up-front modeling followed by more detailed modeling on a just-in-time (JIT) basis throughout the lifecycle. This is exactly the approach which I promoted in the Agile Modeling methodology ten years ago and have applied on projects throughout the world since then. Of course with The Nimble Elephant John Giles goes into far greater detail when it comes to modeling data in an agile manner, and rightfully so.

One thing that I really like about this book is how John makes it clear that patterns can increase not only the quality of your work but your productivity as well. He summarizes seminal patterns work by David Hay, Martin Fowler and others, showing how to apply their patterns in a lightweight and effective manner. I also like the fact that John promotes key concepts such as taking a metadata driven approach using decision tables as well as a business-rules approach. Both of these topics have been given short shrift within the agile canon and with The Nimble Elephant John Giles has started to address this mistake.

Time to get down to brass tacks – Why should you read The Nimble Elephant? If you're an existing agile professional then you're going to find that agile data modeling is an important new skill for your intellectual toolkit. Many agile developers underestimate the value of data modeling and other data skills at their peril. Traditional data professionals will benefit most from this book because it provides them with an entry point into the brave new world of agile software delivery. I highly suggest that both these groups of people give this book serious consideration.

The primary strength of this book is its focus on agile data modeling. It's also its primary weakness. Agile data modeling is only one of many skills required of agile data professionals, let alone agile professionals in general. As John makes clear in Chapter 1 there is far more to modeling than data modeling. As I make clear in my own agile data writings, many of which you can find at www.agiledata.org, agile data modeling is supported by agile database techniques such as database refactoring, database testing, and continuous database integration. This book doesn't cover everything you need to know, no book can, but it will prove to be a key stepping stone in your overall agile learning path.

My experience is that the majority of data professionals could up their game by adopting proven agile strategies, and agile data modeling is clearly one such strategy. I have also found that agile project teams benefit from the insight and skills brought to the table by experienced data professionals who are flexible enough to work in an agile manner. I highly suggest that you pay heed to the advice John has generously shared with us in this book.

Scott W. Ambler

Chief Methodologist for IT, IBM Rational
Founder of the Agile Modeling, Agile Data, and Disciplined Agile Delivery methodologies

When a tradesman starts out, he or she will probably begin by learning the basics of the tools of their trade. Then they get out on the job and apply them. But they never stop learning. New tools and techniques come along and must be taken on board. My late father was an old-time builder; I can still remember him making his own wood glue by boiling it up in a glue pot. Then came along PVC glues, and he chose to move with the times.

Our industry keeps changing, and that's a good thing. But even when we jump into new areas, Simsion and Witt suggest that experienced data modelers

> "... seldom work from first principles, but adapt solutions that have been used successfully in the past."[2]

The use of patterns is part of the lives of data architects, even if sometimes unconsciously. What has changed since the 1990s is the growing list of *published* patterns, and an increasing awareness of their benefits.

I often aspire to being as practical as my dad was, and I guess I am making some progress on that front. He died when I was a youngster, so I tried to teach myself, but I carry the scars of learning the hard way. When I decided I'd like to weld, I figured that at least this time I'd take some lessons before I blinded or electrocuted myself. I was

---

[2] (Simsion & Witt, 2005: 274)

first taught about how the tools work, and the differences between various types of welders. Then I went on to the fun bit – using my newly gained knowledge to actually construct things.

This first section, "Foundations for data agility", is a bit like learning how patterns work, and the differences between variations of patterns. The second section, "Steps towards data agility", is more like the fun bit of applying the patterns to gain tangible benefits where you work, but I would encourage you to hang in there with the first section, as it may well equip you to enjoy the application of the tools even more. And the last section, "A bridge to the land of Object Orientation", is optional – it is aimed at traditional data modelers who wish to expand their horizons by tapping into the object-oriented market.

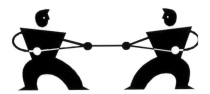

The speed versus quality war isn't new

THE NEW CIVIL WAR

If you walk around the "agile" camp, you could be forgiven for thinking there's a civil war. I've encountered articles such as *"We Don't Need No ... Architects"*. The author actually holds the view we *do* need architects, but that they need to change their ways. Nonetheless, perhaps the title warns us that some in the agile community perceive a disconnection between architects and the agile practitioners.

In fact, I would suggest that, for some people, they believe there really is a war going on. The agile developers are motivated by a less-is-more attitude. Well, less of some things (like documentation) and more of others (like working code). The Agile Manifesto[3] states that its followers have come to value:

- **Individuals and interactions** over process and tools
- **Working software** over comprehensive documentation
- **Customer collaboration** over contract negotiation
- **Responding to change** over following a plan.

Some of these statements can be sufficient to trigger stress-related symptoms from some such as architects and project managers. One overreaction is to condemn the agile enthusiasts as wanting no process, no documentation, no contract, and no plan. This is unfair. The list above, taken from the Agile Manifesto, is immediately followed by the explanation that

> *"... while there is value in the items on the right, we value the items on the left more."*

---

[3] http://agilemanifesto.org, December 2011

But even this emphasis worries some. A project manager grounded in years of carefully managing the progress of fixed deliverables against a fixed plan just doesn't want to hear from people who enthusiastically embrace change in the middle of a project. And a data architect with years of experience may well carry scars from fast-to-market developers who get praised for their work but then move on and leave others to try and integrate their system within the enterprise.

TRADITIONAL CONFLICTS

You could be forgiven for coming to the conclusion that the thing that architects and agile developers have most strongly in common is that they despise each other's views! But the pressure on architects, including data architects, isn't new. It's not just about "agile". While a growing appetite within corporations for agile software development has added to the pressure, and perhaps made the debate a bit more public, the undercurrent to deliver more with less without compromising quality has been around a lot longer than the Agile Manifesto.

In traditional waterfall developments, you can't start coding until the data model and the subsequent physical database design is done. And if the data modeling appears on the project manager's critical path, the pressure is on.

Or maybe, as a data architect you've been tasked with getting a team together to develop an enterprise data model. Maybe it's as part of an IT strategy initiative (which may make the demands even higher, if they want an "as-is" model reflecting today's realities, as well as a "to-be" model for the future). Or maybe it's the foundation for development of an enterprise data warehouse. And by the way, the coding for the warehouse starts next week.

You get the picture! Let's have an enterprise data model, and let's have it now. And by the way, it had better be a high-quality model, reflecting best practices, and able to be extended in any way we might desire in the future. And don't tell me later you got it wrong and need more time to correct it. And definitely don't tell me that the money we've invested in working code that's based on your model will need to change. Sound somewhat familiar, even if a bit exaggerated?

Sometimes there are more incentives for getting it right than others. I remember clearly one IT project where I had design responsibility. The client was in a remote location. And I mean remote. From my normal work place in Australia's south east required a flight of well over 3,000 km (2,000 miles) to the northwest mining region, mainly over desert with little or no sign of human habitation. I'd done the traditional waterfall thing – spent time on site getting requirements, followed by the client signing-off on design, and then development started against the specifications. Now it was time to go back for on-site training, only to be told by some participants that the management I had interviewed initially didn't actually understand the day-to-day realities, and my solution would therefore never work!

At this point in the book, the agile evangelists would smile and say, "What did you expect?" Fixed statements of requirements, based on interviews that proved to be flawed. No surprise to them. Simple solution – I should have gotten together an agile team and developed in a co-location environment. But this was 1980, and getting the development team to work on-site in heat and humidity was challenging. Not to mention the possibility of them having an encounter with venomous snakes and scorpions on the land, and a visit to the beach exposing them to sea snakes, stone fish, and sharks. And no, I am not paid bonuses by any tourism authority!

Seriously, though, there has always been pressure to deliver quality (right the first time). And to do it fast. It's just the publicity surrounding agile methods seems to have increased the pressure.

Demands for agile data modeling

Different organizations may have their own definitions of the roles of "data architect" and "data modeler". I don't want to get too side-tracked into debates on these terms, so as a broad, sweeping statement, perhaps you may be comfortable if I say that most, if not all data architects will, from time to time, do data modeling, while the responsibilities of a specialist data modeler may be more focused. Either way, I suspect most people with either title will be interested in data modeling, and this book is aimed at those responsible for contributing to an agile project's data model, no matter what their title.

ARGUMENTS ALONG A CONTINUUM

A husband likes watching football. His wife likes watching cooking shows. He wants to watch more of his shows, and less of hers and vice versa. We have a classic zero-sum game – one person's gains equate to the other person's losses. A tension exists along a single-dimension continuum.

If the couple were going to be a bit more creative in their conflict resolution, maybe they would find a new type of show that interests them both. Or they might simply buy a second television set. By looking for a solution outside of the apparent I-win-you-lose way of thinking, all may gain.

Graeme Simsion and Graham Witt put a strong argument for sound data architecture. At first glance, they seem to be asking just the question you might expect from the agile enthusiast when they challenge

> *"... the wisdom of devoting a lot of effort to developing the best possible data model, rather than just accepting the first adequate design."* [4]

But the answer they give to their own question might unsettle the agile true believer. They argue that there is real leverage from investment in sound data models, stating:

> *"A well-designed data model can make programming simpler and cheaper. Even a small change to the model may lead to significant savings in total programming cost."* [5]

While recognizing a better model may save effort in reprogramming, the agile developers may well argue that you can't design a solution for a problem that has yet to be clearly discovered, let alone articulated. And I think most of us would agree that trying to get absolutely watertight requirement specifications before the clients see at least a few iterations of the solution is difficult, if not impossible, in all but very simple cases.

So we appear to be left with a "zero-sum" tension. Some agile approaches openly endorse a "barely sufficient" attitude, while many data architects encourage the best possible design up front.

There's another debate, too, between what some call heavyweight processes and lightweight processes. On the heavy end, you may encounter the disciplined processes typified by Defense Department standards, ISO 9000, Capability Maturity Model (CMM) frameworks, and the like. On the other end of the scale are a variety of agile approaches such as Scrum, Feature Driven Development (FDD), or perhaps a more controversial one, eXtreme Programming (XP).

In their excellent book, *Balancing Agility and Discipline*[6], Barry Boehm and Richard Turner look at the positions on the discipline/agility continuum, and provide some sound advice as to the "sweet spot" that may be found for a variety of project profiles.

---

[4] (Simsion & Witt, 2001: 8)

[5] (Simsion & Witt, 2001: 9)

[6] (Boehm & Turner, 2009)

But I refer to their book to highlight an extremely important issue. While it may be true that the tension between discipline and agility may be somewhat along a continuum, with a shift towards one approach necessitating a shift away from the other, this may not necessarily be true for the data architecture versus agile modeling tension.

My mother was a keen cook. And I was a keen consumer of her cooking. She took pride in the fact that her cakes were fresh – fresh eggs, fresh milk (do you remember when the cream floated on top of the milk?), and fresh butter (definitely not margarine). I clearly remember her response when the idea of "instant cakes – just add water" first hit the supermarket shelves. She emphatically declared you had to make a choice. You could have good, or you could have fast, but not both. In her mind, it was not a continuum. It was two extremes with no room for compromise in between.

In contrast, Barry Boehm and Richard Turner suggest there are many "sweet spots" between the extremes of discipline and agility, when it comes to the process continuum. But does this apply equally to the data architecture versus agile modeling dimension? Edward de Bono, the originator of the phrase "lateral thinking", suggests that sometimes we can get a breakthrough by looking beyond what can sometimes be a one-dimensional debate. Maybe we can have speed _and_ quality (sorry, mum) if we take a creative, new approach?

THE NEED TO AVOID COMPROMISE

It has already been noted that Graeme Simsion and Graham Witt encourage the development of a sound data model before you start coding. Barry Boehm and Richard Turner pursue a different line of reasoning, but in some circumstances may come to a similar conclusion. They note that as agile projects go further into more and more iterations, simple designs that served well initially may result in "architecture breakers" i.e., design decisions that:

> "... _cause breakage in the design beyond the ability of refactoring to handle_" [7]

They suggest that while maybe 80% of architectural imperfections might not cause major headaches, the other 20% of flawed architectures can cost enormously, and would be better off being tackled by a Big Design Up Front (BDUF) approach.[8]

---

[7] (Boehm & Turner, 2009: 40)

[8] (Boehm & Turner, 2009: 219)

So even in the agile camp, we have cautions as to the dangers of some architecture elements being left for iterative discovery. That wouldn't be a problem if we knew exactly where to find the 20% of trouble-makers, and having found them, knew exactly what their requirements were. But as the agile folk will tell you, we're back to the same old problem. Based on imperfect knowledge, some things simply cannot be fully known until we've made a start.

We seem to be in a lose-lose situation. If we get the data architects to back down and abandon their principles, we might encounter the so-called architecture breakers when it's too late to gracefully adapt to new knowledge. But if we get the agile practitioners to back down and wait for architectural perfection before we start, they and the business will roast us.

We could try to meet half-way, by holding things up a little bit while we get a not-too-bad architecture, and then deliver some tangible value in an agile manner. Or we might try this exact same half-way approach and end up with a half-baked architecture that was broken in the worst possible places, and a development approach that is agile in name only, is cumbersome, and delivers little value.

Sound depressing? Well, it may turn into reality if we don't find some circuit breakers.

Modeling ain't enough

You've probably seen it all before. Good data modelers who weren't necessarily that comfortable doing physical database construction, and good database administrators (DBAs) who, likewise, might not be too comfortable doing data models.

The waterfall solution? Have specialists. In the worst cases, the data modelers practice their black art, throw the results over the fence, and never even discover that their highly prized creations have been totally ignored by the DBAs. Now along comes "agile", and it's a game changer. And I suggest that it's here to stay.

MULTIPLE SKILLS, MULTIPLE MODELS

Agile projects tend to have small, tight-knit teams. There is still a valuable (and valued) role for data models. But:

- Team members are often expected to be multi-skilled. For example, those involved in producing data models might well be expected to roll their sleeves up and create the physical database schema. And populate it with test data. And refactor it when it changes over subsequent iterations. And …

- Those examples are arguably all "data" related. That might be a big enough shock for a data modeler who likes to stick solely to practicing their craft. But now the team wants them to get involved in analysis of requirements, discussion on interface design, evaluation of state machine diagrams, and so on. Where does it end? It doesn't!

It's bad enough being expected to be able to read models produced by others (use case models, activity diagrams, and a raft more), but now the data model "specialist" might be asked to contribute to articulating these horrible things. And it's not mile wide-inch deep skills. The expectation is for wide _and_ deep skills.

Before you throw down the book in horror and say it's all too hard, I'd ask you to bear with me a little longer. Our world has changed, but it's really OK. Yes, you're expected to deliver faster, but there is a lot more forgiveness — nobody expects perfection on the first iteration. What's more, we all learn together. You are passionate about data models, and your new-found friends will learn from you, just as you will learn from them, and in a fun environment.

SOME CHOICES

There are still roles for traditional data architects. For example, at the enterprise level, we still need people who will skillfully look after master data management, enterprise data warehouses, data quality, data integration, defining common information models to support service oriented architecture initiatives, and so much more. This book aims to assist these professionals, particularly where there are pressures to deliver enterprise data models in demanding timeframes, through the use of patterns, and through selective application of agile practices.

However, we live in a world where I wonder if the career options for data practitioners may lessen if they are not positioned to also participate in agile practices. I would simply encourage you to consider adoption of agile skills as something that may enrich your current practices, and open new doors. I also encourage you to see this book as a piece of a larger jigsaw puzzle. It aims to fill a gap, namely sharing an agile approach to the application of proven data model patterns. Hopefully it will deliver real value to you as a stand-alone work. I also hope that you will be inspired to look at some of the complementary material available, including:

- Libraries of model patterns. I suggest that the works of Dave Hay, Len Silverston, and Paul Agnew are a good place to start. (See the References section of this book for more details.)
- Descriptions of the extended roles for participants in agile projects. For the "data" types, you would do well to look at Scott Ambler's _Agile Database_

Techniques, as well as his web sites (try www.agilemodeling.com and www.agiledata.org).

- Material to assist in setting some context for agile projects. I reference Barry Boehm and Richard Turner's book, *Balancing Agility and Discipline*. I also recommend a web site that outlines the concept of Disciplined Agile Delivery (http://public.dhe.ibm.com/common/ssi/ecm/en/raw14261usen/RAW14261USEN.PDF), and look forward to the soon-to-be-published matching book.

ITERATIVE MODELING

Scott Ambler talks about a rich variety of models involved in agile projects, of which data models are just one. Data models might not be the center of the agile universe, but he (and I) believe they are still important. But we might ask at what stage of an agile project we might assemble data models (or any models for that matter)?

Scott talks of "architectural envisioning". This starts at the beginning of an agile project. Maybe some outline data architecture work might appear at this stage.

In contrast, the whole thrust of agile is to not load up the start of the project with things that are not needed yet, and may never be needed. So we traditional data modelers are going to have to learn to be comfortable with the reality that the final model may not appear until the project is approaching completion. (But that can happen in a waterfall project, too – it's just that it's seen as failing!)

There is some wiggle room, though. Scott shares that there are times when some "look ahead modeling" might be appropriate, where you see the topics of the upcoming iterations may benefit from a bit of preliminary explorative work. And one of the themes of this book is that even the early models that have tightly limited scope can potentially leverage the accumulated wisdom encapsulated in published data model patterns. Agile goals are to keep things light-weight. Many of these proven patterns have an elegance that achieves the agile goals of simplicity while also delivering flexibility for extension and enterprise integration. A win-win. And that's the next topic.

Can patterns really help?

THE PROMISE OF SPEED

To break free from this risky dance along a one-dimensional continuum, where one's gain is another's loss, we need to think outside the box. Where the debate is over how much agility versus how much architecture, I believe there are some rays of hope, at least within the domain of *data* architecture, and the specialized contributions of data modelers. Within this scope, I suggest that one area of breakthrough is the judicial application of data modeling patterns.

The theory goes something like this. There are some data modeling patterns that have proven themselves over time to be pretty "universal" (thanks to Len Silverston for that term), and are solid, dependable, and perhaps most importantly, surprisingly extensible for adaptation to unforeseen needs. Len Silverston, one of my data modeling patterns heroes, suggests that if you walk into almost any enterprise, you might fulfill something like 50% of their enterprise data model from these common, industry-neutral patterns. Better still, you might get closer to 75% of the very specific needs of a given enterprise just by grabbing industry patterns. I'm not on commission, but I heartily recommend books such as Len Silverston's (and Paul Agnew's) three-part series titled *The Data Model Resource Book*[9], and Dave Hay's publications, starting with his ground-breaking book from the 1990s, *Data Model Patterns: Conventions of Thought*[10], and more recent publications such as *Enterprise Model Patterns: Describing the World*[11].

According to the theory, the use of patterns can deliver quality data architectures, and deliver them fast, keeping both the data architects and the agile developers happy. That's the theory, but does it really work?

First, let's look at a real-world story about speed. Then we'll look at another story about quality.

Here's the setting. I was doing a bit of part-time consulting for several clients. The phone rings. It's Damien, a good friend and a real professional who is helping an Australian bank work through what I might call a business process reengineering (BPR) exercise. It's a major initiative, spanning many months and involving key people, from the very top down. In one stream, though, they had hit a roadblock, and realized that while the emphasis was on business _processes_, the problem required the perspective of an enterprise _data_ model. Could I help?

OK, so the company doesn't have anything that resembles an enterprise data model, and you need one to provide perspective for the problem? I'd love to help, but what's the timeframe? Damien answers that the development of the enterprise data model won't place huge demands on my time. He wants me to start straight after lunch next

---

[9] (Silverston, 2001-a; Silverston, 2001-b; Silverston & Agnew, 2009)

[10] (Hay, 1996)

[11] (Hay, 2011-a)

Tuesday, and deliver the finished model by midday the following day. Thanks a lot, friend. Haven't you heard the saying that we can do the impossible, but miracles do take a bit longer?

I will expand on the story a bit later, but for now, it's sufficient to say that in a moment of sheer madness (but with some clear articulation relating to expectations), I took on the assignment, and delivered on time. Well, delivered enough to break the deadlock. I did have to come back subsequently and fill in some quite large gaps. But I couldn't have done either the initial brainstorming exercise or the follow-up detailing without patterns. Too good to be true? Well, you'll have to wait for later in the book to get the full story. But for now, hopefully it's an appetizer to suggest some pretty "agile" data modeling can be achieved if we use patterns.

THE PROMISE OF QUALITY

The story above is intended to say we can move with speed. Now to the second story, this one looking at quality. And I think you'll find it amusing as well as instructive.

I was responsible for the logical data model for an emergency services response support system. There are a number of spots in the world that get hit by wildfires – including south western USA, Greece, and Australia. While the community is deeply grateful to a vast army of volunteers, the government also shoulders responsibility for responding to not only fires, but coastal oil spills, outbreaks of contagious disease in farm animals, and so on. While in my part of Australia, the most common threats are from wildfires, the systems must be able to be adapted to almost any threat. The system specified flexibility as a primary requirement.

The person responsible for testing the final system quite reasonably stated that he wasn't going to tell us the scenarios intended to test flexibility. If we knew ahead of time, he argued, we could make sure we were able to cope with those "unexpected" scenarios. So he kept them a total surprise.

Now it's crunch time. We're testing the system for adaptability. In real life, our emergency services use both fixed-wing planes and helicopters for fire surveillance and water bombing work. The tester suggested that management have just decided to use helium blimps for surveillance. He asked how long would it take for the developer to produce an estimate of the time required to reconfigure the system to capture details of a few blimps, including characteristics such as air speed, maximum flight distance, radio call sign, and carrying capacity?

The developer was a bloke[12] with a cheeky sense of humor. He suggested the tester go and get a cup of coffee while he worked on the estimate for the reconfiguration time. The tester returned, hoping for an estimate on time. He got the working solution instead!

The next test demonstrated that the tester also had quite a sense of humor. We have a variety of penguins that are so tiny they couldn't peck your knee if they tried. Cute little things. With that as background, instead of testing the system's ability to respond to disasters such as toxic spills, the tester painted a scenario of needing to respond to a "penguin stampede". I understand that maybe a buffalo stampede in Northern America might be a serious threat, but a penguin stampede? Ah, well, a bit of fun, and the system again proved adaptable and robust for more than a decade, in large part due to the quality of the data architecture. The flexibility does sometimes come at a cost, and this was true in this system – the more abstract nature of the data model demanded a higher caliber of programmer. So it's not a silver bullet story. But hopefully another to whet your appetite.

A TOUCH OF REALITY

So what does reality look like if these stories appear to be "too good to be true"?

First, it takes an enormous effort to consolidate the lessons of experience into a library of reusable patterns. I am sure that if you speak to Dave Hay, Len Silverston, Paul Agnew, and others about data model pattern development, or chat with our colleagues

---

12 Aussie (Australian) slang for a male.

from the object-oriented (OO) side of the fence, they will agree that producing their "patterns" books was a mammoth task. But if *you* can find all the patterns you need already sitting on the shelf, their pain is your gain. However, if you find you need to develop some new patterns, it can still be a hard slog, and this time the effort is yours, not theirs.

Second, it does take time to gain familiarity with the libraries of patterns, and it takes experience as a data modeler to evaluate variations to baseline patterns. The existence of proven patterns is a great leap forward, but it does not eliminate the need for modelers.

But there really is good news, too. There's a possibility of a win-win between patterns and agile methods. On the one hand, I am suggesting that the use of patterns can deliver sound data architecture to an agile project (or for that matter, any initiative that requires a data architecture), and at an acceptable speed. On the other hand, if appropriate patterns cannot be easily located, sometimes agile projects can be the research laboratory for discovery and proving of data models that can be the foundation for the next generation of patterns.

Notation: Yet another civil war?

Note: *For those who are comfortable with entity-relationship diagram (ERD) notations and also with the Unified Modeling Notation (UML) class diagram conventions, please feel free to skip this section.*

As a generalization, the data architecture community is perhaps more comfortable with entity-relationship diagrams, and a number of the developers in the agile community are likely to be more comfortable with UML class diagrams. Are these preferences grounds for yet another civil war?

There are multiple notations for entity-relationship diagrams (ERDs), including Information Engineering, Barker, IDEF1X, and so on. There have also been multiple notations for OO class diagrams. But when three of the OO leading lights (Grady Booch, Ivar Jacobsen, and James Rumbaugh) all ended up working for the same company, the Unified Modeling Language (UML) emerged, and has now become widely accepted as the single notation for class diagrams (plus several other types of diagrams). So while there used to be differing views on the best OO representations, that seems to be no longer an issue.

While the OO internal war has ended, one could be forgiven for concluding a war still exists between traditional data modelers and the OO class modelers. Does this have to be so?

Just to get one bit of noise out of the way, the UML defines notations for several types of diagrams (use case diagrams, sequence diagrams, activity diagrams, and many more). It is the UML class diagram that the debate seems to be about when it comes to the world of data modelers.

One view is that class models are intended to model OO classes, while data models are intended to model data – I suspect that there will be little disagreement on that motherhood sort of statement! If we take that as a given, it follows that certain aspects of a class model, such as "operations", are not only best handled by UML class diagrams, but in fact, an ERD has no place for capturing these specifications.

So one might agree that a data model cannot be used to express all that a class model may wish to define. But can a class model capture everything you want to do in a data model? If you want to define aspects such as primary and foreign keys, you might choose to stick with a data model. Or you might choose to follow the approach articulated by Dave Hay in *UML & Data Modeling: A Reconciliation*[13] to adapt the UML notation for data models.

Even without the precision and extensions recommended in Hay's approach, I think that much of the data aspects of the UML class modeling notation can be used as is to define at least conceptual, if not logical data models. Maybe it's not what the UML was designed for, but the UML seems to be growing in popularity, and maybe data modelers should be at least somewhat comfortable with the bits of UML that can help reflect aspects of a data model. To that end, I have included some basic explanations of UML class modeling notation, and I am using this notation in the book. I had to use one notation, so I hope I haven't offended too many by this choice.

But I will try to just get one recurring argument against UML class diagrams out of the way. Some argue that because the UML notation is richer (e.g. it can define operations), it is therefore too hard to use, or even that this expressiveness actually makes it impossible to construct a lean data model. I suggest you can simply suppress the bits of additional expressiveness you don't want, a bit like using traditional data model notation when you may choose to put aside definitions of unique indexes, at least until you need them.

---

[13] (Hay, 2011-b)

Dave Hay's books, *Enterprise Model Patterns*[14], and *UML & Data Modeling: A Reconciliation*[15] provide substantial recommendations on the use of the UML notation for representation of data models. However, my light-weight attempt to try and bridge the ERD-to-UML class model gap in a manner sufficient for my purposes follows. Below we look at some very basic aspects of ERD notation versus the UML class modeling notation, starting with an inspection of a simplified model using one of many ERD notations.

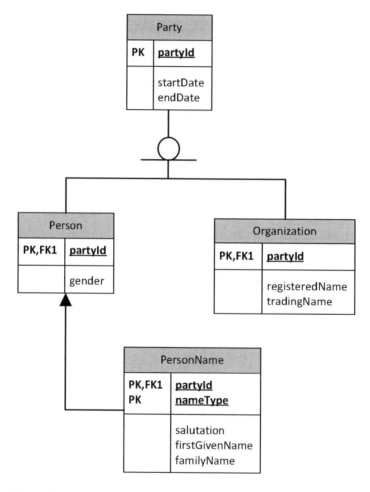

Figure 1: Sample of ERD notation

- Each rectangle represents an "entity", which may well become a physical table in a relational database management system (RDBMS). The name of the entity

---

[14] (Hay, 2011-a)

[15] (Hay, 2011-b)

appears in the first box within the rectangle. For example, the Party entity represents a collection of all parties of interest (maybe parties who play roles such as customers, employees, suppliers, and so on).

- Within each entity are attributes. Those used to identify each row in the entity appear in the middle box within the rectangle, and are labeled as participating in the "PK" (primary key) set of columns. The other box at the bottom of the rectangle may hold other informative attributes. For example, let's assume a person was born with a name of Cassius Clay, but later chose to have a "stage name" of Muhammad Ali:
    - One row in the Party Name entity might have a Party Id of "123", a Name Type of "Birth Name", a First Given Name of "Cassius", and a family Name of "Clay".
    - The same person might have another row with the same Party Id (it's still the same person), but with a Name Type of "Stage Name", a First Given Name of "Muhammad", and a family Name of "Ali".
- The lines linking Party to Person, and Party to Organization, signify the Party entity is a generalization, with Person being a special type of Party, and Organization being another special type of Party. Any aspect of the generalized entity applies to all the specialized entities. For example, because a Party has an attribute called "Start Date", this attribute is applicable to both people and organization units. (For people, the start date may represent the date of birth, and for organizations, the date of incorporation). Conversely, aspects of a specialized entity are unique to them. For example, people have a gender, but organizations don't!
- The line linking Person to Person Name is a "relationship". In this case, each Person may have many Person Names, but each Person Name must belong to only one Person. Depending on the notation used, optionally and cardinality of the relationship are displayed on the line.

There is plenty more we could say about ERD notations, but for the sake of brief comparison, we now look at the UML class notation.

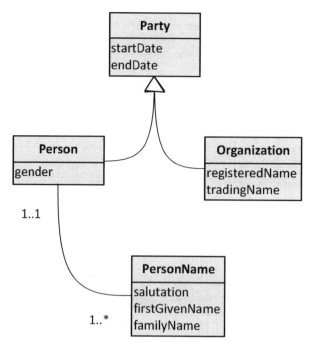

Figure 2: Sample of UML notation

- In a similar manner to the notation of the ERD, each rectangle represents a collection of real-world things that are being modeled, but this time each collection is called a "class" instead of an "entity". As for the ERD notation, the Party class represents a collection of all parties of interest (customers, employees, suppliers, and so on).

- Again, within the rectangle is a box of attributes. The main difference is that each object in a class is assumed to have its own unique object identifier, and the OO community perceives that there is no need for it to be shown as a primary key. There will be more explanation of object identifiers later in the book. For now, for those data modelers familiar with surrogate keys, you will not go too far wrong in assuming each class defines a surrogate key, but just doesn't display it.

- The lines with a hollow arrow-head that link Person to Party, and Organization to Party, signify the Party entity is a generalization, or "superclass", with Person being a special type of Party, and Organization being another special type of Party. In a similar manner to the ERD notation, any aspect of the generalized class applies to (is "inherited" by) all the specialized classes.

- The line linking Person to Person Name is an "association" (similar to an ERD relationship). In this case, each Person may have many Person Names, but each Person Name must belong to only one Person. The association can have a name, and each end can have a role name. This is not shown in the diagram above. Each end can also define multiplicities consisting of a minimum number of occurrences and a maximum number of occurrences, separated by two dots (e.g. "1..*"). The multiplicities appear at both ends. Some examples of notation descriptions follow:

- o "1" (or "1..1", or blank) – Exactly one.
- o "0..1" – Optional (zero or one).
- o "*" (or "0..*") – Many (zero or more).
- o "1..*" – At least one, but may be more.

There are differences, and there are similarities. The reality is that the UML class notation appears to be increasingly used to portray conceptual and logical data models. Rightly or wrongly, that is the notation used by default for the rest of this book, and as a reflection of this decision, it might have been noted that the class names and attribute names follow a convention that is reasonably common in the object-oriented world. In many earlier naming standards, compound words used an underscore as a separator – e.g. Person_Name, or First_Given_Name. The convention used in this book presents compound class names (such as "PersonName") with their name elements identified using the so-called UpperCamelCase style, where each element in the compound word begins with a capital letter. In a somewhat similar manner, compound attribute names (such as "firstGivenName") use lowerCamelCase, where the first element uses a lower case first letter but all remaining elements begin with an upper-case letter.

Consolidating the chapter for you

SUMMARY:

- It's legitimate for data architects to want quality. Why rush today to create tomorrow's problems even faster?
- It's legitimate for agile developers (and the business) to want speedy delivery of working software. Why take all year to design the perfect solution if the delay will mean you're not in business by then!
- Data architects are under pressure from more than the agile camp. It sometimes feels like everyone is demanding fast delivery of sound data architectures (for integration, transformation, business intelligence, etc.)
- There is still a role for traditional data architecture skills, and the application of ideas from this book can improve your effectiveness. That's good, but if you have specialized in data modeling in the past and now want to be welcomed as a full team member in agile projects, you'll need to roll your sleeves up, broaden your skill base, and expect greater involvement across iteration after iteration.
- Off-the-shelf proven data model patterns may go a long way towards bridging the speed versus quality divide.

APPLYING THIS TO YOUR SITUATION:

- Within your company, what data issues exist due to lack of compliance with the overarching enterprise data architecture (assuming one exists)?
- What upcoming (or recently launched) initiatives are you aware of that may be pragmatic, short-term fixes, but with a danger of long-term grief?

The "patterns" movement

When designing homes and commercial buildings, architects and engineers often use patterns. And before some of you react and say, surely John isn't going to go down the well-worn track of comparing information systems design and construction with the building industry, relax. The reason for mentioning the topic is the work of an architect by the name of Christopher Alexander. In 1977, he co-authored a book, *A Pattern Language: Towns, Buildings, Construction,* about patterns within architecture. He dared to suggest that non-professionals familiar with the basic patterns of architecture could design buildings, and even towns, themselves. Perhaps understandably, some qualified architects didn't like his line of thinking. The thought of novices generating designs for themselves without an architect's involvement (and fees) was threatening. Heaven forbid!

Another patterns book emerged in the 1990s that gave recognition to the foundational patterns language work of Alexander. This time it came from the ranks of information systems professionals. It was titled *Design Patterns: Elements of Reusable Object-Oriented Software,* and was produced by the so-called "Gang of Four" (Gamma, Helm, Johnson, and Vlissides)[16]. This highly praised work was squarely aimed at object-oriented (OO) programmers.

---

[16] (Gamma, Helm, Johnson, & Vlissides, 1994)

For our purposes, however, we want to focus on data modeling patterns. Examples might include fine-grained patterns for modeling hierarchies, or coarser-grained patterns for modeling parties of interest. If you haven't encountered these and many more patterns, one of the better known and highly regarded books, also from the mid-1990s, was Dave Hay's *Data Model Patterns: Conventions of Thought*[17]. Then in the 2000s, Len Silverston (later joined by Paul Agnew) produced the three-volume series titled *The Data Model Resource Book*[18]. The breadth and depth of the Silverston/Agnew series makes it almost a reference library in its own right. And the patterns movement continues, including more recent works by Dave Hay, yet again[19].

Then we can go back to the OO community, not to get into the details of programming patterns, but to look at what they have also published that complements the books by Hay, Silverston, and Agnew. Examples include *Enterprise Patterns and MDA* [Model Driven Architecture]: *Building better software with archetype patterns and UML*, by Jim Arlow and Ila Neustadt[20], and *Analysis Patterns: Reusable Object Models* by Martin Fowler[21], just to name a couple.

Suffice it to say, there are many published patterns. It is not the goal of this book to add to the commendable library of published patterns. Rather, the aim is to sort through these published patterns, identify the ones that are likely to help in speedy ("agile") delivery of sound data models, and share some lessons of experience in applying them. But this book does introduce one pattern, or maybe we might call it a meta-pattern. I prefer to call it a "pattern of patterns". When you observe the use of published patterns as they are linked to solve real-world problems, a higher-level pattern emerges as to how they fit together. This can be a starting point for agile delivery of consistent and well-architected overarching models.

---

[17] (Hay, 1996)

[18] (Silverston, 2001-a; Silverston, 2001-b; Silverston & Agnew, 2009)

[19] (Hay, 2011-a)

[20] (Arlow & Nuestadt, 2004)

[21] (Fowler, 1997)

Levels of aggregation in data model patterns

  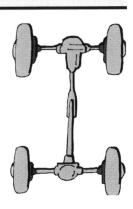

Years ago I had a few acres on some rough, steep country, and I wanted a vehicle I could use to get around on the hills. If I was a mechanical engineer type (and I most certainly am not), I might have chosen to design the entire vehicle, starting from high-level design of the engine and drive train, right down to individually designing the nuts, bolts, and spring washers.

I am sure that sometimes engineers do take the time to design a nut and bolt for a specific task. Maybe if you're designing a lunar vehicle, or something to navigate around Mars, you might make the effort. But most of the time, the engineer will make choices on topics such as whether the nut and bolt are to be mild steel or stainless steel, whether the thread is to be metric or British/Imperial thread, and what bolt diameter and length. In the data modeling world, I call the patterns for these "nuts and bolts" modeling pieces <u>elementary</u> patterns. An example of a data modeling elementary pattern might be one standard approach to resolution of a many-to-many relationship. (For those not familiar with this pattern, I will shortly provide a brief explanation.)

Let's get back to my example of wanting a vehicle that was capable of getting around anywhere on the farm. I have decided I am not going to waste my time designing each nut and bolt. But if I am still very keen (or maybe very stupid), I might design a purpose-built gearbox, clutch, differential, carburetor, fuel pump, and so on. Again, there will be times engineers will do just this. I had a good friend whose job it was to design and build tailored gearboxes for racing cars. But for a vehicle that's going to bounce around the paddock[22] at low speeds, and occasionally grind its way over the rocks I didn't see in the long grass, I reckon a stock standard gearbox from the wrecker

---

[22] Common Australian term for a field.

will probably do. To again return to the data modeling parallel universe, I call ready-to-use patterns that can be picked off the shelf and bolted together <u>assembly</u> patterns. One widely published example is the Party/Role pattern. Some other examples of assembly patterns include Account, Product, and Agreement/Contract.

Finally, I have decided my paddock vehicle will use standard assembly components. But again, I have choices as to use of proven patterns or a custom design for the overall vehicle. As a crazy example, I could decide I want a fifth wheel in the middle to protect the vehicle from the enemy – the rocks that jump up without warning and wreck bits of the underside. Alternatively, I could choose between a number of standard choices for the drive train. To make a point, let's say I had chosen a standard rear-wheel drive set-up, and it included (in alphabetical order) the following assembly components:

- Clutch
- Differential
- Engine
- Gearbox
- Universal

Based on my fairly rudimentary knowledge of these things, there is a certain order they would be expected to appear. And it's not in alphabetical order! A rear-wheel drive car has some standards for how these things fit together – engine, clutch, gearbox, universal, and then one differential at the back. For a part-time four wheel drive (4WD), one solution might include two differentials – one between the back wheels, and one between the front wheels – and a transfer case in the middle. And if it's a full-time 4WD, you might find a third differential in the middle instead of the transfer case.

These are all examples of how assembly patterns (clutch, gearbox, differential) can fit together in predictable ways. Each gearbox reflects an assembly pattern, as does each differential. But there is an overarching pattern, or "pattern of patterns", for assembly of the assemblies. In the context of data modeling, this book refers to this framework as a standard <u>integration</u> pattern. As an example, this might be reflected in the observation that the Party entity may be connected to the Agreement entity via a Role entity – maybe there might be an agreement for my wife and I to buy your home, with me as one party in the role of purchaser, my wife as another party, also in the purchaser role, and you as a party in a vendor role.

Fine-grained "Elementary patterns"

Using the analogy of a paddock vehicle, we have introduced the concept of elementary patterns, the "nuts and bolts", in data models. These are the building blocks used to create the next level of patterns. The example given of an elementary pattern was an approach to resolution of a many-to-many relationship. Maybe we have a Person entity, and a Skill Type entity, as displayed below. Each Person may have many Skill Types (e.g. Alex can Weld and speak French). Conversely, each Skill Type can be held by many Persons (e.g. Welding is a skill held by Alex and Brooke).

Person	skill acquisition	**SkillType**
name		skillTypeCode
gender	0..* 0..*	skillTypeDescription

Figure 3: Many-to-many association

The diagram above portrays a many-to-many association between a Person and a Skill Type. Unfortunately, a many-to-many relationship cannot be directly implemented in a relational database management system. Further, we may want to hold some attributes about the relationship, such as the date the skill was acquired and the level of proficiency. A simple example of creating a resolution entity follows.

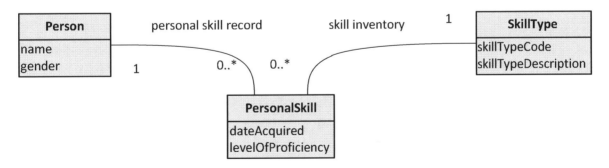

Figure 4: Many-to-many resolution

Here the Person Skill entity holds the suggested details for the resolution entity, and we have eliminated the troublesome many-to-many relationship. The intent here is not to delve into the whys and wherefores of relational systems not being able to cope with many-to-many relationships, while object-oriented systems can. Rather, the purpose of providing the example is just to demonstrate one common elementary pattern that experienced data modelers may quite reasonably take for granted.

Another common elementary pattern relates to hierarchies. Let's assume the Acme corporation has an organizational structure where departments are made up of sections, and sections are made up of work centers. We could model this hierarchy as follows.

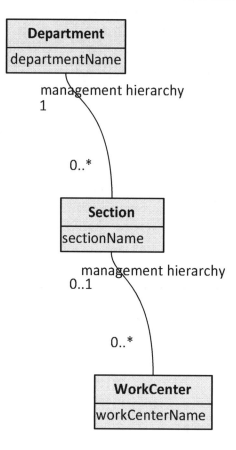

Figure 5: Specific hierarchy

This may be fine as long as the organizational structure is stable. But if new levels are introduced, we may need to change the data model, and worse, possibly rework the implemented software based on the new data model. A more generic structure such as the one shown below may provide an alternative that is more adaptable to change.

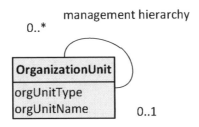

0..*   management hierarchy

0..1

Figure 6: Generic hierarchy

This model is a reflection of the self-referencing/recursive elementary pattern. In it, each department, work center, or whatever, is just one type of Organization Unit. They all "fit" into the generic Organization entity, and the hierarchy between each entry is managed by the self-referencing "management hierarchy" relationship. I highly recommend reading Silverston and Agnew's *The Data Model Resource Book Volume 3*[23], if you are interested in a very thorough and very approachable treatise on this pattern. But for now, this brief set of examples may be sufficient to introduce you to the concept of elementary data model patterns.

But do these elementary patterns help in real life? They most certainly do. Taking the recursion pattern above as an example, I have several times encountered enterprises with relatively complex organization structures that change frequently. The simplicity of the above model allows the developers to have implementation stability in this domain. And perhaps equally important, people who use the model to get a perspective of the enterprise are not confused by unnecessary clutter – without this pattern, the model will have to explicitly identify each organizational hierarchy level. Using the simplicity of the recursive model, they can focus on more important things.

Medium-grained "Assembly patterns"

Applying the paddock vehicle analogy once again to the topic of data modeling patterns, we had elementary patterns (the "nuts and bolts") that were basic building blocks to be used in the construction of assembly patterns (gearboxes, differentials, etc.).

---

[23] (Silverston & Agnew, 2009: 133-186)

Back to the data modeling universe, one example given for an assembly pattern was the Party/Role pattern. This pattern is widely published, and for good reason. It can be applied to many organizations and industries. It can provide a consistent approach to handling data for people and organizations if they play common roles (e.g. people as customers and organizations as customers). And it has the potential to reduce data duplication if one party can play multiple roles. I could possibly continue the list of benefits of the pattern, but you may be better off reading the works of others. Silverston and Agnew's Volume 3 patterns book dedicates one whole chapter to the Party pattern, and another to the complementary Role pattern![24] A significantly simplified version of this pattern follows.

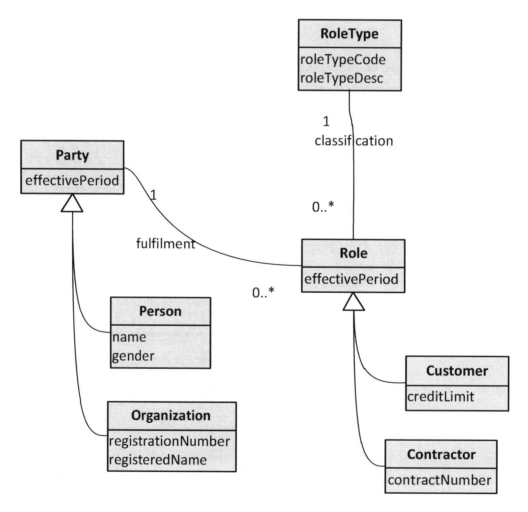

Figure 7: Simplified example of the Party/Role pattern

---

[24] (Silverston & Agnew, 2009: 35-65, 71-124)

The diagram presents Party as a generic superclass that represents people *and* organizations. The subclasses have their own special attributes; a Person may record their name and gender, while an Organization may record its registration number and name. In this version of the Party/Role pattern, the Party has one attribute that applies to the Person and Organization classes, namely the effective period. To keep things simple, the start point for the "effective period" of a Person might be their date-of-birth, and for a company might be their date of incorporation. This is subtly different from the effective date of a Role. For example, the period during which a Party in the Role of Customer is of interest to us may be recorded as the effective period of their Customer Role.

The Role class is shown as having an association with the Party. A few things we might note are as follows. First, the Role class is also subclassed, and this simple example shows Roles for Customer and Contractor, again with their own specialized attributes. Next, we can observe that the relationship is from the Party to the Role, not from Person to Role or Organization to Role. This implies that both individuals *and* corporations can be customers, which is exactly what is required, in many cases. Last, it is a one-to-many relationship. One Party can be both a Customer and a Supplier. Going even further, over different periods of time, one Party may fulfill the Contractor role repeatedly, and we can record each occasion. That's a very brief introduction to this Party/Role pattern.

One of many examples from my own experience in the use of this pattern is related to a private school. They effectively had a contact list, or address book, of *people* in some way related to the school. This, not unexpectedly, included teachers, students, and their parents. The list went on and on, including cleaning staff, medical professionals to be contacted in case of emergencies, tradespeople, politicians, and local government officials, etc. That's just some of the people on the list; also in the contact list were *organizations* (the local council, the hospital, the volunteer fire brigade, and on and on and on). With the Party pattern including attributes for addresses and phone numbers, much of the contact list was able to be accommodated.

But things got much worse. The same person may be a teacher *and* a parent. Or a parent *and* a mature-age student. Or all three! And maybe they were a trained first-aid officer and needed to appear under that part of the list. And even something as simple as "parent" wasn't simple at all. There were students whose biological parents were separated and remarried, but who now had children from the second marriage also enrolled as students. And maybe the person paying the fees wasn't a parent. I'm sure you get the picture. Fortunately, the Party/Role pattern, along with its inherent ability to record interrelationships between parties, very elegantly managed all this data.

We have looked briefly at one assembly pattern, the Party/Role pattern. Just like a car has components such as the gearbox, the clutch, and the differential, so too there are many data modeling assembly patterns. A few of the more common ones are portrayed graphically below, with the image in the center intended to communicate that a suitably qualified person can bolt together these assembly components to create one final product.

Figure 8: Some common assembly patterns – ready for integration

It must be noted that each icon represents an entire, rich set of entities, attributes, and relationships. It's a bit like having an icon for my car's clutch, gearbox, and differential. Each assembly has a level of complexity hidden by its outer shell. But at a coarse-grained level, we have a palette of assembly patterns we may choose to mix and match together.

Coarse-grained "Integration patterns"

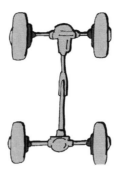

We return again briefly to the paddock vehicle example. We've got a selection of assemblies (gearboxes, clutches, and the like), but we now have to integrate them. Whether we want a two-wheel drive or a four-wheel drive, we are going to need an engine, and a clutch, but the number of differentials will vary, and the way they are joined will also vary.

In the data modeler's world, let's assume we have a rich selection of assembly patterns as portrayed at the end of the last section (accounts, agreements, tasks, and of course our trusty party/role pattern), but for any given modeling assignment, we need to select and link them appropriately.

One data modeling job I had related to transfer of ownership of properties. In a simple case, Alex Anderson owns the house at the corner of Main and High streets, and Brook Brown wants to buy it. Alex has no loan, and Brook doesn't need to borrow. It's a cash purchase. Lucky Brook!

In a perhaps more typical scenario, the financial institutes are involved. Chris and Dan jointly own the house at 1 Station Street, but the EzyLoan bank has a mortgage. Ed and Fran want to buy it, but have to borrow. Just to go one small step further, maybe the bank isn't happy about lending them the money, but Fran's parents, Glen and Hilary, are willing to stand in as guarantors.

This might not sound too complicated. But even a simplified diagram to represent the signed contracts/agreements, and who signed them, starts to get pretty horrible. A crude attempt follows.

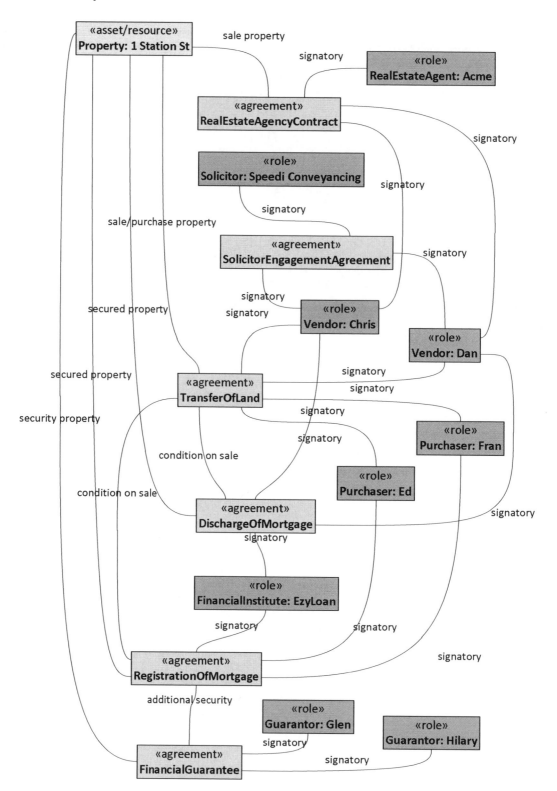

Figure 9: Sample objects for a land transaction scenario

Considering that that's only a small slice of samples, the modeling may sound daunting, especially when I've only touched on a handful of agreement types such as transfer of ownership, registration of a new mortgage, discharge of an old mortgage, and guarantee in the case of loan default, plus a few contracts for engagement of estate agents and solicitors.

But my client had over 200 types of agreements! If we explicitly modeled each type of agreement, and explicitly modeled the role types involved, we would have quite a large task ahead of us. A model with 200 classes, one for each agreement type, would have what our OO colleagues call a "bad smell" – it just seems to have something wrong. Instead, I would be hoping for a simple, elegant model that has the flexibility to accommodate these 200 agreement types, plus more that are sure to be discovered. Big is not better. A compact model is. Thankfully, we were able to use the palette of assembly patterns, and integrate them in a way that was meaningful for this domain. The resultant framework is displayed below.

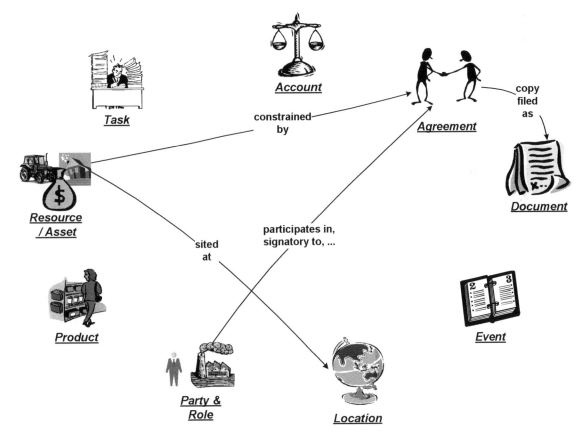

Figure 10: Integration pattern / land transaction scenario

This is obviously a very high-level model. But remember that each colorful icon actually represents a complete, rich assembly pattern with all the detail and rigor you would expect from a logical data model. All the parties (Chris, Dan, Ed, etc.) and their roles (vendor, purchaser, mortgagor, etc.) are gracefully managed by the Party/Role pattern. All the agreements (and I mean all 200 of them) can have all their fundamental properties handled by the Agreement pattern, with possible subclassing when and if required for specialized needs, and documentary hard-copies can be handled by the Document pattern. The properties (houses, land, shops, etc.) are treated as Resources/Assets, at a geospatial Location. And to tie it all together, we have a few foreign key links, for example, between Ed in the role of purchaser related to the Transfer Of Land agreement, to which Ed is a signatory. Too easy!

We will go into more detail, but this hopefully gives you a taste of how the assembly patterns can start to fit together to form the beginnings of integration patterns.

Consolidating the chapter for you

SUMMARY:

- Elementary patterns are the "nuts and bolts" of data modeling. They include items such as ways to resolve many-to-many relationships, and to construct self-referencing hierarchies. They are handy (and even essential) design patterns, but they are too technical to excite most business people.
- Assembly patterns represent the building blocks that span the business and data modeler worlds. Business people can understand them – assets, documents, people and organizations, and the like. Equally importantly, they are often the subject of published data model patterns that can give the modeler proven, robust, extensible, and implementable designs.
- Integration patterns (or "patterns of patterns") provide the framework for linking the assembly patterns in common ways.

APPLYING THIS TO YOUR SITUATION:

- Has your company invested in a library of data model pattern books such as the publications by Dave Hay and Len Silverston (see the list of referenced books at the back of this book)?
- Have your modelers been proactively encouraged to gain working knowledge of these published patterns?

We've looked at some varying levels of aggregation of pattern components. For my paddock vehicle, we had the elementary patterns for the "nuts and bolts", the assembly patterns for gearboxes and differentials, and the integration patterns for how all the assembly bits could be joined together. I had choices as to whether I would design the assembly components, or just go for off-the-shelf components. Similarly, I can choose to do a bottom-up data model from first principles, designing my own elementary pattern components. Typically, though, I will welcome the existence of off-the-shelf patterns.

But there are more choices. For example, having decided I would simply take an off-the-shelf differential from the local car wrecker, I may choose a regular differential or a limited-slip differential. And I could choose an off-the-shelf clutch and manual gearbox assembly, or an automatic gearbox; with three, four, or five gears. These are variations *within* the same assembly type. If you have looked at some of the patterns books, you may encounter a number of variations on the same theme.

Dave Hay has a chapter on patterns for "The Laboratory"[25], and Martin Fowler has one titled "Observations and Measurements"[26]. Fowler has a chapter for "Inventory and Accounting"[27], while Jim Arlow and Ila Neustadt have one on "Inventory"[28] and a

---

[25] (Hay, 1996: 157-172)

[26] (Fowler, 1997: 35-55)

[27] (Fowler, 1997: 95-132)

[28] (Arlow & Neustadt, 2004: 267-301)

separate one on "Money"[29]. Hay has one on "Accounting"[30], Silverston has one on "Accounting and Budgeting"[31], and so on. And lots of authors have published data model patterns on party and role, with some authors providing multiple variations! So just as you can decide on an off-the-shelf gearbox, there are so many variations that it's not enough to say you are going to use the one, standard "observation" pattern. There isn't just one.

But before you start feeling discouraged and say it's all too hard, let me encourage you. Len Silverston and Paul Agnew's book, *The Data Model Resource Book, Volume 3*[32] gives some great perspectives on how and why variations can add richness. For example, a less normalized model may be well suited for communication to non-technical executives, while another level of modeling (of what is essentially the same pattern) can provide implementation benefits for the developers. The rest of this chapter aims to share my experiences relating to selecting variations of patterns, and making your own adjustments. Hopefully it complements the excellent work of Len and Paul.

The detail behind the facade

Earlier, we used simple icons to represent assembly patterns such as agreement, task, or event, and noted that behind the icon there is a rich world of modeling detail. We now take the Party/Role pattern as one example, and poke around under its covers. First, we look again at the simplified model.

I don't want to go into an elaborate description of the Party/Role model – so many good books have done this already. However, a short description may be warranted for those not already familiar with this pattern. Remember, I am not trying to explain the internal *mechanics* of individual patterns, but rather, I wish to share with you how they can be *applied* to improve agility and quality.

---

[29] (Arlow & Neustadt, 2004: 411-432)

[30] (Hay, 1996: 117-156)

[31] (Silverston, 2001-a: 259-298)

[32] (Silverston & Agnew, 2009:7-14)

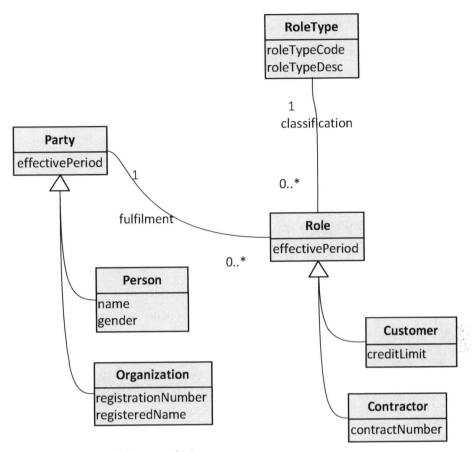

Figure 11: Simplified example of the Party/Role pattern

In this model, the Party class represents a "party of interest". For a retail company, this might include its customers, suppliers, and employees. Each Party might have properties (not shown) such as contact phone numbers and addresses. Some parties of interest (e.g. customers) may be individuals, while others may be organizations. The attributes that are distinct for people (such as gender) can be assigned to the Person (sub)class, while the attributes that are common for all parties can be assigned to the Party superclass and inherited by the Person subclass (and the Organization subclass, too).

One Party may play several roles. For example, Jo might be an employee who also holds an account with the company as a regular customer. The Role class can record the effective from-and-to period Jo was an employee, and also the effective from-and-to period Jo was a customer.

That's the helicopter view. Now let's look at the pattern in some more detail.

As stated, there are plenty of variations to choose from when it comes to Party and Role. Below is just one that I happen to have used a number of times, and that is at least partly influenced by a local standards organization. I am more than happy to have you mentally substitute your favorite Party/Role pattern. Please just accept this as one example.

Your reaction might be a bit like mine if I see my car's gearbox opened up – there are too many bits, and how will I ever be able to understand their purpose? Yes, there's quite a bit of detail there. But it does add some flexibility. For example:

- Each Person can have multiple Person Names. In the earlier sample data set for selling and buying land, Chris was one of the vendors. Maybe Chris was given a birth name of Christine; or maybe it was Christopher – it's a good thing we have a gender attribute to help us when the name is gender-neutral (and, of course, when it is appropriate to even record such information). Maybe Chris is also a writer and has a pen name as well as a birth name. Each Party can record one or several names. This might be true for Speedi Conveyancing also. Maybe they have a trading name plus a formal, registered company name.

- I've spoken above about Chris being a vendor. To be more precise, Chris is a Person, and one Role played is as a vendor. Maybe Chris and Dan are not only selling their house at 1 Station Street, but they are also buying a house, and hence acting in a purchaser role, as well. Don't you hate it when you have to fill in forms with your name and address repeatedly? At least in a database built using this model, you would only need to be identified once as a Person, then for each Role you play, you simply link the role details to your one "Person" record.

- Speaking of addresses, we sometimes have many. Maybe Speedi Conveyancing has a head office address, a branch office address, and a post office box. And in this model, the concept of "address" is pretty generic. For example, it also includes email addresses (and even phone numbers!).

- And each address may be used in multiple ways. For example, the physical address of the Speedi Conveyancing branch may be also a postal address – people may send mail there, even if there is also a post office box. Similarly, a phone "address" may be used for voice calls *and* for faxes.

- Finally, those with a relational background may be used to having one identifier for each instance i.e., the primary key. This model permits a Party to have several identifiers. Maybe for Chris, this might include a social security number, a driver's license, and a passport number. In some countries, some of these may be the same, but in other countries, several identifiers are issued for a person, depending on the agency.

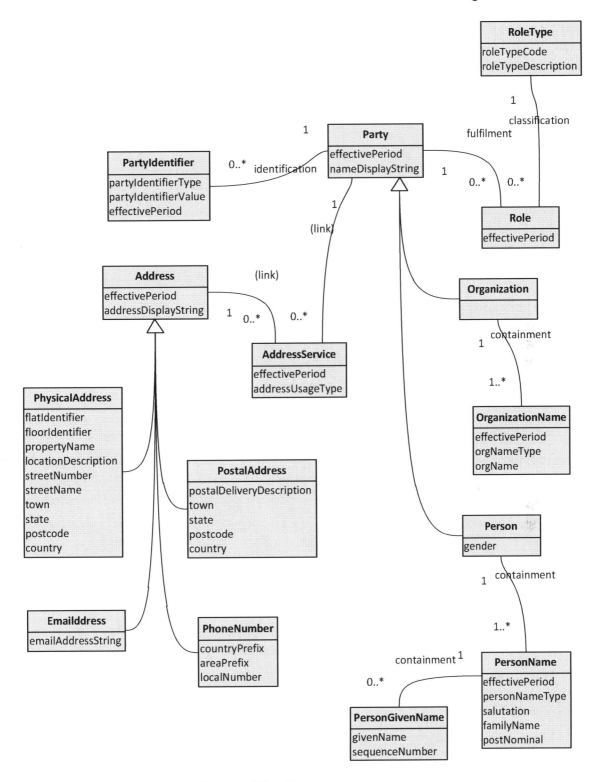

Figure 12: Party details – name, address, and identifier

You may love or hate this model. It has some strengths, but also some weaknesses. Hopefully, it makes the point that there's a bit more than meets the eye to the Party/Role baseline pattern.

Variation via custom extension

I've seen examples where a logical model similar to the Party/Role model above was pretty well mapped directly to a physical implementation. Several of my clients found the "standard" model rich enough to meet all their needs. In fact, one client, who worked in a licensing and registration area, felt the standard model was too complicated for their needs, but took my advice that it might stand them in good stead in the longer term. As it happened, I bumped into one of the programmers a few years later and asked how the project had gone.

She laughed. She said that on the first iteration, some of the programmers felt so strongly, they actually expressed a hatred for my model – they were not familiar with the level of abstraction, and felt uncomfortable and stretched, and quite rightly noted that it required additional effort in the first iteration. Then she told me that on the second and third iterations, the *business* required extensions in scope for the Party/Role domain (along with many other changes to other domains), but there was absolutely no *reprogramming* required for the Party/Role bits. The developers now loved the model!

If only all stories had such a happy ending. But sometimes even the richness of "proven" models may be insufficient, and the pattern must be extended. For example, one of my clients had responsibilities for emergency service responses. They needed a "directory" of contact addresses for a large number of parties. So far, so good. The standard Party/Role model, with all its address details was looking fine. But some of the contacts were not just phone numbers and email addresses; they included radios in fire trucks, planes, helicopters, and personal radios. No major obstacle – just do a little extension to the Address logical class by adding a Radio subclass.

Then the challenges began. They needed some way to capture rules for the prioritization of contact mechanisms – which one to try first, and if that failed, what to do next. Len and Paul have an entire chapter devoted to "Contact Mechanisms: How to get in touch"[33]. Unfortunately, I encountered this need for an extension *before* they published Volume 3. So to demonstrate a real-life example of pattern extension, I will walk you through the model I built on top of the baseline Party/Role model.

---

[33] (Silverston & Agnew, 2009. 303-410)

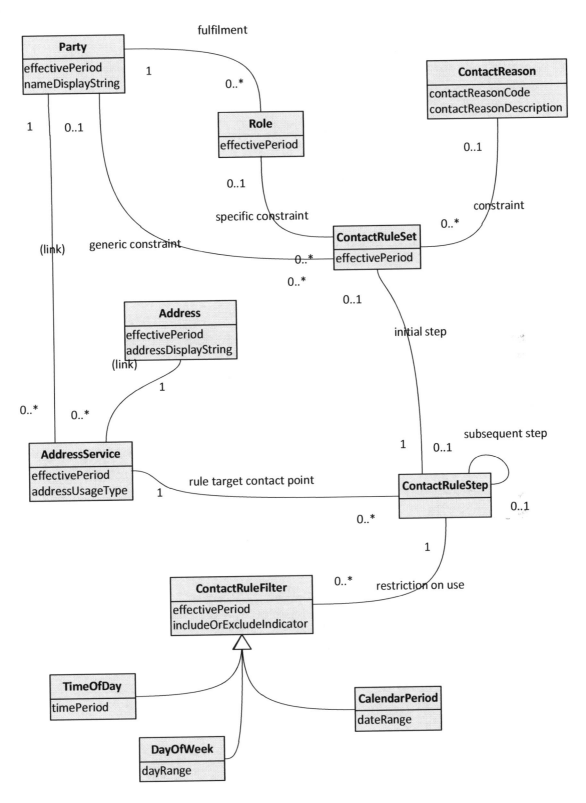

Figure 13: Party contact rules

Let's say Chris is a fire-fighter and has two mobile phones (one personal and one issued by her employer), a personal radio, a radio in the fire truck, a work phone, a home phone, and an email address. That's not too far-fetched in this connected world. All of this data is happily captured by the standard Party/Role (and Address) model. Now we start to build up the contact rules.

As a Person (Party), Chris might have a Contact Rule Set that defines how to contact her in a personal emergency, independent of the roles she may play. The Contact Rule Set is linked to the Party instance via the "generic constraint" association, rather than to a specific Role. Due to the intended usage of this Contact Rule Set (personal emergency), it is linked to a "Personal/Emergency" Contact Reason – the individual contact provides her personal mobile and her home phone, and she doesn't want those details made available for general use – just for emergencies.

This Contact Rule Set is fairly simple. The first Contact Rule Step references the Address Service for Chris' personal mobile phone. If there is no answer, the second Contact Rule Step references Chris' home phone. And if that also fails (again, no answer), the third and last Contact Rule Step suggests you try the home phone of Chris' parents. Note that the contact Address Service for steps in *Chris'* rules can refer to Chris' parents, boss, partner, or anyone – it doesn't have to be an address registered personally for Chris.

Chris has a regular "day job" as well as having responsibilities for emergency response in the case of a wildfire. The "day job" Role is as an Employee, performing environment protection officer duties. Attached to the Role (via the "specific constraint" association) we have one Contact Rule Set, with no special Contact Reason – it's just the set of rules for any contact with Chris in her baseline Role. The first Contact Step in this Contact Rule Set references Chris' work phone. If this fails (i.e., Chris doesn't answer), we go to the subsequent Contact Rule Step – in this case, Chris' email address. If we still don't get a response in a timely manner, Contact Rule Step number three says we should try Chris' work-issued mobile phone, and failing that, the last Contact Rule Step in this Contact Rule Set suggests we try Chris' manager's mobile. And maybe the boss has said to only use this step during regular business hours – a Contact Rule Filter entry.

We now have one Contact Rule Set for Chris' personal emergency use, and one for contacting Chris for any reason in her regular job. During the fire season, Chris typically plays a very senior Role as an "Incident Controller". In this Role, Chris has a totally different Contact Rule Set. Actually, two sets – one for typical activities related to that role, and one for emergency situations (e.g. an approaching storm likely to bring lightning and start new fires, and likely to fan going fires).

While the standard Party/Role/Address pattern was more than capable of providing the foundations for these requirements, some extensions were required. The fairly simple model shown above was able to manage the wide number of requirements for registration of how to contact a person via a chain of contact methods, constrained by the reason, the role, and time of day, day of week, and periods of planned absence.

It's interesting to note that I have encountered other examples of the need for this type of pattern extension to the Party/Role pattern. One client's business was related to monitoring the media on behalf of a number of clients, giving early notification of articles of interest. For example, maybe a politician with a certain portfolio wants to know about bad press before he or she has a microphone pushed under their chin for comment on a story they otherwise might not have been aware of! So the media monitoring company needs to have a number of contact points for their clients, with rules relating to the order in which contacts are to be attempted. It's the same pattern extension.

And yet another client wanted to improve public relations. They wanted to record people of interest to be notified of things such as changes to government policy. That involved pushing out information from the department to specified members of the public. Conversely, if the public expressed views, the system was intended to facilitate finding the right department employee, and being told how best to contact them.

Finding the patterns and gaining familiarity with them and their variations takes time, but I recommend investing in some of the publications referenced throughout this book. Given that you have access to a library of patterns, the key message is this: Often the richness of mature patterns will meet all your needs, but not always; however, they can still provide a platform for extensibility, and that extension may itself turn out to be a reusable pattern.

Variation via inheritance

Variations via custom extensions can be hard work. You're breaking new ground, even if (hopefully) a number of the pieces your new solution touches are components in other, regular patterns. A way that gains more leverage from reuse can be through the use of generalization/specialization. But let's try and get some language barriers out of the way first:

- In traditional data modeling terms, we speak of supertypes and subtypes. The supertypes typically define what attributes and relationships are common for all of its subtypes. The subtypes define what is distinct for them.

- In the OO world, we have superclasses and subclasses, or generalizations and specializations. The association between them is often referred to as an inheritance association.

Different terms, but without getting into the finer points (such as inheritance of behavior), for our purposes, I am suggesting they are close enough to the same.

With that behind us, we may note that for the emergency services scenario given in the previous section, we started with a standard model that was able to record a number of different types of addresses, but not radio "addresses". We simply created the Radio class as a subclass, alongside Physical Address, Postal Address, Email Address, and Phone Number. The new Radio class "inherited" all the richness of the generic Address superclass, such as its ability to link to a number of parties. Inheritance can be a great way to introduce variations to a model with minimal effort.

A second example relates to the Role and Agreement classes. We looked earlier at the scenario of wanting a system to record details of agreements relating to the transfer of ownership of properties, mortgages, and the like (200 types of agreements in total). We also presented a slice of what a model might look like if we explicitly modeled all types of roles and agreements. At the other end of the scale, we optimistically hoped a generic model might handle everything we needed. Maybe one generic Agreement class, supported by an Agreement Type class to classify the 200 types of agreements, might suffice. The reality is that the generic model might comfortably accommodate some types of roles and agreements, but some might have specific needs. This mixing of solutions (inheritance versus creation of a "type" reference class) is addressed succinctly by Silverston when he states, for a given model he has portrayed,

> "While the subtypes represent a complete set of possible classifications [for that model], there may be more detailed subtypes that are not included in the data model; instead, they may be included in a TYPE entity. In this case, subtypes are shown in two places on a model: as a subtype and in a TYPE entity that shows the domain of allowed types for the entity."[34]

For the sake of an example, we might assume that roles such as vendor and purchaser could be accommodated generically, but solicitors and real estate agents might need to record license or registration numbers. (It is arguable that a generic Party Identifier class might better manage data such as license or registration numbers, but for the sake of the example, we are keeping it simple.) And of course, some of the agreements might

---

[34] (Silverston, 2001-a: 10)

have their own peculiar requirements. Let's say that the mortgage agreement needs to record the loan-to-value ratio cap (e.g. the loan cannot exceed 80% of the property value), but the generic agreement class can handle the other types of agreements we have encountered so far. The resultant model might look something like the following.

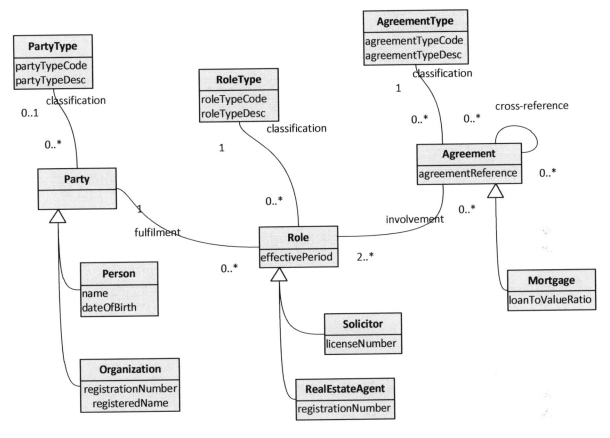

Figure 14: Specialization through inheritance

By applying inheritance to basic patterns, often much of the clutter can disappear into the generic base pattern, with only those parts requiring specialization appearing as subclasses. And new subclasses can be easily added. This whole approach worked really well for the client with 200 types of agreements. And for more on the specifics of subclassing roles, Silverston and Agnew[35], or the TM Forum's "Frameworx" generic model, are two places to start.

---

[35] (Silverston & Agnew, 2009:56-65)

Variation when linking patterns

We started considering variations to patterns by looking at how we might perform custom model variations <u>within</u> one pattern (if we choose to see Party and Role as a single pattern, rather than two separate patterns). We then considered how we might extend one pattern by using the concept of inheritance.

Now we want to look at how we might handle variations when we want to associate classes belonging to <u>separate</u> patterns. As an example, we look at how we might model relationships between parties via associations (again, this is within one pattern, namely the Party pattern), via links between the Party pattern and the Role pattern, and via Party-to-Role-to-Agreement links.

The following pages go into some detail on alternative patterns. The purpose is to provide a level of insight into the mechanics of pattern variations, not to teach patterns or to debate their relative merits. Other authors have already done this.

<u>Note</u>: *If you find the worked samples below too detailed for your interest, you may wish to skim over the material to get an overall feel for the topic. A high-level understanding of pattern variability may help steer you towards agile data modeling, but you may choose to ignore the specifics of this particular set of pattern variations.*

For the first scenario, let's assume we want to record relationships between parties involved in a school. We want to record parent/child relationships, partner relationships (such as traditional marriage or de facto relationships), and teacher/student relationships.

I know that there are complications regarding parent/child relationships, e.g. natural parents, foster parents, guardians, etc. I also recognize that there are a number of variations on types of relationships between partners, but for the sake of simplicity, I am asking that you please allow me to limit the examples, in this case, to what might be classified as "traditional" marriage. Further, let's please assume that a person will only be married to one other person at a time. If you've ever seen the old musical comedy film, "*Paint Your Wagon*", you will realize this may not always be true!

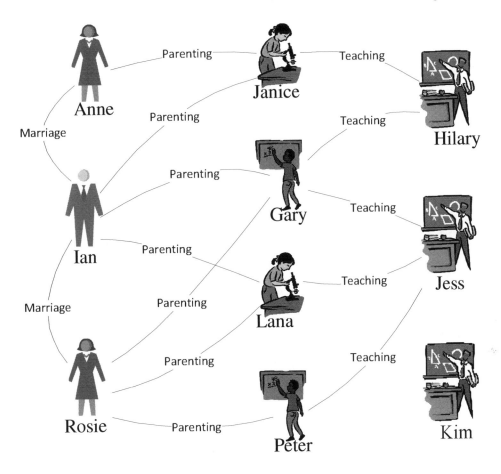

Figure 15: Party/Role sample objects for a school scenario

The scenario can be described as follows:

- Ian and Anne married, and had one child, Janice.
- Ian and Anne were later divorced.
- Subsequently, Ian remarried and had two more children (Gary and Lana) with his new wife, Rosie.
- Rosie had also been married before, and had one child, named Peter, from her earlier marriage. As far as the school is concerned, its records do not contain details of Peter's father.
- Hilary is a teacher at the school, and has Janice and Gary as students.
- Jess is another teacher, and who also teaches Gary, plus Lana and Peter.
- Kim is also a teacher at the school, but currently has no assigned students.

PARTY RELATIONSHIPS – IMPLIED AGREEMENTS, IMPLIED ROLES

One way we can model the database for recording these relationships is as follows.

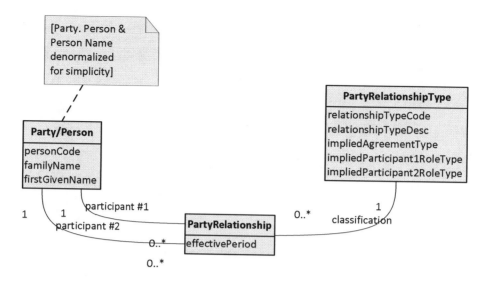

Figure 16: Party relationships – implied agreements, implied roles

If we assume a simple relational implementation of this model, and make some fairly crude assumptions about primary and foreign keys, we might have tables with the following rows.

Party

Person Code	Family Name	First Given Name
AnneG	Green	Anne
IanW	White	Ian
RosieB	Black	Rosie
JaniceW	White	Janice
GaryW	White	Gary
LanaW	White	Lana
PeterG	Goldman	Peter
HilaryH	Hughes	Hilary
JessJ	Jenkins	Jess
KimK	Kidd	Kim

Table 1: Sample "Party" table

PartyRelationshipType

Relationship Type Code	Relationship Type Description	Implied Agreement Type	Implied Participant1 Role Type	Implied Participant2 Role Type
Parenting	Parenting	Birth cert.	Parent	Child
Teaching	Teacher / Student	Enrollment	Teacher	Student
Marriage	Husband / Wife	Marriage cert.	Husband	Wife

Table 2: Sample "Party Relationship Type" table

PartyRelationship

Relationship Type Code	Participant1 Person Code	Participant2 Person Code	Effective Period
Marriage	IanW	AnneG	1990-1999
Marriage	IanW	RosieB	2001 onwards
Parenting	AnneG	JaniceW	
Parenting	IanW	JaniceW	
Parenting	IanW	GaryW	
Parenting	RosieB	GaryW	
Parenting	IanW	LanaW	
Parenting	RosieB	LanaW	
Parenting	RosieB	PeterG	
Teaching	HilaryH	JaniceW	2010-2011
Teaching	HilaryH	GaryW	2010-2011
Teaching	JessJ	GaryW	2010-2011
Teaching	JessJ	LanaW	2010-2011
Teaching	JessJ	PeterG	2010-2011

Table 3: Sample "Party Relationship" table

In spite of the relative simplicity in these three tables, they can easily accommodate the complexity of the hypothetical scenario, plus much more.

Len Silverston and Paul Agnew talk about two types of roles, namely "contextual" roles and "declarative" roles.[36] Based on the above scenario, we might say that, in the _context_ of the teaching relationship between Jess and Gary, we can conclude that Jess fulfills the role of a teacher, and that Gary fulfills the role of a student. Based on other relationships, we can also, for example, conclude that Ian is a husband and also a father.

If this data were held in a relational database, we may join the tables together. The information we might imply from the context of the stated relationships is displayed in italics in the hypothetical join result below.

View - PartyRelationship

R'ship Type Code	[Implied Agree't Type]	Participant1 Person Code	[Implied Role]	Participant2 Person Code	[Implied Role]	Effective Period
Marriage	Marriage cert	IanW	Husband	AnneG	Wife	1990-1999
Marriage	Marriage cert	IanW	Husband	RosieB	Wife	2001-present
Parenting	Birth cert.	AnneG	Parent	JaniceW	Child	
Parenting	Birth cert.	IanW	Parent	JaniceW	Child	
Parenting	Birth cert.	IanW	Parent	GaryW	Child	
Parenting	Birth cert.	RosieB	Parent	GaryW	Child	
Parenting	Birth cert.	IanW	Parent	LanaW	Child	
Parenting	Birth cert.	RosieB	Parent	LanaW	Child	
Parenting	Birth cert.	RosieB	Parent	PeterG	Child	
Teaching	Enrollment	HilaryH	Teacher	JaniceW	Student	2010-2011
Teaching	Enrollment	HilaryH	Teacher	GaryW	Student	2010-2011
Teaching	Enrollment	JessJ	Teacher	GaryW	Student	2010-2011
Teaching	Enrollment	JessJ	Teacher	LanaW	Student	2010-2011
Teaching	Enrollment	JessJ	Teacher	PeterG	Student	2010-2011

Table 4: Sample generated view with implied agreements and roles

---

[36] (Silverston & Agnew, 2009: 35-65, 71-124)

There is a problem with this design, though. If, at a point in time, Jess has no relationships recorded with students (maybe during extended leave for a training sabbatical), we do not have a _contextual_ role from which we can imply Jess is still actually a teacher. That is, unless we _declared_ Jess to be a teacher, independent of relationships. This issue is already obvious for Kim, who is largely not visible. This brings us to the next design to support this requirement.

PARTY RELATIONSHIPS – IMPLIED AGREEMENTS, EXPLICIT ROLES

The previous model had implied agreement types and Party roles defined via attributes in the Party Relationship Type class. It was a simple, compact model – everything required for defining party interrelationships tied quite directly to the Party class. And often, that is all that is required. However, if, as noted, we want to declare explicit roles for parties, we need to involve elements from the Party pattern and its close cousin, the Role pattern.

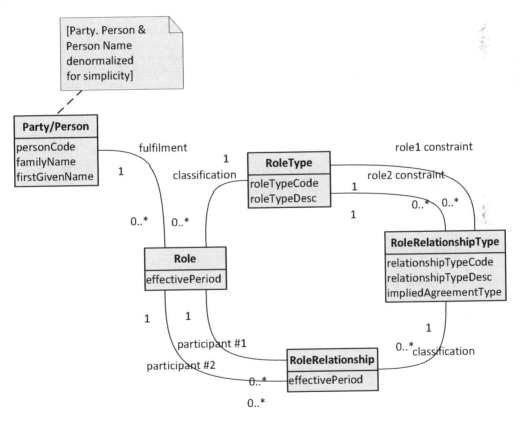

Figure 17: Party relationships – implied agreements, explicit roles

In addition to the Party table as already portrayed, we now have the following sample data.

RoleType

Role Type Code	Role Type Description
Husband	Husband
Wife	Wife
Parent	Parent
Child	Child
Teacher	Teacher
Student	Student

Table 5: Sample "Role Type" table

RoleRelationshipType

Relationship Type Code	Relationship Type Description	Implied Agreement Type	Role1 Type	Role2 Type
Parenting	Parenting	Birth cert.	Parent	Child
Teaching	Teacher / Student	Enrollment	Teacher	Student
Marriage	Husband / Wife	Marriage cert.	Husband	Wife

Table 6: Sample "Role Relationship Type" table

The above two tables represent reference data. Now we start to look at the explicit, declared roles each Party (Person) plays. These roles can be declared, even if relationships do not exist related to those roles, as is true for Kim, the teacher.

Role

Person Code	Role Type Code	Effective Period	(Comments)
AnneG	Wife	1990-1999	#1. Explicit ("declarative") recording of Anne's role as a "Wife". Until we look at the associated Role Relationship data, we don't know who she was married to from 1990 to 1999, but we do know that she was married. This explicit role was implied by the "context" of a simple "Marriage" relationship in the previous model.
AnneG	Wife	2005 onwards	#2. Explicit ("declarative") role - Anne has informed the school that she remarried in 2005, but has not informed the school of her new partner's name. I.e., no relationships were provided to allow "contextual" implication of the role. This information could not be recorded if the previous design was used.
AnneG	Parent	1997 onwards	#3. Anne's first (and only) child was born in 1997. The lack of an end date for this role may be seen to reflect the observation that you're still a parent long after the kids have grown up!
IanW	Husband	1990-1999	#4. Ian's first marriage. For the link to Anne's mirrored role of "Wife" in this marriage relationship, refer to the Role Relationship sample data.
IanW	Husband	2001 onwards	#5. Ian's second role of "Husband", this time as part of his marriage relationship with Rosie – but again we do not know of Rosie without looking at the Role Relationship entry.
IanW	Parent	1997 onwards	#6. Ian became a parent when Janice was born in 1997. To demonstrate some of the flexibility within this data structure, the one "Parent" role is linked to all three of Ian's children, even though born to two different mothers. This contrasts with the "Husband" role where a new role instance is recorded for each of Ian's two marriages.

Role   **(Continued)**

Person Code	Role Type Code	Effective Period	(Comments)
RosieB	Wife	2001 onwards	#7. As far as the school's records are concerned, Rosie became a "Wife" in 2001 as a result of her relationship with Ian. In the scenario we are using, she was married before, when Peter was born, but for her own personal/private reasons she has not provided these marriage details to the school.
RosieB	Parent	1995 onwards	#8. Rosie first became a parent when Peter was born in 1995. She subsequently had two more children from her marriage to Ian.
JaniceW	Child	[1997 onwards][37]	#9. The "from" date in the Effective Period column reflects the date-of-birth.
JaniceW	Student	2002 onwards	#10. Janice is recorded as becoming a student at the school in 2002. At the time, this explicit "declarative" student role could have been implied from the contextual relationships with teachers. But the teachers might have left and their student records deleted, or the teachers' records could still be on the files, but the teacher/student relationships removed. The fact remains that Janice has been "declared" to be a student from 2002 onwards, independent of any supplementary contextual role implications.
GaryW	Child	[2002 onwards]	#11. As in comment #9, the effective period could be derived.
GaryW	Student	2007 onwards	#12. As in comment #10, the declared start date for the role may be prior to the recorded current teacher assignment(s).

---

[37] The Role's Effective Period value is enclosed in square brackets to indicate that it is not required to be captured as fundamental data. In this example, and other subsequent role dates, the "start-date" for a Child is really their date of birth, and this value should be derivable from a more complete model of the Party.

Role   (Continued)

Person Code	Role Type Code	Effective Period	(Comments)
LanaW	Child	[2004 onwards]	#13. As in comment #9, the effective period could be derived.
LanaW	Student	2009 onwards	#14. As in comment #10, the declared start date for the role may be prior to the recorded current teacher assignment(s).
PeterG	Child	[1995 onwards]	#15. As in comment #9, the effective period could be derived.
PeterG	Student	2000 onwards	#16. As in comment #10, the declared start date for the role may be prior to the recorded current teacher assignment(s).
HilaryH	Teacher	2001 onwards	#17. Hilary is recorded as becoming a teacher at the school in 2001. Earlier, this explicit "declarative" teacher role may have been implied from the contextual relationships with students, but these relationship records have been removed. The fact remains that Hilary has been "declared" to be a teacher from 2001 onwards, independent of any supplementary contextual role implications.
JessJ	Teacher	2002 onwards	#18. As in comment #17, the declared start date for the role may be prior to the recorded current student assignment(s).
KimK	Teacher	2003 onwards	#19. This is most definitely a "declarative" role. There are no teaching assignments recorded to provide a "contextual", implied role. Maybe Kim is a new teacher, yet to be assigned students, or maybe Kim is an emergency teacher, recorded on the school's database, but perhaps the school has decided to never record the very short-term student assignments, or …

Table 7: Sample "Role" table

That's the set of explicit roles. Now we have to link them together to record their interrelationships:

RoleRelationship

R'ship Type Code	Participant1			Participant2			[R'ship] Effect. Period
	Person Code	Role Type Code	Effect. Period	Person Code	Role Type Code	Effect. Period	
Marriage	IanW	Husband	1990-1999	AnneG	Wife	1990-1999	1990-1999
Marriage	IanW	Husband	2001 onwards	RosieB	Wife	2001 onwards	2001 onwards
Parenting	AnneG	Parent	1997 onwards	JaniceW	Child		
Parenting	IanW	Parent	1997 onwards	JaniceW	Child		
Parenting	IanW	Parent	1997 onwards	GaryW	Child		
Parenting	RosieB	Parent	1995 onwards	GaryW	Child		
Parenting	IanW	Parent	1997 onwards	LanaW	Child		
Parenting	RosieB	Parent	1995 onwards	LanaW	Child		
Parenting	RosieB	Parent	1995 onwards	PeterG	Child		
Teaching	HilaryH	Teacher	2001 onwards	JaniceW	Student	2002 onwards	2010-2011
Teaching	HilaryH	Teacher	2001 onwards	GaryW	Student	2007 onwards	2010-2011
Teaching	JessJ	Teacher	2002 onwards	GaryW	Student	2007 onwards	2010-2011
Teaching	JessJ	Teacher	2002 onwards	LanaW	Student	2009 onwards	2010-2011
Teaching	JessJ	Teacher	2002 onwards	PeterG	Student	2000 onwards	2010-2011

Table 8: Sample "Role Relationship" table

For the previous pattern variation (based on direct Party-to-Party relationships), we generated a view of the complete data. We have done likewise here, but one difference is that the roles that were implied by context in the first models are sourced from explicit role declarations in this model. There is another difference I wish to highlight. By joining the pieces of information together, we can now view declarative roles, even if they have no contextual joins to other parties. This can be observed in the last two rows of the following table.

View - RoleRelationship

R'ship Type Code	Participant1		Participant2		[implied Agreement]	Effective Period
	Person Code	Explicit Role	Person Code	Explicit Role		
Marriage	IanW	Husband	AnneG	Wife	Marriage certificate	1990-1999
Marriage	IanW	Husband	RosieB	Wife	Marriage certificate	2001 onwards
Parenting	AnneG	Parent	JaniceW	Child	Birth certificate	
Parenting	IanW	Parent	JaniceW	Child	Birth certificate	
Parenting	IanW	Parent	GaryW	Child	Birth certificate	
Parenting	RosieB	Parent	GaryW	Child	Birth certificate	
Parenting	IanW	Parent	LanaW	Child	Birth certificate	
Parenting	RosieB	Parent	LanaW	Child	Birth certificate	
Parenting	RosieB	Parent	PeterG	Child	Birth certificate	
Teaching	HilaryH	Teacher	JaniceW	Student	Enrollment	2010-2011
Teaching	HilaryH	Teacher	GaryW	Student	Enrollment	2010-2011
Teaching	JessJ	Teacher	GaryW	Student	Enrollment	2010-2011
Teaching	JessJ	Teacher	LanaW	Student	Enrollment	2010-2011
Teaching	JessJ	Teacher	PeterG	Student	Enrollment	2010-2011
Teaching	KimK	Teacher				
Marriage			AnneG	Wife[38]		

Table 9: Sample generated view with implied agreements, explicit roles

---

[38] Note that for this entry, Role1 is blank, whereas in the previous entry for the Teacher, it was Role2 that was blank. The positions are determined by the arbitrary assignment of role types in the Role Relationship Table. If rather than Teacher/Student and Husband/Wife, the definitions were Student/Teacher and Wife/Husband, the positions would have been reversed here.

As demonstrated by the sample data, this variation of the pattern permits the capture of declarative roles, even if expected relationships are not recorded at a point in time (refer to comments #1 and #19 in sample for the Role table above). Further, this variation will facilitate the specialization of the Role class to allow subclasses of Role to capture details relevant only to that type of role. For example, the "Teacher" role may carry government departmental certification/approval details.

The downside, though, is that this pattern variation means we might end up explicitly declaring a whole heap of roles that could easily have been implied by the simpler Party-to-Party relationships variation. So if we don't need the additional power of this variation, maybe we should return to the previous one.

Conversely, even this pattern variation, with its extended functionality, may prove to be limited if we want to:

- Explicitly define agreements rather than imply them via relationships. This requirement may be highlighted, especially if we want to subclass the Agreement class to define additional properties for particular types of agreements.
- Involve more than two parties in one relationship.

PARTY RELATIONSHIPS – EXPLICIT AGREEMENTS, EXPLICIT ROLES

One real-world example I encountered had a need to associate several parties to an agreement related to recording mortgage details. If you encountered the situation with several common parties for (say) a first mortgage and a second mortgage, but only one of the mortgages involved guarantors, the model seemed to handle the associations more elegantly by having an explicit Agreement class (with mortgage as a type of Agreement) and multiple parties involved via their explicit roles. The resultant pattern variation looked something like the following. (Note the many-to-many association between Role and Agreement that in my "relational" implementation samples that follow, is resolved by the Role Agreement data set.)

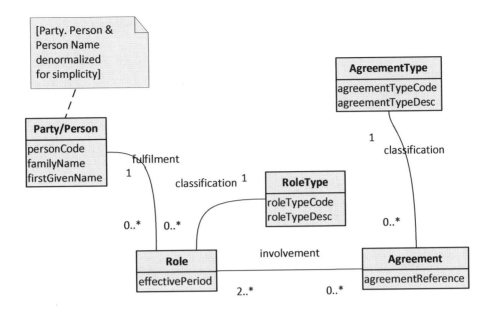

Figure 18: Party relationships – explicit agreements, explicit roles

For our hypothetical school scenario, we might have data something like the following:

AgreementType

Agreement Type Code	Agreement Type Description
MarrCert	Marriage certificate
BirthCert	Birth certificate
Enroll	Enrollment

Table 10: Sample "Agreement Type" table

We start by looking at some simple marriage agreements that involve only two parties, and hence do not need the power (and relative complexity) of this variation.

Agreement

Agreement Reference	Agreement Type Code
MC001	MarrCert
MC002	MarrCert

Table 11: Sample "Agreement" table

To link the parties (in appropriate roles) to the agreement, we introduce the many-to-many resolution named "Agreement Role".

AgreementRole

Agreement Reference	Person Code	Role Type Code	Effective Period
MC001	IanW	Husband	1990-1999
MC001	AnneG	Wife	1990-1999
MC002	IanW	Husband	2001 onwards
MC002	RosieB	Wife	2001 onwards

Table 12: Sample "Agreement Role" table - marriage

For Party-to-Party relationships that involve only two parties, and where there is no business requirement to hold details for explicit instances of agreements, there is probably very little incentive to use this pattern variation. It really appears to add no significant value. But now, let's ease towards scenarios involving more than two parties. We start with a relatively simple one. In the previous two pattern variations, we recorded that both Hilary and Jess had a teacher/student enrollment relationship with Gary. Let's assume that Gary is a special needs student, and the enrollment form assigned two teachers as part of a signed agreement requiring the consent of both parents. This could be easily represented by the following data set.

AgreementRole

Agreement Reference	Person Code	Role Type Code	Effective Period
Enr006	HilaryH	Teacher	2001 onwards
Enr006	JessJ	Teacher	2002 onwards
Enr006	GaryW	Student	2007 onwards
Enr006	IanW	Parent	1997 onwards
Enr006	RosieB	Parent	1995 onwards

Table 13: Sample "Agreement Role" table - enrollment

Similarly, a simple birth certificate could record the parents, the doctor, the registrar taking the birth certificate and entering it on the register, and so on. And of course the newborn child! Assuming we have now obtained more details about Peter, including his father, Robert Goldman, a possible data set follows.

AgreementRole

Agreement Reference	Person Code	Role Type Code	Effective Period
BC008	PeterG	Child	
BC008	RosieB	Parent	1995 onwards
BC008	RobG	Parent	[39]
BC008	SandyS	Registrar	
BC008	TerryT	Doctor	

Table 14: Sample "Agreement Role" table - birth

Not that we may necessarily want to, but the data structure could record polygamous marriages where several people were married in one ceremony, complex birth certificates with IVF donor details, and so on. The structure has significant flexibility, but the business may choose to limit its application.

PARTY RELATIONSHIPS – CLOSING COMMENTS

When do you use these variations? Several of my clients have found the simple Party-to-Party model more than sufficient. Conversely, another client (a land titles registration organization) needed explicit agreements, and also needed explicit declarative roles (identifying who declares themselves to be a solicitor, a real estate agent, a home finance institution, etc.).

Another client was of particular interest. They are one of Australia's largest construction companies. They build and maintain railways, dams, hospitals, mine facilities, etc. – no matter what it is, if it's big and you want it built, they will do it. They

---

[39] The "effective date" from which Robert Goldman become a parent *could* be entered as "1995 onwards", but maybe he had become a parent in an even earlier relationship. The real world can get complicated, and sometimes it can be a challenge to model a data structure capable of reflecting those complexities that are relevant to the problem at hand.

wanted to record simple Party-to-Party relationships where the roles and agreements could be implied by context. They also wanted a register of explicitly declared roles, particularly for companies that supplied services to them. And they absolutely needed to record the details of specific agreements, and the roles of those involved. In summary, they wanted to use all the variations we've looked at, plus more.

One solution could have been to force all relationships to be recorded using the most powerful and flexible variation available. It obviously would accommodate everything, but may be overkill for the simpler scenarios. The chosen solution was to use all variations, and effectively create consolidated views from the relational union of data from separate sources. Some sources had implied roles and agreements, some had explicit roles and agreements. But all could be combined to deliver a unified view of customers, suppliers, and employees, plus the myriad of other roles of interest.

Variations in the real world

Theory is fine. We need motivated people to do research and write papers. I suspect many of us who lived through CODASYL and hierarchical database systems are probably grateful for Ted Codd's 12 rules on what a relational database should look like. But, we also need to balance theory with the hard, cold reality of delivering value in the workplace.

I've already shared a little about usage of the Party/Role pattern. In some cases, the pattern was used "off-the-shelf". In other cases, it was customized to meet unusual needs. Even in these cases, though, the foundational pattern proved to be extremely robust.

Party/Role isn't the only pattern, of course. We've already touched briefly on the fine-grained self-referencing/recursive elementary pattern. A very common form of this pattern involves one-to-many hierarchies. However, when I was consulting at a government organization, I found that they needed to classify plants, fruit, seeds, and the like according to *several* classification schemes, ranging from the formal botanical ones to clashing and overlapping schemes spanning multiple state jurisdictions. So something as basic as a classification for "apple" ended up being a sub-classification in several classification schemes.

A variation on the recursive pattern that catered to many-to-many relationships is described by Silverston and Agnew[40]. This solved the classification problem and gave a

---

[40] (Silverston & Agnew, 2009: 222)

level of flexibility the client had wanted but wasn't sure could be delivered. Similarly, another client in the telecommunications industry wanted to classify their products with many-to-many classification schemes. The same pattern variation applied.

That's just one more pattern. The next chapter provides a framework for understanding model types, and is followed by a section that takes a number of real-life experiences and draws out tips and techniques that you may choose to selectively apply to your world.

Consolidating the chapter for you

SUMMARY:

- We can often refer to a common pattern simply by its name (e.g. the Party/Role pattern), but behind this simple facade are rich details with the potential to shape implementation.
- The baseline published patterns can be extended by bolting on additional detail for your situation. In this case, the core pattern remains largely unchanged, but just has some interesting new bits hanging off the side!
- Another common way to extend the baseline patterns is to flesh out their generic superclasses with your own specialized subclasses.
- The above two bullet points focus on tailoring *one* pattern to meet your needs. Yet another way you can apply generic patterns to your unique situation is to link a *set* of patterns in new ways.

APPLYING THIS TO YOUR SITUATION:

- Start by identifying a number of assembly patterns that at face value, have a good fit with your enterprise. Then lift the covers on each one and see what distinct aspects of your enterprise might necessitate refinement to the baseline patterns.

Different types of models

So we want to build some pattern-based models to assist our agile OO colleagues. Fine. But what sort of models should we deliver? Conceptual, logical, or physical models? Industry, enterprise, domain, or specific IT system models? Abstract or concrete models? Generalized or specialized models? Data models, object models, or class models?

Getting confused?

The first bit of good news is that, thankfully, I think there is a fairly simple way through this maze. I suggest that you might read this chapter to lessen the possibility of others misunderstanding what you should deliver, and to assist in presenting a reasoned position as to why you might take a certain approach.

The second bit of good news is this chapter is short and tries to avoid wandering into heavy academic debates.

CONCEPTUAL, LOGICAL, OR PHYSICAL?

OK, let's get one thing out of the way up front - you're not going to get a universally agreed upon definition as to what constitutes a conceptual, logical, or physical data model. Dave Hay[41] and Len Silverston and Paul Agnew[42] likewise note that there are divergent opinions as to the meaning of these terms, and offer pragmatic, useful ways of classifying models.

---

[41] (Hay, 2011-a: 40)

[42] (Silverston & Agnew, 2009: 13)

So, for the sake of taking a position, I am going to suggest the following:

- A <u>conceptual</u> model captures the ideas behind the way the business sees itself, expressed in terms the business can understand. Although there is debate (yet again) on the level of detail to be included (e.g. no attributes or just the major ones to help understanding of entities), I think all agree it doesn't and shouldn't get bogged down in endless detail.
- At the other end of the scale is a <u>physical</u> model that defines an IT system implementation, and reflects aspects of the chosen technology platform (Oracle, SQL Server, or whatever).
- In the middle is a <u>logical</u> model. It attempts to provide a bridge between the conceptual model world and the physical model world. It should reflect the concepts of the business *and* provide enough detail that it can influence and shape the physical implementation.

A subsequent chapter ("Chapter 10: Challenge the Concepts of the Enterprise") goes into a lot more detail on the interaction between logical and conceptual models. Suffice it to say that the main thrust of this book is to deliver logical models that faithfully represent the conceptual or "business" view, but just as importantly, add real value in the development of physical implementations.

SCOPE

There are <u>industry</u> models that offer consistency and facilitate data interchange amongst partners in a given industry, such as banking. A little less ambitious is the development of an <u>enterprise</u> model that represents your entire organization. Even more focused are models that portray the essence of a given <u>domain,</u> such as human resource management, contract management, or the records related to a laboratory. And then there are models whose stakeholders are little more than participants in one <u>IT system</u>. Dave Hay's book, *Enterprise Model Patterns*[43], describes these varying levels and provides worked examples of models.

All of these levels have a valid and valuable role to play, but it's not black and white. To take an example from the agile world we want to serve, an agile project may be charged with delivery of one IT system for a small number of sponsors. It would seem an IT application model might be sufficient. But let's assume a wider-reaching enterprise or industry model exists - maybe it can do two things. First, it may give the agile project a running start at articulation of their own model. And second, many "stand-alone"

---

[43] (Hay, 2011-a)

systems eventually need integration, and wider-scoped models may ease this path. So while one might expect this book would focus on a single-application model, I am, in fact, suggesting that an **enterprise** view that is well architected (and that in turn may reflect an industry model) is the ideal default starting point.

LEVELS

The world's population can be classified in many ways. You can produce statistics based on some measure of wealth, or by first language, by country of birth, and so on. In addition, some classification schemes that have the potential for wrongful discrimination (such as age and gender), may still be valid when organizing patients for placement in hospital care. Any or all may be valid and helpful in varying circumstances.

Model levels can also be classified according to different "level" dimensions. For example, in *Enterprise Model Patterns*[44], Dave Hay nominates 4 levels of abstraction, from the most abstract (level 0 for templates and metadata) through to level 3, for models aimed at specific industries.

Len Silverston and Paul Agnew also define 4 levels in *The Data Model Resource Book, Volume 3*[45], namely levels 1 to 4 (as compared to Dave's levels 0 to 3), but these reflect levels of specialization to generalization. They explicitly avoid classification according to how abstract or concrete a model might be.

Just as we noted above that we can classify people according to different classification schemes, it may be helpful to be familiar with alternative ways of classifying patterns, including the approaches of Hay, and Silverston and Agnew.

To cut to the chase, these dimensions help us think about where our models fit. Using Dave's classification scheme, the models that I suggest are helpful in an agile world may come from any of his levels, but perhaps more often from the enterprise component patterns (Level 1) and functional area components classified as Level 2. If you are lucky, maybe your organization aligns with one of his Level 3 industry patterns. Or if we use Len and Paul's scheme, I am suggesting the patterns we might find the most helpful for driving agile implementation are the generic ones at Level 3 or even 4.

---

[44] (Hay, 2011-a)

[45] (Silverston & Agnew, 2009:7-14)

If that's all too confusing, the summary is simple. For agile projects, where the requirements typically emerge over progressive iterations, I recommend we lean towards **generic** models that can adapt, rather than specific models targeted at today's understanding.

STYLE

We've already spoken about model notation, and very briefly introduced notation for the UML, but there's something even more fundamental than notation - that's the decision about *what* we are modeling. I suspect that many of the readers of this book are experienced data modelers, and could reasonably expect that the intent is to use patterns to model data for agile projects in a manner that is well-architected and fast. That is, it is assumed that we deliver <u>data models</u>, not <u>class models</u>, even if we use an object-oriented (OO) notation.

By the way, some people use the term class model and object model interchangeably. Within the UML, however, there is a difference between a class diagram and an object diagram. UML class diagrams are more closely aligned with the entity-relationship diagrams data modelers know and love. Object diagrams are a graphic way of presenting examples of instances. So for example, you might have a Customer class and a Product class in a class diagram, but in an object diagram, you might show "Acme Incorporated" as an example of one Customer buying a "Platinum Widget" as an example of one Product.

In many agile projects, the developers will be using an OO language. Further, they are likely to be using a multi-tier software architecture. They might have a database tier for storage of data related to their objects. Above that, they might have a business layer tier that is built on top of a class model. And of course, we might expect to find at least one more tier to handle the user interface.

If our job is to do nothing more than contribute to the database tier, then developing a data model for that tier is fine. If to do this you wish to use the UML notation, Dave Hay's book, *UML and Data Modeling: A Reconciliation* describes one approach in a lot of helpful detail.

However, if we are expected to design the class model for the middle tier, that's a different kettle of fish. It's a bit of a leap from developing data models to developing class models, but certainly not impossible. You will first need to understand the underlying principles of OO concepts, not just understand some aspects of the notation.

Dave Hay recognizes

> *"... the different thought processes that are behind the UML"*[46]

He openly and honestly shares that it requires some effort to accommodate these concepts. The last section of this book is intended to facilitate experienced data modelers to make the paradigm shift to OO thinking, and almost by accident, introduces some more UML notation along the way. In "Chapter 17: Object-orientation - A Data Modeler's Primer", I provide an alternative way to move between class and data modeling, based on personal experience.

So for this book, what position are we taking? You might be surprised, given my statement that we want to deliver class models to agile projects, but apart from using UML notation, the bulk of this book talks about **data models**, not class models. For the purposes of understanding how patterns can help, and how to interact with our agile colleagues, I have chosen to avoid mixing these messages up with class modeling. But at the end of the book, I do give you the option of making the shift if it suits your purposes.

The way forward

CLEM

In a moment of inspiration (or madness – you can decide), I thought of a new acronym to describe the style of model we are aiming at. It's a CLEM model!

It's <u>Canonical</u>. In this part of the book, I have been trying to sort out terms like conceptual, logical, or physical, and data or class models. And now, here I go and introduce another term that is open to misunderstanding! Sorry. But I will simply use the term to mean we want our model to be the central, standard, recognized model upon which we base other models in our enterprise.

So, for example, if the agile developers want a class model for their business layer, and the data people want a physical data model for their database, if they both base their view on the one sanctioned "canonical" model, we might get less of an "impedance mismatch" between the two. For a much more detailed look at this topic, you may want to refer to *Building the Agile Database* by Larry Burns[47].

---

[46] (Hay, 2011-b: 7)

[47] (Burns, 2011)

Canonical models are well known for their ability to assist in the mapping of data from one form to another. So if the model we produce to support the agile project is well architected, it should also help in the specification of interfaces, e.g. XML message payloads for service oriented architecture (SOA) infrastructure.

So to put it simply, the model we want to produce should be a reference model for multiple purposes.

It's <u>L</u>ogical. To achieve the goal of delivering a "canonical" model, it must have more detail than a conceptual model, and it must be platform independent, unlike a physical schema for specific platforms. A logical model fits the bill.

And to meet the "agile" requirements of speed and quality of delivery, we should be able to assemble this model from the patterns of logical components published in a variety of sources.

It's an <u>E</u>nterprise model. Not because the agile project has that scope, but because we are using proven patterns that are generic in nature and should be better able to integrate with other initiatives within the enterprise.

And of course it's a <u>**M**</u>odel. I have deliberately not called it a data model or a class model – it's just a "model". Hopefully, the subtle implications of this decision will become clearer after you've completed the section on building a bridge to the land of object orientation (Chapter 17: Object-orientation - A Data Modeler's Primer)! The key point in avoiding calling it a data model is that, as a canonical model with multiple possible uses, we might actually need it to be a class model. Nonetheless, for now we can focus on the data aspects of the model and leave this debate to a little later.

You may be relieved to know that I'm not going to keep on referring to producing a CLEM model. It probably succinctly summarizes what we want, but to keep things a bit more comfortable, I will simply talk about how we can quickly and confidently produce a logical data model. I do want to assume we are aiming at it reflecting enterprise concepts, and I do want to keep the options open for class modeling, but that comes later. For now, let's have fun seeing how best to produce a quality (logical) data model.

Consolidating the chapter for you

SUMMARY:

- One way of classifying models is to label them as conceptual, logical, or physical. Definitions vary, but within this book, we are striving to use patterns to develop *logical* models that (1) are somewhat faithful reflections of business concepts, and (2) provide guidance for physical implementation.
- Even if a model is targeted at a specific, small part of the business, there may be merit in it reflecting wider enterprise views.
- It can be challenging to achieve a balance between specific models highly tuned for a given requirement versus generic models that are flexible and possibly better able to adapt to yet unknown requirements. One way to respond is to apply proven, flexible patterns to your specific needs!
- The Unified Modeling Language (UML) is, when all is said and done, a notation. It has strengths and weaknesses, but it is gaining momentum and *can* be applied to capture the essence of data models, at least at the logical level we are focusing on here.
- Although much of the rest of the book will talk of producing a data model, we want to keep the option open to produce a class model.

APPLYING THIS TO YOUR SITUATION:

- Do you have mission-critical software (in-house developed and commercial packages) that does not have a readily available logical data model? (<u>Note</u>: I can understand commercial package providers being reluctant to share their data model, but with appropriate safeguards for their intellectual property, it can often be obtained, especially if it is made a requirement as part of the package evaluation phase. What I have more problems with are the software vendors who cannot provide a logical model of their package because they do not have one! Maybe that's a discussion for another day.)

If you have access to a number of the published patterns, you've got a kit bag of some of the basic tools for producing agile data architectures. The previous section took us a little further by providing some perspective on the *types* of patterns that are available and how to *vary* them for specific needs. That gives you some skills in selecting, or adapting, the right tool for the job.

Let's now have a look at some of the ways we can use, and build on, these "pattern" tools in real-world situations to achieve the data agility others want from us, while retaining the high standards of data architecture we are so passionate about.

CHAPTER 5
Test the Levels of Generalization

A little bit more on generalization

In the earlier section, "Variation via inheritance", we introduced some of the basics of generalization/specialization via the inheritance mechanism. Or if you prefer, this can be seen as OO lingo for good old data modeling supertypes and subtypes.

Something we didn't cover was (UML) generalization sets, or in data modeling terms, partitioning of the supertype into overlapping sets of subtypes. An example might help.

Let's say that a national health scheme wants to divide people into males and females for certain medical reasons. (In spite of the proposition of males carrying a baby to full term, as portrayed by Arnold Schwarzenegger in a film titled "*Junior*", I think we're some way off from that, let alone seeing it as common. So there still are some aspects of medicine that are genuinely gender-specific.) And let's also assume that the national health scheme also needs to differentiate between its own citizens, and those that are visiting the country. A possible model follows.

Note that one set of generalizations has a discriminator label of "gender", and the other set is labeled "nationality". In this model, any one individual can be a male or a female, _and_ also can be a citizen or a non-citizen of that country – the two sets are overlapping.

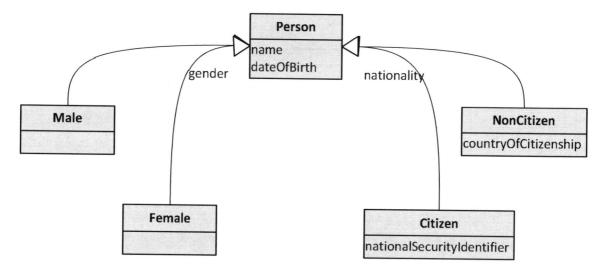

Figure 19: Generalization sets

Another observation is that the diagram demonstrates no different attributes or associations for the Male and Female classes. This might be because it is an incomplete model and these details have not been exposed in this diagram. Or maybe it is because there really are no differences that the enterprise considers as important to be noted. If the latter is the case, an alternative model might be to define a "gender" attribute in the Person class.

More could be said on the topic of generalization/specialization. Some possible sources, if you're interested, include detailed coverage in Simsion and Witt's *Data Modeling Essentials*[48], and a more summarized perspective appears in Martin Fowler's *UML Distilled*[49].

Whetting your appetite

Generalization can deliver quite amazing results. I remember clearly the risk I took with one project. A major restructuring of the entire wool industry in Australia was proposed, and an IT solution to support it was mandated. Before my involvement, the delivery date was set for the 30th of June, the end of the financial year. I suspect that the date was shaped more by optimism than realism. It just seemed too neat a date to have come from a project manager's detailed plan!

---

[48] (Simsion & Witt, 2005: 111-143)

[49] (Fowler, 2003: 45-46, 75-78)

The first I even knew about the project was when it was a bit over 8 months to the target completion date, and the IT manager sensed trouble brewing. Don't you hate it when you get called in to sort out a looming train wreck? The manager was a good friend, so in a moment of weakness, I agreed to help.

I had a quick look at the intended data architecture. It had something like 600 entities, most of which were highly specialized. You may have heard the statement that a camel is a horse designed by a committee? Well, what I found was a data model that had several groups working on different domains. The consolidation that had been performed prior to my arrival was largely an exercise in putting the domains side-by-side and calling it the enterprise model. Unfortunately, each domain overlapped with the other domains, and there was a sad shortage of overarching patterns.

The organization was about to engage a team of developers, but the manager wanted a review of the data model first. That's where I came in. I swallowed hard, and made a tough call. I shared my opinion that there was no way the solution as designed could be developed in the remaining 8 months. Instead, I suggested that half of the remaining development time be set aside to get the architecture sorted out, and in the remaining 4 months, we would assemble a small team of top-ranking developers to deliver in 4 months what I believed a larger team could not deliver in 8 months.

Pretty courageous? Maybe. Pretty stupid? Definitely. But we did deliver it, and on time, with a tiny team of three developers plus myself! At the heart of the success, though, was a generalized model. It was cut down from the original 600 entities to 120 entities, and that included all of the reference tables, system control tables, etc. That's an 80% reduction in tables. The model was more abstract and the coders required a higher skill level, but with fewer tables, the total coding effort was significantly reduced.

That does raise an issue, though. The proponents of agile approaches quite understandably note that "agile" works better when the team has a high skill level. Boehm and Turner go so far as to say that while a team can carry a few novices, it needs a core team of more experienced people.[50] But my view of this particular project was that we achieved what we did by not only having good people, but by first taking the time to generalize the underlying data architecture.

Another story I wish to tell follows; I wish I could take the credit for it. A visionary public servant who had exceptional passion and creativity and was willing to move mountains shared it with me. (By the way, don't believe the stereotypes some may

---

[50] (Boehm & Turner, 2009: 48, 54, 55)

present for public servants as little cogs in a big machine who aren't willing to rattle the cage. I have been privileged to work with some really inspiring government employees.) Unfortunately, the vision my friend had originally articulated got somewhat diluted by less far-sighted developers. The system reached a point of 1,300 screens for the core data entry. A new change request that was going to be too big and too hard to accommodate hit the team. Thankfully, vision won out. The solution was reengineered based on generic data patterns, and the subsequent replacement system now required 6 screens to do the work of 1,300. And the cost of the *total* rebuild based on generalized entities was less than the estimated cost of the *one* requested extension.

Too much of a good thing?

Where does generalization stop? Dave Hay ends his earlier book on data modeling patterns with an entertaining model of "Thing"[51], plus half a dozen more entities to handle the thing's attributes, relationships, and so on. Such a model is provocative. It challenges us to question when we've gone too far with generalization. Let's look at an example with some real-life stories.

Many organizations keep track of their company's fleet of vehicles. The model for the fleet management system might include classes as displayed below, where the Vehicle is the superclass, and Car and Truck are subclasses that specialize the generic Vehicle class.

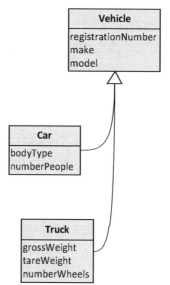

Figure 20: Sample low-level generalization #1

---

[51] (Hay, 1996: 254-256)

The same company might also have a register of sundry plant and equipment. That might be accomplished with a data model something like the following.

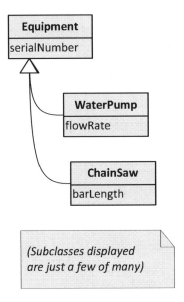

Figure 21: Sample low-level generalization #2

These two samples have used generalization to an extent. Maybe we can push the generalization to a higher level. Perhaps the accountants wish to see vehicles *and* plant and equipment all as depreciable assets.

The wildfire response system I worked on had hundreds of different types of resources that had to be managed, from trivial items such as rake hoes, to expensive "multiple personality" radios, to aircraft worth millions. To them, vehicles and equipment were all just resources. Many of the aspects of these vastly divergent resources had common requirements for management. A small slice of one model that might have been considered follows.

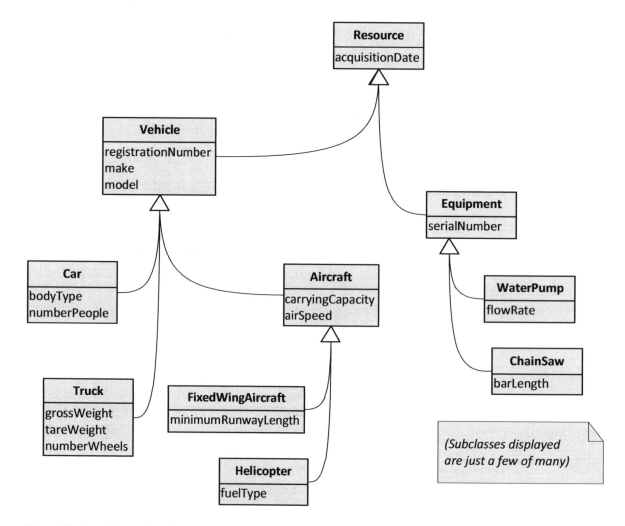

Figure 22: Sample medium-level generalization

This model was getting closer to the requirements for consistent management of resources, but the question was asked, "Are human resources, and the organizations that supply them, just resources, too?" Within this context, the answer was, "Yes". The emergent model follows.

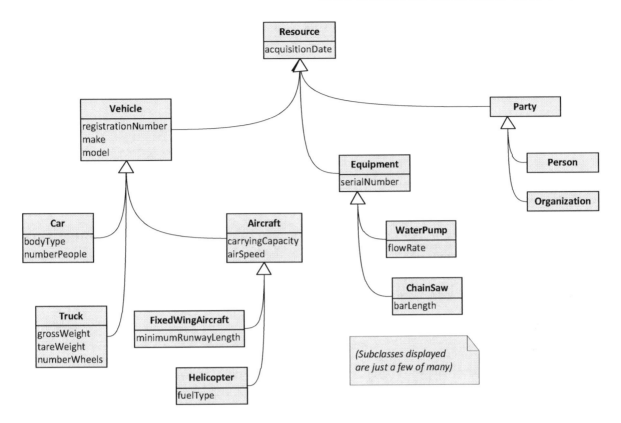

Figure 23: Sample high-level generalization

Many organizations might see human resources and physical plant and equipment as starkly different, and resist subclassing them under a generic resource class. However, the emergency services response organization felt justified in treating them all as resources that could be assigned to incidents such as the outbreak of a wildfire or spillage of toxic chemicals.

This level of generalization may be uncomfortable for you and your organization, but it is shared to demonstrate how we can, in some cases, gain benefits by looking for ever higher levels of generalization. Now we head in the opposite direction, seeing if we can abandon some superclasses and just have their specialized subclasses as base classes in their own right.

The TM Forum is a consortium that originally had a focus on the telecommunications industry, but has expanded to provide more generic IT frameworks. Their information framework defines the core components of an information architecture. Given the telecommunications origins, it is not surprising to find "Product" as a central class. One model they *could* have proposed to the community might have looked something like the following, where every product is either a physical, tangible object (like a mobile phone handset or a spare battery), or an intangible service (like the ability to connect to the Internet or to make an international phone call).

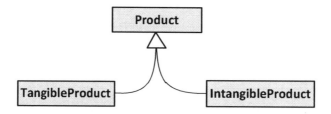

Figure 24: Specialization by inheritance

Inheritance (i.e., superclasses and their subclasses) is a very common way of handling generalization and specialization of similar but different classes. Another way to achieve results that are somewhat comparable is to link the classes by associations. The TM Forum model for handling tangible and intangible products is something like the following.

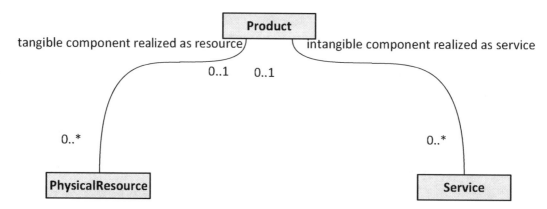

Figure 25: Specialization by association

If we treat Tangible Product and Physical Resource as synonyms, and do likewise for Intangible Product and Service, we still have fundamentally different models. No longer are the tangible products/physical resources a subclass of product; they are a separate class in their own right. According to the inheritance model, one instance of a product can be either one tangible product, *or* it can be one intangible product. Using my adaptation of TM Forum's "Frameworx" information model, one product can be "realized" by zero, one or more tangible physical resources and/or zero, one or more intangible services. For example, one telecommunications product might be "realized" as a mobile handset plus a spare battery (both physical resources), as well as the intangible services that allow the customer to make calls, retrieve voice messages, send SMS messages, and so on.

The TM Forum's model is rich and extensive. I recommend you take a look at it, especially if you are in the telecommunications industry. It is a framework, and as with any collaborative effort, some bits are elaborated in greater detail than others. Nonetheless, it is worth a look if you have the opportunity. However, the real reason I introduce it is to provide a sample of how what could have been modeled via inheritance was modeled with the "subclasses" as first class citizens, abandoning the idea of a superclass (in this case, Product).

Trying to get the balance right

A very specialized model is better able to represent tight business rules at the data level. It may be more readable for a non-technical audience – for example, you can easily find the "Customer" class, rather than having to understand the Party/Role construct. Moreover, it may have better response time performance. Perhaps.

On the other hand, a highly generalized model may be more stable and require less change over time. While its adaptability (a good thing) means it is less able to represent business rules by its primary data structure, its abstractions may actually facilitate implementation of business rules in a data-driven construct. And while a business user may be less comfortable when they first encounter it, the technical people who have to implement the solution may already be very comfortable with well-known patterns. They may actually find it easier to read.

Getting the balance right can be challenging. Some of the considerations were briefly introduced above. For a much more in-depth consideration, I highly recommend Len Silverston and Paul Agnew's *The Data Model Resource Book Volume 3*. The entire book grapples with worked examples of alternative models at different levels of specialization versus generalization, with a concise summary of relative merits also provided[52].

In the context of this chapter, we look at opportunities to use inheritance. A well-chosen superclass can provide a central place to assign responsibilities that are common to many other classes. In a complementary fashion, the identification of subclasses can be a means of corralling those things that are special and unique to a subset of the domain. However, the take-away lesson is that whenever you draft a model with a first-cut level of generalization, it may be worthwhile deliberately challenging that level. On the one hand, try looking for opportunities to make the model even more generic. Search for superclasses that can represent otherwise unrelated classes. And when you've done

---

[52] (Silverston & Agnew, 2009: 10)

that, do it again, seeing if you can find even higher levels of generalization. And then, very seriously challenge each step to see if you've gone so far that the gains of generalization are delivering diminishing returns, but the losses of specialization are mounting up.

On the other hand, try looking for opportunities to throw away generalizations that are not delivering value. Take the model with its first-cut levels of generalization and see if you may benefit from deliberately abandoning some of the superclasses, ending up with a model that works better for you.

Graeme Simsion, in his book *Data Modeling Theory and Practice*[53], convincingly argues that there is no one "right" model. There can be several workable models, each with relative merits. I encourage you to test the levels in your model and see if the standard patterns can be either combined into higher levels of generalization (as happened with the emergency services response model), or conversely take a standard pattern's subclasses and see if they can be beneficially divorced from their superclass.

Consolidating the chapter for you

SUMMARY:

- A handy mechanism when defining inheritance hierarchies is the ability to label separate concurrent hierarchies (known by some as generalization sets).
- A concise, elegant model that uses generalized patterns may require a higher skill level for developers, but has the potential to reduce development and maintenance costs.
- Generalization is a balancing act. If you go so far as to end up with the "Thing / Thing Type / Thing Characteristic" model, you've probably gone way too far. And if you've gone the other way to the point where you have a multitude of specific, denormalized classes with little or no generalization, it might work for communication with the business, but it is unlikely to be effective for implementation.

APPLYING THIS TO YOUR SITUATION:

- Take a look at some of the data models in your company and consider how they might be improved (or otherwise) if some of the specific classes were generalized. Conversely, consider the merits of abandoning some generalized classes and only retaining the subclasses, as specific, independent classes.

---

[53] (Simsion, 2007: 8-9)

Albert Einstein:

> *"We can't solve problems by using the same kind of thinking we used when we created them."*

Thinking outside the box

You have probably encountered phrases such as "thinking outside the box" (or thinking outside the square). To some, this is but one of many annoying and over-used terms. But the background is a bit more interesting, so just in case you haven't seen the puzzle upon which the phrase is based, it goes something like this:

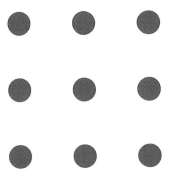

Figure 26: Thinking outside the box – the problem

> *"The aim is to link all nine dots using four straight lines or fewer, without lifting the pencil and without going over the same line another time."*

There may be a number of ways of solving this puzzle, but the solution implied when consultants use the phrase "thinking outside the box" is more like the one presented below:

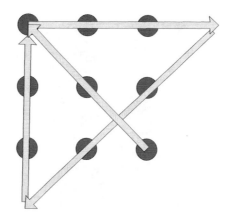

Figure 27: Thinking outside the box – a solution

We can so easily assume that we must keep the lines within the *imagined* border around the 9 dots in this puzzle that we miss this solution. In a similar manner, Edward de Bono's many contributions challenge us to think beyond the boundaries of "conventional" wisdom.

Back to the topic at hand. We have a library of patterns available to us, but it's not uncommon to struggle to find one that is a good fit. Sure, we can build some new ones. But maybe if we think creatively, we will be able to adapt an existing pattern to our needs.

I remember one consultant who did just this. He was a senior member of the consultancy and commanded a good hourly rate. When he presented a simple, elegant solution, the client reacted by saying, "We paid you good money, and all you've done is deliver something really obvious." To which he replied with a smile and a touch of dry humor, "Yes, it appears it was obvious to me, but not to you." Ouch!

Let me share a concrete example of an "obvious" solution. A client of mine had been put in a corner by some legislation. The client was a government body, and the legislation said they must ensure that no individual was deemed to be in control of too many media organizations (TV stations, radio stations, etc.).

The act of parliament defined what was meant by "control". It included being on the board. It also included rules relating to share holdings. In a simple case, a person with direct personal shareholding of 20% of a radio station would be deemed, by this legislation, to have a controlling interest. Or, if they were a director of a company that *in turn* had a 20% shareholding in the media outlet, they were in "control". Or if they were in control of a company that had (say) a 15% shareholding, and also were in control of a totally separate company that had (say) another 5% shareholding, by adding them together they were in control. Maybe this company (controlled by adding 15% plus 5%) might not have been a media company, but it might have had a 20% shareholding in one – they were again deemed to be in control. You get the picture!

This government department had access to all the data it needed on directorships, shareholdings, etc., but it was perplexed as to how to store the data and apply the rules. We could have designed a custom data model from first principles. We might have defined entities for Company, Director, Shareholder, and so on. Alternatively, we could have looked for an existing pattern that seemed to be a close fit, and tried to adapt it - which is what we did. We started with a bill-of-material pattern similar to that described by Dave Hay[54] and Len Silverston[55]. Companies can be seen to be made of shareholders, just as cars are made of assembly components. We thought there might be some commonality.

The traditional bill-of-material pattern can be used to reflect a data model for a manufacturing company. Perhaps they make cars. They may have raw materials such as nuts and bolts, gears, washers, metal and plastic door handles, and the like. They can put these raw materials together to construct assemblies such as gear boxes and differentials. And of course, they can put the assemblies together to make finished products, in this case, cars.

A somewhat crude simplification of the patterns, using fairly specific classes, might look something like the model on the following page.

---

[54] (Hay, 1996: 57)

[55] (Silverston, 2001-a: 101)

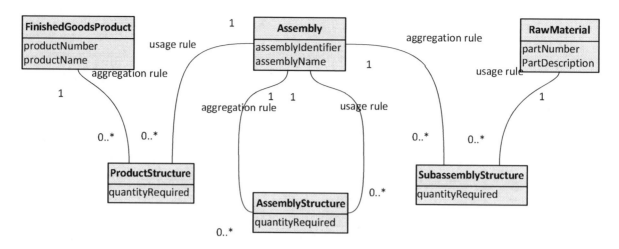

Figure 28: Simplified bill-of-materials pattern

To understand the model, let's take the manufacture of several types of a car as an example. The Finished Goods Products (those ready for sale) might include the standard sedan, the family wagon, and the sports sedan version. Assemblies (things ready to put in place as components of the finished goods) might include the 6-cylinder engine, the 8-cyclinder engine, the 6-speed manual gearbox, the 5-speed automatic gearbox, and so on. The Raw Material types might include all sorts of nuts and bolts, panels, gaskets, etc.

An instance in the Product Structure class defines how many of what type of Assembly item is required in a particular version of a Finished Goods Product. So for example, one 6-cyclinder engine might go into the standard sedan, whereas one 8-cyclinder engine might be required for the sports sedan. And five magnesium alloy wheel sets (one spare) might also be required for the sports sedan.

Similarly, the Assembly Structure class defines how many of what type of sub-Assembly goes into another Assembly – the pistons, carburetor, block, etc. that go into the engine, and the (sub-)Assembly bits that go into the carburetor. Eventually, we get to the Subassembly Structure defining what Raw Materials are required to go into the (sub-)Assembly items.

Len Silverston and Paul Agnew[56] make the point that we can have more generic patterns to support the same business need. A higher-level pattern might look something like:

---

[56] (Silverston & Agnew, 2009: 7-14)

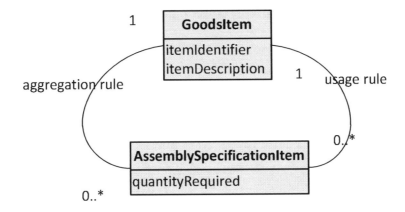

Figure 29: Generalized bill-of-materials pattern

In this more generalized pattern, Goods Item represents the Finished Goods Products, the Assembly items, and the Raw Material items from the previous model. Similarly, the Assembly Specification Item is the generalized class to represent Product Structures, Assembly Structures, and Subassembly Structures.

So how does this relate to the data model for managing the control of media companies by people in the community? Just like cars are "goods items" made up of smaller goods items (that are made up of even smaller ones, …), we could view companies as being "made up of" shareholders that sometimes are themselves companies made up of shareholders, until we eventually reach individuals.

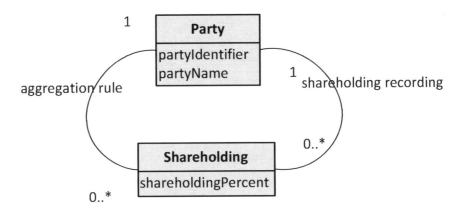

Figure 30: Adapted bill-of-materials pattern

For example, let's say that Acme Limited has the following shareholders:

- Excelsior Incorporated as a 60% shareholder.
- Mr. and Mrs. Smith, each as 20% shareholders.

In turn, maybe Excelsior Incorporated has the following shareholders:

- The same Mrs. Smith, this time as a 50% shareholder.
- Mr. Green as a 25% shareholder.
- Acme Limited as the remaining 25% shareholder. Yes, one shareholder in Excelsior is a company that is part-owned by Excelsior!

The real world of corporate ownership is quite complex. But the key message is that by taking a proven bill-of-materials pattern that works well in the manufacturing industry, we can adapt it to the world of company shareholdings. A delightfully simple solution to what might have been seen as a difficult problem. (Well, there actually was a bit more to it. The programmers among you might see the challenge in self-referencing loops of ownership, often nested several levels apart. Unfortunately, in this case I was the programmer as well as the data modeler - I had to take my own medicine! But the model, as presented, was the core of the delivered solution.)

A multi-faceted challenge

In the previous case study, one pattern was adapted to suit the needs of one problem domain. We now look at a problem domain that required the adaptation of several interdependent patterns.

The client was another government department. In this case, they were charged with the responsibility of managing the state's mineral and petroleum resources. In my corner of the world, the government owns the gold, silver, oil, gas, and the like, even if these assets are on or under *your* land. The government grants permits to mining companies, who pay levies into the common purse (and compensate you for the impact on your land).

To encourage companies to invest in mines, the agency responsible sought to make available as much information as possible on what resources exist and where. One challenge was the vast diversity of the information. For example:

- Sea bed soundings are created when a boat pulls a large matrix of devices floating on the sea surface, each one emitting loud sounds whose echoes are measured. Vast amounts of data are generated and stored in purpose-built computer records.
- Rock core samples are taken during explorative drilling. The 3-dimensional position of the core sample is recorded, along with information about the sample. I guess if the sample was pure gold, there would be quite a bit of excitement. The

sample results I saw were, to me, boring and meaningless. But I am told the information is actually of great worth.

Dave Hay has patterns for storing laboratory results[57]. Martin Fowler has similar patterns[58], but with an emphasis on medical test results. While this client did have some laboratory records (for example, chemical analysis of core samples), many of the result types were arguably beyond the intended scope of the published patterns. Nonetheless, with a bit of gentle reshaping, the laboratory patterns proved to be more than capable of adapting to fit the requirements. And as a good friend of mine often says, when gentle reshaping doesn't work, just get a bigger hammer!

The need for pattern adaptation didn't stop at the laboratory pattern. We needed to record locations. Many patterns reflect a two-dimensional view of the world's surface, and can't cope with altitude or depth. Also, many don't care about recording the time dimension (i.e., recording locations and their historic changes). For this client, locations had to not only record the three spatial dimensions (latitude, longitude, and elevation), but also the "fourth dimension" of time. For example, an open-cut mine and its contents change over time, and the reserves of oil and gas in the sea-bed also change over time as adjacent wells draw down on the reserves. In this case, we didn't actually need to adapt a pattern beyond its intended use – all we had to do was to put aside the simpler location patterns and locate one that suited our requirements.

Finally, there are patterns for records and document management. They work well for paper and electronic records, but this client's records included physical "records" such as actual samples of rock, minerals, and soil. We generalized the "document" pattern and called it "storable object". That arguably wasn't the most creative or best name, but sometimes finding a good name for an abstract concept can be contentious. The good news was that the document management pattern proved to be easily extensible to meet our broader scope of requirements.

The conclusion? The laboratory pattern and the document management pattern were quite easily stretched to accommodate the needs of analysis and storage (respectively) of field samples, and a more sophisticated location pattern than is commonly needed was easily added to the mix.

---

[57] (Hay, 1996: 157-172)

[58] (Fowler, 1997: 35-55)

Some suggestions

Adaptation of proven patterns can most certainly be an effective and efficient way to identify solutions for new domains. However, a couple of cautionary suggestions follow.

CHECK FOR OVERWEIGHT BAGGAGE

First, sometimes the uptake of a pattern from one domain and deployment in an unintended domain can result in some unwanted functionality from the pattern's home-ground being carried across and cluttering the solution in the new domain.

In the example of applying the manufacturing's bill-of-material pattern to a share registry domain, one bit had to be cut out. In traditional manufacturing, you cannot have assembly recursion. For example, you can have a washer being a part in a distributor. The distributor, in turn, can be part of the overall fuel management system. However, it doesn't make sense for the fuel management system to be a component of creating a washer.

Conversely, in the share registry system, it is quite common for ownership recursion. For example, company A might own shares in company B, who in turn owns shares in company C, and then we discover that company C owns shares in company A. The constraints that *prevented* bill-of-material recursion had to be stripped out of the standard bill-of-material solution and replaced with mechanisms to *detect* recursion and prevent it from going into an infinite loop when determining diluted ownership.

When you apply one pattern to another domain, you may be well served by challenging the baggage the pattern carries and seeing if some can be left behind. The story goes that the United States' standard railway gauge of 4 feet 8 inches was chosen because that was the gap between the railway tracks used by the English who shaped parts of early America. Why did the English use that standard for their railways? Because the tools used for making horse-drawn carriages were the same tools used for locomotive-drawn train carriages. Fine, but why have a standard at all for horse-drawn carriages? Because the old roads had deep ruts, and everyone had to use the same wheel gap. OK, but why *that* specific size? Because that was the standard of the conquering Romans. Now we're getting closer – the Roman chariots were made as narrow as possible while still accommodating a fat horse's rear end.

So the story line goes that the railway gauge standard used in the United States is based on the width of an overweight horse's backside. Standards are good, but they do need to be challenged from time to time.

TO A MAN WITH A HAMMER, ...

The second suggestion relates to being overly enthusiastic about your favorite pattern. There is a quotation that states:

"To a man with a hammer, everything looks like a nail". [59]

Even if you have a screw you want to put into a piece of wood, hit it hard enough with a hammer and you may have some success. Similarly, when we find a pattern that comfortably fits in a number of scenarios, it is tempting to see if we can force it to fit in places it doesn't really belong. I encountered a consultant who was a key player in developing a generic model for tasks, or "work". It had great potential to be usefully applied, for example, to the management of the out-of-office field workforce who built infrastructure for the company, and who also assisted customers at their premises. That was a good fit for the "work" model, but he went further.

He quite rightly argued that the installation of a product for a customer involved "work". For example, installing a specific music player in a specific car takes work. That's true, and the consultant wanted to enforce the recording of who did the installation and how long they took. He had found a place for his "work" model to be used.

The problem was that all the business wanted to know was what serial number player was installed in what vehicle. The proposed data model mandated the capture of the work involved and would not allow product instances to be recorded unless the work that created them was first entered and stored. This might have been fine in some cases, but not all. For one thing, the company had many records of installed products with no record of the work involved in delivery and installation.

Even more fundamentally, the company didn't want to be forced to always record "work". This consultant argued that even the sale of a consumable from a company outlet involved work, even if it was the effort involved in picking the product off the shelf and ringing up the sale on the cash register. There was no way the company would ever agree to demanding that such "work" must be captured, but he fought hard and long to keep his beloved "work" pattern applied even where it didn't fit.

We all need to be resourceful in seeking ways proven patterns can be creatively applied to new domains, but we also need to be careful our enthusiasm doesn't color our judgment.

---

[59] Variously attributed to Abraham Maslow and Mark Twain

Consolidating the chapter for you

SUMMARY:

- When you encounter a problem with no obvious matching pattern, you may find a pattern intended for a different purpose that can be applied.
- Be aware that you may have to refine the pattern to make it fit.
- If you have to try too hard to force it to fit, maybe it doesn't!

APPLYING THIS TO YOUR SITUATION:

- Consider some of the areas where you may have developed custom models because you couldn't find appropriate patterns. Revisit these model fragments and see if adaptation of models intended for other purposes may be beneficial.

There is often tension between the short-term tactical and the longer-term strategic perspectives.

I once worked in a country area that hosted several open-cut coal mines. They used the coal to generate electricity, so the coal companies held the view that they might as well use their own power (at cost-price) to drive their coal-face dredges. That seems pretty sensible, when compared to buying another type of fuel and transporting it huge distances.

There was one problem, though. They drew the power for their equipment from the same grid used to supply the general population. When big machinery started up, you would get a brown-out for a few seconds. Even worse, when it shut down, enormous power surges hit the grid. We measured a voltage spike of something like 1,500 volts for 3/50 of a second. (We did have a lightning storm that night, so I suspect we can't blame the coal companies for that enormous spike!). That might not sound like a long time, but it was more than enough to blow the brains out of our computers.

The *strategic* solution may have been to ask the coal mines to invest in separate power grids for their equipment. Even if we thought that they would jump at the idea of spending millions duplicating power lines just to make us happy, we needed a *tactical* solution, and we needed it now.

I am sure that surge protectors have come a long way in the last three decades, but back then, the equipment we tested just wasn't up to the task of handling 1,500 volt spikes... and believe me, we tried several makes and models. Then along came a local bush carpenter[60], Jack, who solved our dilemma.

Let me paint a picture of Jack. He was a likeable country lad who would fearlessly turn his hand to anything. Maybe he didn't have formal trade skills, but that never slowed him from trying his best to please. For example, one office had a whiteboard that was too big, and another had none. Jack lifted the whiteboard off the hooks holding it at each end, and took it outside to halve it. I still remember looking out the window as he first cut from the top as far as he could reach, then from the bottom. It was a pity the two cuts didn't line up. Out with his trusty hammer ("To a man with a hammer, ..."), and one blow smashed the middle of the whiteboard between the two cuts. He returned with one half and hung the end with a hook on the wall. The other hook now belonged to the other half. There's no problem too hard to a man with a hammer. A three-inch roofing nail pounded through the whiteboard and into the wall, and the job was done.

So perhaps you can understand my hesitation when he volunteered to fix our computer power problem. A few hours later, he came back from his farm workshop and proudly assembled his solution. To his credit, it was beautiful in its simplicity. He had welded a frame to house his creation, with a piece of rusty old corrugated iron as weather protection. Under the iron were:

- An enormous electric motor to be run off the low-quality grid. It was a big, old beast that was bullet proof. No power surge would upset it.
- A fly-wheel that probably weighed more than me, driven by the big old motor.
- An oversized electric generator. The flywheel would drive the generator that would produce our power.

As Jack explained, a spike wouldn't harm the motor, and a brown out wouldn't have any noticeable effect on this huge steel fly-wheel. Out of the other end came enough power to run several arc welders, let alone one small computer. Job done. Terribly inefficient, but timely and pragmatic, especially as the solution only needed to be in place for several months.

In the architecture world, we are often expected to be guided by long-term IT strategies. Then we look over the fence to see what's happening in the agile camp, and it looks like they are deliberately scaling back deliverables to just what is needed now.

---

[60] A person whose skill is in improvisation rather than any particular formal trade skill

Who's right?

The YAGNI view

DIFFERING OPINIONS

Within the agile community, there is a phrase whose acronym is YAGNI – "You Ain't Gonna Need It". The principle is to implement things when you *actually* need them, not just because you foresee that you *might* need them. There are some solid arguments for taking this stance. For example:

- Delivery of something that is not needed may consume time that *could* be used to deliver something that *is* needed, now.
- The code is tighter and easier to maintain if it is not bloated with features that may be required later (or, in fact, may never be required).
- By the time a future feature is actually needed, its specifications may have changed and any work done now might have to be redone.

Just as there are strong arguments for YAGNI, there are arguments against it.

- Where known future requirements mandate certain architectures, to ignore them now may result in what Boehm and Turner call "architecture breakers"; i.e., where simple design decisions now can avoid architectures whose postponed inclusion are "beyond the ability of refactoring to handle"[61].
- Compliance with standards may mandate inclusion of features not immediately required.

A blog I inspected[62] from the XP (eXtreme Programming) community had many views put forward by experienced developers, and the views held were largely in favor of the YAGNI approach. They also typically agreed that unthinking application of YAGNI, particularly where it was never intended to be applied, had dangers. Some issues that were raised reflected a good deal of humor. With a little artistic license on my part to reword their comments, some of the challenges to the application of YAGNI are listed below.

- There is a difference between "you ain't gonna need it ever" versus "you don't need it yet". An example given is leap year computation. Maybe it's another two

---

[61] (Boehm & Turner, 2009: 40)

[62] http://c2.com/xp/YouArentGonnaNeedIt.html

years to the next Leap year, but you know it's coming, and you know how to program for it, so do it now.

- When packing for a car trip, it's easy to clutter the boot[63] with lots of things you aren't going to need. "Travel light" is a good motto, but in Australia, if you are heading to the outback[64], people have died because they haven't taken some things they *hoped* they would never need. The list of suggested items for outback travel is quite daunting. So there's a difference between "you ain't gonna need it" versus "you probably won't need it but we recommend you take it anyway, 'cause if you find you do need it, you're in real trouble". In IT terms, you hopefully don't need a backup-and-restore mechanism right now, but it's better not to wait until you really need it to start developing it.

One comment suggests a difference between upfront *architecture* that is well positioned to accommodate reasonable future expectations (recommended) as compared to upfront development of *code* that may not be needed yet, but that has a place in the architecture for when/if it is required. Even with architectures, though, there is the danger of over-engineering for what may never eventuate. So how do we achieve balance? Perhaps a few stories might give some insight.

A LIGHT-HEARTED REQUEST FOR OVER-ENGINEERING

The ideas behind YAGNI typically present a picture of overzealous developers who want to give users more than they need, or even want. One amusing story turns this around the other way – a user who wanted much more than proposed. I was responsible for the data architecture behind a system to facilitate online auctioning for the sale of livestock a quarter of a century ago – long before Internet auctioning.

One of the goals was to try and make the system available to all, whether in remote parts of Australia, or at a sale yard where bidders were also competing for the purchase of livestock in the traditional manner. To support the latter group, auction rooms were created where registered bidders could participate by pressing buttons something like those used in hospitals for patients who wish to call for a nurse.

---

[63] In Australia, the compartment at the back of a car is called a boot, and sometimes what we put in the boot is a trunk (a suitcase). I am told that for others, the compartment is called a trunk, and they may put a boot (shoe) in it. Ah, the wonders of the so-called "English" language!

[64] The "outback" is an Aussie term for the remote, hot and dry parts of Australia (arguably most of the country!) that are "out the back of beyond". Similar phrases include "out the back of Bourke", referring to a town that is itself quite remote, hot and dry, being serviced by camels a century ago.

After one bidder accidentally dropped his bid-button nose-first onto the floor, and unintentionally ended up winning the bid, an alternative bid mechanism was required. The country lad informed me that most participants were pretty good shots with a rifle – so could the bid buttons please be replaced with electronic rifles as seen in country fairs? Surely we could provide TV screens which displayed the livestock available for sale, and bidders could "shoot" at the ones you wanted to buy?

Thankfully, he was only having a bit of a good-humored go at me, but I did admire his creativity. Maybe you've encountered some serious requests for features that make you wonder "Surely they must be joking?".

ARCHITECTURE ACCEPTED, BUT PERCEIVED OVER-ENGINEERING BLAMED FOR PROBLEMS

One of my clients managed loyalty systems, a bit like the frequent flyer points earned with your favorite airline, but much more complicated, and aimed at corporate purchasers. For example, a loyalty system aimed at the automotive repair business might offer bonuses for the purchase of more than five dozen of a certain brand of spark plugs. The next month, the participating suppliers might offer bonuses for more than $2,000 worth of oil, filters, and brake pads from three different suppliers, as long as the total purchases included at least 10% in value from each of the three suppliers. And the next month, who knows?

Not only were the ways to earn bonuses changing frequently, but the form of the bonuses changed, too. This month, it may have a cash value. Next month it may be a ticket in a drawing for a holiday for two. And the following month, the bonus might be a tankful of fuel for your car. With the way fuel prices are going, it may not be long before that may be worth more than a holiday for two!

These are just examples from the automotive repair industry. The client ran loyalty schemes for other industries, as well. To cope with the changing formulae, and a requirement that these formulae be modifiable by the users without programmer involvement, a design was chosen that included a domain-specific language. This delivered against the stated user requirement, but one developer felt maybe we should have pushed back against the user and had a less flexible solution.

It can be a balancing act. A simpler solution delivered now may actually turn out to be expensive if rules that could have been managed by a domain-specific language needed to be hard-coded. Conversely, a highly generic domain-specific language designed to handle many more bonus and payment scenarios than likely to ever be encountered could unnecessarily raise the costs. Only time will tell, and even then that will only be true if efforts are made to try and measure the chosen solution against emerging reality.

For what it's worth, however, this one developer did blame over-engineering as the source of some of the problems encountered. Was he right? Maybe. But the next story shows another side to the controversy.

ARCHITECTURE REJECTED ON THE GROUNDS OF PERCEIVED OVER-ENGINEERING

Another client manufactured made-to-measure shower screens, wardrobe doors, security doors, and the like. As you may be aware, not all buildings are perfectly square, and not all walls are perfectly vertical. Sometimes an off-the-shelf security door will fit well; at other times, the opening may be narrower at the top, and the opening may be a bit skewed. This company only supplied products for the cases where non-standard, tailored solutions were required.

In this life, mistakes are made. For this company, mistakes in calculating cutting sizes for the components were costing them real money, both in wasted materials and the costs of failed attempts to install things that didn't fit. The stated requirement was a rules engine that integrated with other systems. Inputs for each order were to include the model number and the client site measurements, and the outputs were to be a list of all components and their exact sizes.

As in the example above for the loyalty scheme, a domain-specific language was proposed. The total time to (1) design the solution, including the domain-specific language, (2) create the database for storage of the rules and storage of the order details, (3) build a prototype user interface, and (4) populate the rules engine with sample data, was two days. Well, two calendar days. A bit more than 16 hours were spent on this job!

The client loved the working prototype, and the software house was commissioned to build the production solution. Now here's the sad bit. The lead developer assigned was in a different part of the company, and he didn't understand the concepts behind domain-specific languages and the engine that had been developed in two days. Nor did he *want* to seek understanding. He simply wrote off the solution as being over-engineered, and redeveloped the engine, with specific code for each of dozens of models. And I understand that it took him weeks to build.

The moral of the story? Perceived "over-engineering" of a data model can be rejected unnecessarily by developers who don't make the effort to, or simply don't want to, understand the design.

The enterprise view

We've taken a look at the arguments for avoiding unnecessary complications, especially the introduction of "features" before they are needed. Conversely, we've also (hopefully) accepted that there are times when a little engineering that reflects a measure of foresight might be a good investment. Now we move to the central theme of this chapter – when you are developing a data architecture for just one domain within an enterprise, should it try to align with the overall enterprise information architecture? And wouldn't doing so be blatant over-engineering for the problem at hand?

This question is based on the premise that the organization already has an enterprise-wide information architecture in place. If it doesn't, the next chapter will give some advice as to how you might be able to construct at least a framework for an enterprise model that is surprisingly robust, yet quick to construct.

HOW BIG IS THE ENTERPRISE?

I did some work for a well-known and respected church-based charity. How big was their enterprise? As a matter of principle, they kept a clear separation between their church activities and their social concern outreach. Any money donated to their social arm never ended up supporting the salaries for their church leaders, nor for the building funds for their churches. While I was not personally affiliated with their organization, I deeply respected the conscious separation of the two functions. The enterprise information model I was exposed to focused primarily on their social outreach, reflecting the effective existence of two organizations within one.

I have also seen a similar separation within the telecommunications industry. This is not only related to the ethics of separation of wholesale and retail operations, but in Australia, separation may be a legislative expectation, rather than just a self-imposed ethical division. However, in contrast to the church-based charity, where there could be two enterprise models in the one organization, there may be value for the telecommunications company in having one logical enterprise information architecture based on industry standards, even if it is arguable that the two arms of the company are really distinct enterprises.

In the above two examples, one could debate whether the church and its social concern initiative were two organizations or one. Similarly, within the telecommunications industry, there are debates about functional separation of wholesale and retail operations versus structural separation where each operation is a separate, registered company. Similarly, I've seen a government department that was so enormous that various largely-autonomous sections within it have, at various times, expressed the desire for an "enterprise" model just for them. From the perspective of just one section within the department, they *are* the enterprise.

In another setting, the department as a whole has expressed the desirability of having a unifying enterprise model. Conflicting views? Possibly, but less of an issue if (a) all "enterprise" models are constructed on common, proven patterns, and (b) if the modelers share with each other. But that's another story.

We have just looked at how one enterprise may have sections that want their own "enterprise" model – an enterprise within an enterprise. Conversely, I've seen separate organizations that see themselves as part of the same industry group. Let's take one scenario. What used to be a government utility has been partially privatized. The retail aspects of the original "enterprise" have been spun off, but some of the wholesale aspects involving core infrastructure remain somewhat under government control. In such a case, to facilitate data sharing, the privatized retail organization may seek the articulation of an "enterprise" model that spans both organizations.

At the risk of being seen as a bit too vague, can I suggest that the boundaries of *your* "enterprise" may sometimes turn out, for practical purposes, to be quite different from those set by (for example) the incorporation of the company? I encourage you to consider whether or not finer-grained (or coarser-grained) definitions of your enterprise may deliver value.

CAN A PROJECT-BASED MODEL BENEFIT FROM THE ENTERPRISE MODEL?

Now we face a different question. If a specific project (e.g. an agile project) has a scope that is tightly targeted at one small part of the enterprise, should the model I develop for them be constrained to reflect the shape of the enterprise information architecture? There may be some more obvious reasons why the answer might be "Yes". Perhaps the domain you're working in is intended to have its data integrated with data from other parts of the enterprise. That would be a good reason. But what if it is seen to be largely a stand-alone system and/or at least short-lived?

John Zachman, in the foreword of Len Silverston's 2nd volume of patterns, states:

> *"Even if you are implementing a single application – that is you are not attempting to build an Enterprise-wide model – you are still way ahead of the game using one of Len's models. Because his models are enterprise-wide in nature, he has already anticipated other applications' semantic requirements for the entities you are embarking on implementing. If you use his more broadly defined, enterprise-wide structures, you will save yourself the time and cost of having to scrap and rebuild your application later or the untold frustrations that arise in management when*

the data in your application is not consistent with the data in ensuing applications." [65]

It's not my place to dictate to you what you should do, but I offer one suggestion. From my experience, even when a solution is expected to have a somewhat independent life from other systems in the enterprise, it can benefit from the thinking that has gone into the enterprise view. Something as simple(!) as adopting the enterprise definition of a "product" or a "customer", and the model for holding such data, might deliver real value to your "stand-alone" project.

You don't have to boil the ocean to get alignment with the enterprise model.

First, the parts that are central to your world may be taken from the enterprise model and adapted, if necessary. That way, you may discover some good components to help you hit the ground running. For "free", you will also be consistent with the enterprise model. You may be surprised to discover how many areas of your domain model have already been described in an enterprise model. Even if it's only 50%, that's a good start. In addition, good corporate citizenship might mean providing feedback on your discoveries, as candidates for improving the enterprise world view.

Second, you might choose to look at where your world view touches the edges of others. You might not need to hold data for these touch points (perhaps other than as transactions), but understanding how your solution might be seen when it interfaces with others can potentially influence a mutually beneficial solution.

Last, there's a whole world out there you don't have any interest in – at least not for today. So for the challenges of your current project, if you've got alignment with the enterprise on the data you store and the interfaces you build, you can save time by ignoring whatever is beyond your touch points. That way, you hopefully end up with a better solution for your needs, invest in the corporate good, and keep your sanity by not stressing about the larger world.

On a more recent project, we leveraged the company's logical enterprise model (which happened to be a specialization of an industry model) for the product and service catalogue domain. This baseline framework was extended for the local project's needs, and our experiences were fed back into the enterprise model. All were winners.

---

[65] (Silverston, 2001-b: xiii-xiv)

The story gets even better... Another project had a partial overlap with the catalogue project's domain. They, like the first project, wanted to seek alignment and consistency with the enterprise model. The solution for them was to get access to not only the data structure of the first project's product and service catalogue, but also to the actual data. It was more than they needed, but they took it all, and used it totally unchanged.

The key message I would like to communicate is that the first project had no idea of the second project's subsequent need for data sharing – they were separated by perhaps a couple of years. But because both aimed at alignment with the enterprise model, they consequently achieved alignment with each other, and the second project was able to make huge gains by adopting the common bits of the first's data structure, in all its details.

Making peace

We've looked at how there are times when the "You Ain't Gonna Need It" (YAGNI) approach brings some much needed common sense to projects otherwise threatened by scope creep. We've also looked at how sometimes a solid architecture based on the enterprise view can deliver significant return on investment.

I am confident that the agile enthusiast could very quickly assemble an array of stories proving the value of the YAGNI approach. Likewise, I am sure that the architects of this world could demonstrate times when they have foreseen needs and saved significant rework costs. Given that this book is working towards pattern-based strategies for bringing the best of information architecture quality to the table to support agile delivery, let's look at some real-life examples of patterns contributing to the needs of both groups.

WHEN YAGNI IS CHALLENGED BY STANDARDS

One project I was involved with required the building of a system to manage highly configurable product and service definitions. Len Silverston describes an approach he calls "product features"[66], and Dave Hay articulates a similar approach that he calls "characteristics", which he applies to several modeling constructs[67]. The properties of each type of product (color, size, make and model, etc.) are defined in data rather than

---

[66] (Silverston, 2001-a: 76-80)

[67] (Hay, 2011-a)

as fixed columns in tables. This offers greater flexibility in the configuration of definitions for new products and services.

The specific requirement was to develop a design-time repository for this configuration data so that it could be published to a number of run-time commercial-off-the-shelf (COTS) systems that implemented what I might call the Silverston and Hay approach. There were many aspects of the project that favored an agile approach. YAGNI looked good. However, we were not starting with an empty whiteboard for our data architecture. There were already a number of expectations regarding the structuring of this product configuration data. The solution had a solid foundation, as it was based on the TM Forum's "Frameworx" standard. Where this base framework needed to be extended, instead of just looking to today's needs, the data architect consciously considered other patterns and standards.

Was this level of compliance with standards needed initially? No. But it did prove to be a good choice when, for example, the desirability of exposing the configuration data using the XML Metadata Interchange (XMI) standard arose. We had to have some design for the repository. Why not use helpful elements of a widely accepted standard?

OVER-ENGINEERING, OR REALISTIC VISION?

A mechanism for pricing that allowed product prices to vary according to attribute values was needed. For example, a red, small widget costs $10, a red large one costs $12, and a blue, small widget is priced at $9. In this limited example, the price varies according to the color and size selected. The design solution was based on decision table constructs, an idea that goes back decades. According to some of the standards known at one stage in the project, the products characteristics (color, size, location, level of warranty support, etc.) were highly variable by product line, but the outcome was always a price. However, the data architect noted that similar mechanisms were required for other outcomes – the wording of the product description as it appeared on the bill being one example, which likewise could vary depending on color, size, etc.

Strict application of the YAGNI principle would have resulted in the initial decision table only catering for prices. However, it was really quite simple to include configurable variables for result types (price, bill literal, discount, ...). That additional functionality was built in from the outset, and was very shortly put to work. Did that justify the risk of including this extra flexibility, or could it have been added later when the precise requirements hit the project? I suspect there are arguments that could support either approach. The only thing I feel somewhat confident in concluding is that some decisions are going to lack confidence! But for what it's worth, I tend to lean towards a bit of extra flexibility in the architecture, even if it is not deployed immediately in code. And my observation is that some agile developers, and some architects, seem to agree on at least that much.

Resolving differences of opinion can be difficult. One way of handling the situation is to avoid it – simply make sure you don't have the visionary architects and the pragmatic agile developers on the same team. A better way is to tap into the energy and wisdom of both groups[68].

Consolidating the chapter for you

SUMMARY:

- There is a difference between "you ain't gonna need it ever" versus "you don't need it yet".
- While over-engineering is a real problem, so is under-engineering. You need to distinguish the difference between over-engineering and clever engineering that may actually save you lots of effort.

APPLYING THIS TO YOUR SITUATION:

- Next time you have to make a design decision, deliberately include some visionaries *and* some hard-nosed pragmatic people on the same design review panel. It is sure to generate some heat, but if people are encouraged to respect and understand the divergent views, a great outcome is possible.

---

[68] Edward de Bono's book *Six Thinking Hats* has some tips on facilitating a creative outcome among people with different thinking styles.

Setting the scene

As noted in the previous chapter, an enterprise data model can be a great way to capture strategic thinking for our "to-be" data architecture, which in turn can prove to be valuable to a project, even if the project is aiming at minimal functionality in the code delivered in each iteration. If your enterprise doesn't yet have a strategic enterprise data model, don't despair. This chapter will help you develop a vision of how you can assemble at least an initial framework surprisingly quickly. Conversely, if you are fortunate enough to have an existing enterprise model, you may still get some ideas that will contribute to its refinement and improvement.

In "Chapter 2: Understanding Pattern Aggregations", we looked at a classification scheme for the levels of granularity encountered in data model patterns. Using an analogy of a car, we looked at the elementary "nuts and bolts" patterns, the assembly patterns, and the concept of an overall integration pattern. Below is a copy of that chapter's high-level integration of some quite common assembly patterns (such as Party/Role, Resource, Agreement, Document, and Location) that formed the foundation of an enterprise model for processing real estate transactions.

Each icon represents one *assembly* pattern. For example, a number of patterns books have entire chapters on one topic such as the Party/Role pattern, patterns for Resources/Assets, Agreements/Contracts, and so on. There is a significant amount of detail for each of these assembly patterns.

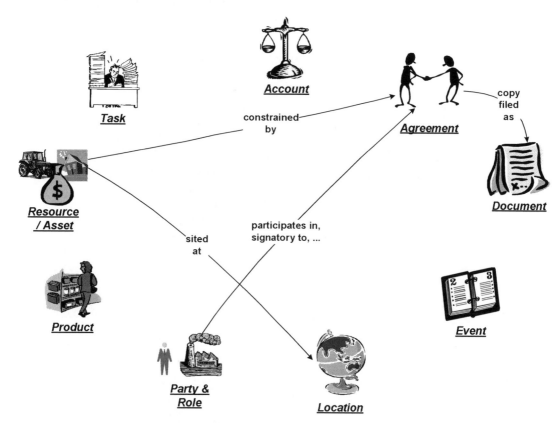

Figure 31: Integration pattern / land transaction scenario

The diagram above presents them pictorially. The lines between them represent selected associations as required for a given problem domain. In the example quoted, data needed to be managed for the processing of real estate transactions. Agreements included transfers of land, recording of mortgages (and discharges of others), agency agreements, and the like. The parties and their roles included vendors, purchasers, real estate agents, solicitors, and more. The resources/assets typically represented the houses and land being bought and sold. And of course, the houses and land have a location.

If you are building a car, you don't start by making the finished car itself, then building (or selecting off-the-shelf) assemblies such as the gearbox, and acquiring the washers, nuts and bolts last. You simply couldn't create the car, then create its components. If you don't start with the elementary bits and pieces such as nuts and bolts, you won't have a gearbox, let alone a car.

That's true for *construction*. For *design*, you may well work the other way around, starting with an overall concept, then designing or selecting the appropriate assemblies, and if necessary, designing specialized elementary bits and pieces.

In a similar way, if we are trying to design a data architecture for a given domain, we can start at the higher level and work down into finer levels of granularity. For example, we might be able to start with this palette of assembly pattern icons, then see if we can draw some associations between them that suit our specific needs. In this chapter, we will have a look at some real-life stories that demonstrate how each enterprise maps to an evolving integration pattern, and then see what lessons of experience may be applied to your situation.

A pattern starts to appear

We look at a domain that is totally different from the real estate transaction domain portrayed above. However, we start with the same palette of nine assembly pattern icons (Account, Agreement, etc.), having removed the lines from the previous example. Our blank palette now looks like the following diagram.

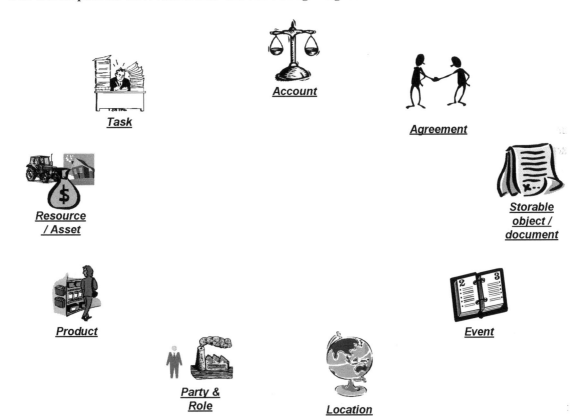

Figure 32: Integration pattern palette

We looked at the government department that manages the state's mineral and petroleum resources earlier. At that time, we were focusing on adapting *assembly* patterns to the specific needs of the department and adding our own new ones. This time, we want to focus on how the assembly patterns *integrate* together.

We start by identifying candidate assembly pattern icons from the palette.

- We are going to need **Resources/Assets** to identify the mineral resources (oil fields, gold deposits, mineral sands, etc.) and link them to their **Location** via a "sited at" association. As noted in an earlier chapter, the Location will need to be able to handle 3-dimensional objects and a time dimension, as well, to maintain a history of old resources that have since been extracted.

- **Agreements** that record the structured data details for exploration permits, excavation licenses, rehabilitation agreements, blasting licenses, and the like will be required. These Agreements absolutely must identify the **Parties/Roles** who "participate in/are signatories to" the Agreements, and typically will have to reference the **Resources/Assets** to which they apply. For example, an exploration license may be signed by an authorized officer of the government and representatives of the exploration company, and it will reference the ore deposit Resource/Asset. Further, a hard copy of the Agreement will be filed as a **Document**, and the responsible document management system must note the **Location** of where it is filed.

- As part of the Agreement, the state body that "owns" the deposit may mandate that field and laboratory test results be kept and made available for later research. For example, a core sample from a drilling is considered a **Storable Object**, and it may be stored in a secure **Location** in much the same way as valuable documents are stored, hence the reason for the generic **Storable Object / Document** class.

- Analysis **Events** invoke some interesting associations. The analyst (a **Party** in a **Role**) may take as input several **Documents** and/or **Storable Object** samples from previous analysis **Events**. They may produce new **Documents** and/or **Storable Object** results that, in turn, may be input for subsequent analysis **Events**. It's a bit of a cycle!

Having identified the assembly patterns we want to use, and their interrelationships, an overall framework emerges:

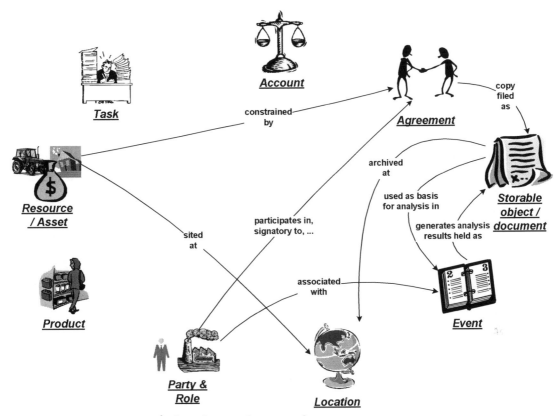

Figure 33: Integration pattern / mineral extraction scenario

Perhaps the first observation might be that many assembly patterns for the minerals and petroleum domain are common with the real estate transaction domain. For example, the Agreement pattern that is used by the real estate transaction domain has to record details of agreements such as transfer-of-land and discharge-of-mortgage, while the minerals and petroleum domain may have exploration licenses and blasting permits. The content is hugely different, but the data structures have much in common, including the associations between Agreements, the Resources they constrain, the Parties in Roles that sign them, and the physical copies of Documents that are held as legal evidence backing up the computer records managed by the Agreement class.

The overall framework of the real estate domain used five of the nine assembly patterns; this domain uses six – the additional one is the Event pattern, for capturing analysis events. The key message is that while a new assembly pattern has been included in this domain, the five assembly patterns that were common to the real-estate transaction domain are largely unaffected, other than the new associations to the Event pattern.

A variation on the theme

We have already looked at several aspects of the assembly patterns for the emergency response domain, but we now look at the associated integration pattern. We start again with the blank palette of assembly pattern icons and see which ones we need and how they might integrate.

- Perhaps the obvious starting point for emergency response is the recording of **Events,** such as the outbreak of a wildfire on a particular mountain (a **Location**), or the spillage of oil off a coastal area (another **Location**). The reporting and evaluation of the **Event** may involve several **Parties**.
- The recognition of an emergency **Event** triggers a series of **Tasks.** For a wildfire, a highly mobile initial response team (a combination of **Resources/Assets** such as trucks and radios, plus the crew, i.e., **Parties** in **Roles**) are immediately selected based on their proximity (**Location**) to the emergency.
- Emergency events typically grow in scale. It may be a wildfire that gains hold, or a spill that spreads. Whatever the case, a series of **Tasks** are identified and assembled into a response plan, and additional physical **Resources/Assets** and human resources (**Parties/Roles**) are assigned.

Again, we can create a framework as the basis of our integration of assembly patterns, as shown on the facing page.

At first glance, emergency response seems to be totally different from real estate transactions or mineral exploration and extraction, and it is. But at a data structure level, the assembly patterns used and their associations, reflected in an emerging pattern for integration of the components, are surprisingly similar.

There is one subtle difference among the assembly patterns. As explained in "Too much of a good thing?" within "Chapter 5: Test the Levels of Generalization", the decision was made to create a "Resource" superclass that had parties ("human resources") as a subclass, as well as the more typical plant and equipment resources as subclasses. So strictly speaking, the diagram above should show the association between the Resource icon and the Party icon as an inheritance.

The reality was that the Party subclass continued to have its own specialized roles as before, other than certain properties that were lifted up to the superclass. The most notable was the generalization of "capabilities". For a fire truck, one of its capabilities might be that it can carry one-and-a half tons of water. For a person, one of their capabilities might be that they can deliver first aid (or operate a chain saw, or use specialized radios, or …).

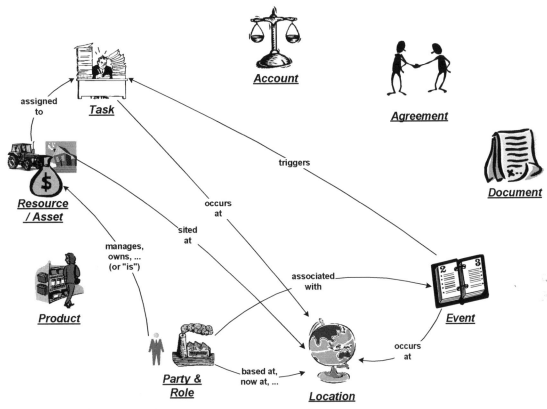

Figure 34: Integration pattern / emergency response scenario

I fully concede that the decision to combine physical assets and human resources under one superclass may be contentious, but my opinion is that it did deliver value in this circumstance. Even if you feel uncomfortable with my view (and that really is fine – put three data modelers in a room and you'll probably get at least four opinions!), what I wish to share is the inherent flexibility of these assembly patterns to be combined or pulled apart, generalized or specialized, or adapted in any manner that assists you. They really are quite powerful.

Complexity or simplicity?

The last real-life integration pattern we look at is for a bank. A very short summary of the assembly patterns identified, and their inter-relationships follow:

- Banks have **Parties** in **Roles** such as customer, guarantor, etc.
- In a bank, you will have **Accounts**. Lots of them.
- They also have mountains of **Agreements**; some are electronic, but many are still in paper form, requiring careful storage of the hard-copy **Documents**.

- Backing up the loans (a type of **Product**), there will often be real property (**Resources/Assets** at a **Location**) used as security.
- **Events** occur and need to be recorded, from customer complaints through on-site valuations of secured properties.

Banks are obviously more complicated than this. However, a few years ago, I worked on one focused area within a bank, and the diagram below captures the essence of the required framework. It looks quite a bit more complicated than the integration patterns we have just looked at. The irony is that the integration model was developed to provide a simple context for problem solving.

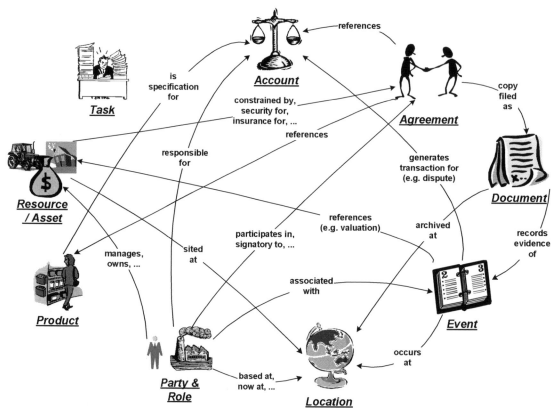

Figure 35: Integration pattern / banking scenario

The background was that the bank had a known problem with recording "securitization". If you don't know what that is, neither did I when I took on the assignment. Put simply (and hopefully somewhat accurately), a bank can sell off some of its loans to investors to raise capital to provide more loans. Let's say a bank has lent $100 million at 7%, and has the loans secured by high quality real estate. Along comes someone with a lazy $100 million in their wallet who can't think how to spend it. They might be happy to hand it over to the bank and get (say) a 6.9% return with the backing of the real estate as effectively *their* security now – they get the loans, and they get the associated security. The other 0.1% might be a margin for the bank to manage the loan portfolio – sending out statements, collecting the monthly payments, and so on. Now the bank has got another $100 million to lend.

The bank's problem was related to keeping records of not only the loans to the individual members of the community, but also linking them to the lender. It's a bit more complicated than that, but that's the core issue. Basically, we looked at the enterprise, fitted together some proven assembly patterns, and quite quickly were able to spot the areas of change required in the record keeping structures. The loan to an individual was an Agreement, with the home used as security as a Resource/Asset. The individual was a Party in the role of mortgagor. All pretty standard stuff.

Now we look at the wealthy individual with $100 million to spare. He or she is another Party, in another Role, who signs an Agreement with the bank. More of the same. The only trick is that you have a link between the wealthy person's Agreement and the hundreds or thousands of Agreements which are, in turn, linked to the Resources/Assets that indirectly provide security for the big loan. The integration pattern displayed above gave the needed perspective to see a (relatively) simple framework for a solution.

An integration pattern emerges

If we combine the real-life scenarios presented above, plus a few more from other domains, an integration pattern starts to emerge. The assembly patterns (Agreement, Party, Location, etc.) often seem to have the same or similar associations, even though they are encountered in vastly different situations.

One of the things you may have noticed is the loose coupling between the assembly patterns. Across widely divergent problem spaces (banking, mineral exploration, etc.) the basic assembly patterns can be linked for significantly different purposes.

In the past, a number of banks had computer systems where parties and accounts were tightly coupled. If you had two accounts, your personal details were recorded twice. If you changed your address, it had to be updated in two places, simply because your personal details were recorded as part of the account record, rather than as a separate but linked "party" record. Similarly, the agreement might hold structured data, and the document may be an associated but separately managed image in a document management system.

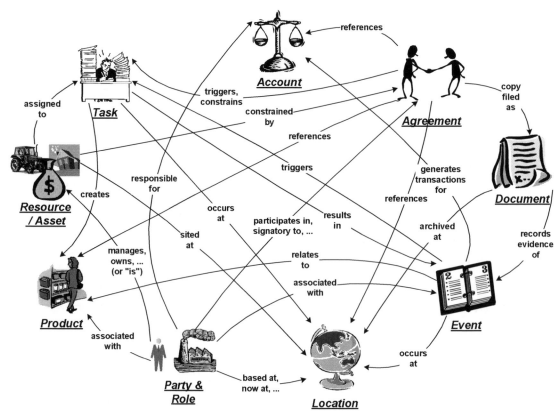

Figure 36: Integration pattern / a pattern of patterns!

It may sound like a subtle difference to separate responsibilities. However, my experience suggests that the benefits of loose coupling between specialized assembly patterns are significant. And having a framework as portrayed above can assist in keeping the coupling loose.

Where to next?

The integration pattern presented in the previous section is clearly a very high-level framework. Of course, it is backed up by a rich library of assembly patterns from multiple sources. But where does it fit in the real-world need to deliver sound data architectures in a timely manner? That's what we will discuss next.

Maybe your goal is to quickly fabricate a solid framework based on proven patterns. Where might you start?

One option is to take the integration framework presented in this chapter, see how much fits your needs, and then get your hands on some of the excellent books with assembly patterns to start fleshing out the details. That might be an approach if you don't already have an enterprise data model as a framework.

Or maybe you are fortunate enough to have an enterprise model at hand. That's great.

But either way, you may be well advised to check this starting-point framework against some of the standards described in the next chapter.

Consolidating the chapter for you

SUMMARY:

- A consistent final outcome can be achieved by starting with a top-down integration view, even if some of the details need a bit of work later.
- One such framework is presented in this chapter, consisting of a set of 9 common assembly patterns and their typical inter-relationships.
- Use of this "pattern of patterns" (i.e., the integration pattern describing links between assembly patterns) can provide a fast start-up skeleton for an enterprise model.

APPLYING THIS TO YOUR SITUATION:

- If you haven't got an enterprise data model, consider using the integration pattern presented in this chapter as a starting point for your model. It may take less time than you thought possible, and deliver value in the very short term. (There will still be lots of hard work fleshing it out, but it can still prove to be a robust framework.)

Standards for integration patterns

Once you have acquired an enterprise data model to reflect your organization's domain, it can be beneficial to cross-check it against the standards offered by others. Although not an official standard, one source I recommend is Volume 2 of Silverston's *Data Model Resource Book*[69]. He suggests that it would not be uncommon to find that 50% of your enterprise model's *components* could be aligned with truly universal patterns, and a further 25% might be defined by industry-specific models[70]. His first volume describes a number of assembly patterns that might address the 50%, and his second volume might address the next 25%, if you are lucky enough to belong to an industry he has modeled. Even if your industry is not listed specifically, Len notes[71] that some of the integration patterns that emerge from looking at specific industries can be helpful in wider contexts.

---

[69] (Silverston, 2001-b)

[70] (Silverston, 2001-a: 1-2)

[71] (Silverston, 2001-b: 7)

Another source of what I call integration patterns is Dave Hay's book on *Enterprise Model Patterns*[72]. My interpretation is that Len and Dave take a somewhat different approach to model level classification. Len has four levels, numbered 1 to 4, ranging from more generalized models to more specialized models. Dave also has four levels, ranging from 0 to 3, where I suggest that Dave's level 3 models for criminal justice, microbiology, banking, and the like are perhaps closer to Len's Volume 2 of industry specific models. Please note that I am not being critical of either classification scheme. Rather, I am trying to communicate that both authors, in their own unique way, are making a contribution to the total knowledge-base of patterns.

In addition to Len and Dave's works, there are several sources of industry models against which you can benchmark your model. Some are commercially available models offered by large vendors of consulting services or data warehouse designs.

Another candidate source is from a consortium of players in your industry. The TM Forum is an example of one such group. While its enterprise framework data model is now moving towards being more generic, its roots were solidly planted within the telecommunications industry. Or if you are in the healthcare industry, you may already use the Health Level Seven (HL7) Reference Information Model (RIM). While the HL7 model was initiated in the USA, in my home country (Australia) it has been keenly and widely adopted.

One anecdote may be helpful in demonstrating the potential of these integration pattern standards. One telecommunications company here in Australia had put in something like five person years of effort to develop their enterprise data model. It is important to note that these five years of effort were expended *before* the existence of either Silverston's industry pattern book or the TM Forum's SID (Shared Information/Data) model.

Now, after publication of Silverston's book and the TM Forum's SID, an ex-employee of that organization finds himself at another telecommunications company that wants a similar enterprise data model. But they have two weeks to prepare it and only enough budget for one modeler. Can I help?

My rather cheeky response was that they could save the cost of my two weeks of consulting by simply buying Len's books! Seriously, though, I did agree to take on the job, with a few conditions to help us all time-box the project and set achievable expectations. I started by telling the story of Len's 50% + 25% perspective, and

---

[72] (Hay, 2011-a)

suggested that there was a chance that 75% of their company might look the same as every other telecommunications company in the world. In theory, that still left a 25% gap that represented what made them unique and gave them a competitive advantage.

Beginning with this assumption, I asked that I limit interviews to define their special requirements to no more than six interviews of no more than 1 hour each, and with their key thought leaders. Why six? I guessed that if I only interviewed two or three people, I would have a very limited perspective, but if I interviewed ten or twenty, I would run out of time. So it was a somewhat arbitrary time-boxing decision.

How did the project go? I did overrun (by four hours – and I didn't charge for it). The client was delighted, and quite frankly, I was relieved. The model was clearly a high-level framework only, but it proved to be sufficient to provide direction for three initiatives that were launched almost immediately after delivery of the enterprise data model. Some further consulting was required to flesh out details in specific areas, but the framework proved to be resilient over the years that followed.

Standards for assembly patterns

We have just noted that high-level standard integration patterns can be used to cross-check your enterprise model. Finer-grained assembly standards might be able to play a similar role. For example, I have had several encounters where an organization was struggling to find a data structure to accommodate complex interrelationships between parties and their roles, only to discover that the standards for the Party/Role pattern could meet or exceed their needs.

Another example relates to the Location pattern. Several government groups in my home state were required to keep records that related in one way or another to locations on the earth's surface, or to be a bit more specific, locations within my home state. Although the groups spanned widely different interests, many used one shared geospatial information system (GIS), and hence the same data structure for geospatial information.

An impressive outcome of this sharing relates to the seasonal wildfires our part of the world has to cope with every summer. You may remember from your school days about triangulation? If you have two known points (in this case, a pair of fire towers where people are employed to spot smoke), and both fire-spotters report smoke and the compass bearings, you can work out where the fire is located. In minutes, by referencing the shared geospatial records, the fire controller has the following information at his or her finger tips:

- Determination as to whether the fire started on private land or public land, as identified by the land titles office. The triangulation works out the position on a map (latitude and longitude) of where the fire started; the reference to the land titles office tells who owns the land. This information is important in our situation, as fires that start on government land are managed by a government-funded agency, whereas fires that start on private land are managed by a volunteer fire brigade. Both bodies obviously work together in a supportive manner and for a shared purpose, but the responsible group varies on a case-by-case basis, depending on whether the fire is classified as commencing on public or private land.

- The type of flora, as provided by a group charged with responsibility for sustainability of the ecology. If the fire started in an area that is dominated by marshes and fern gullies, it's probably not going anywhere fast. Conversely, if it's in a dry eucalypt forest, you've probably got a fight on your hands.

- Another source of information is the weather bureau. Based on a bit of extrapolation from nearby weather stations, they can provide statistics for temperature, humidity, and wind speed and direction.

- Combine the above with a contour map from another department, and if you've got a hot, dry, and strong wind that started near the bottom of a mountain, but is going to blow the fire up the mountain if not stopped soon, you've got trouble, as fire spreads more rapidly uphill than downhill, especially when fanned by wind.

- Now that the coordinator knows the likely rate of spread for possibly multiple fires all started by a series of lightning strikes, the impact needs to be assessed. Are there townships nearby, or maybe reference sites for protected or endangered flora and fauna?

- Finally, the coordinator needs to know the locations of the nearest water sources, emergency aircraft landing strips, and access roads, with all of this data provided by different agencies.

Lives depend on timely consolidation of all this data. And something as simple as all agencies ensuring compliance with agreed standards for interchange of data can make a big difference.

Did I just say that getting agreement on standards was simple? In hind sight, after they are bedded down, standards can look simple. But their development can be challenging, both technically and "politically", and anything *but* agile. Perhaps if some of the principles of agile software development were to be applied to development of standards, a lot more could be achieved?

Join the community

We can benefit by refining our models after we consider the usefulness to us (and the wider community) of the standards of others. We can also contribute to the standards bodies, partly as a result of a desire to be good citizens in our particular part of the world, and partly because there may be merit in shaping the wider standards in a way that is of benefit to our organization, as well as the larger group.

The TM Forum's Shared Information/Data (SID) model not only defines patterns for overall integration, but it also has a number of patterns at a finer level of granularity. One is the "Specification / Characteristic" pattern. For those interested, it defines a very powerful and flexible way of dynamically defining data structures along the lines of the Entity-Attribute-Value (EAV) model.

The architects in a telecommunication company chose to adopt the SID on principle, with the understanding that people within the company had the right to request modification of the standard. Local changes to the standard could have been made to reflect a deliberate and conscious variation where the organization saw benefit in being different, but I observed that the typical changes were potential improvements to the standard.

This particular company is an active and respected member of the TM Forum and was pleased to make contributions. In reality, though, many of the shared refinements were of mutual benefit. If its vendors are encouraged to supply software that aligns with the industry standard, and if the local telecommunications company helps shape the future of the standard, one could hope that the vendors would enhance their products to conform to the new standard. The vendors may have a better tool to sell in the open market, this local company has an improved expectation of future releases delivering the functionality they desire, and the industry body has an improved standard. That sounds good for everyone.

Consolidating the chapter for you

SUMMARY:

- No man is an island, and neither is any organization likely to be totally unique. If you look in the "right" places, you may find that someone else has done at least some of the hard work for you by articulating a generic industry data model.
- Even if no industry data model exists, you may at least be able to find standard patterns for some of the components of your enterprise data model.

- If you cannot find either, or if you find something but it's not quite right, perhaps *you* can be the catalyst for creating and sharing a new/improved standard.
- One can achieve agility through the *use* of existing standards, but their development may be far less than agile!

APPLYING THIS TO YOUR SITUATION:

- See if you can join a consortium of likeminded organizations and work together for your mutual benefit to, for example, facilitate the interchange of data.

I remember being asked to identify the core business of a well-known international fast-food chain. I shrugged my shoulders and gave an answer that seemed blindingly obvious – "fast food". My friend smiled and corrected my wrong perception, claiming their business model actually centered on real estate. They bought commercial property, developed it, and rented it out to tenants. The fast food franchise was merely a way of ensuring their tenants had a good income so that they could, in turn, pay a good rent.

That story demonstrates that the public's view of one enterprise may be vastly different from their internal operating model. That might not matter too much as long as the business itself knows its drivers, but what if the business has imprecise or inconsistent views about its own core values and concepts? That can cause real problems. Unfortunately, discovering wrong concepts can be difficult, particularly if they are well and truly entrenched in the culture of the organization.

Physical models are not the only reality

I continue to be amazed at the number of companies that develop software for the market place who do not have a logical data model. I am not talking about those who have one but feel it represents the heart of their intellectual property, and hence are hesitant to share it. Rather, I am talking about large international software companies who have a glazed look when you talk of a logical data model, and state they've got a physical model, so why would they want more?

I recall one of my clients who mandated the supply of a logical data model as part of their evaluation process for package selection. One of the software companies had never had a logical data model for their own software package, but to be able to be considered, they had to develop one. They then commented (off-the-record) how helpful they had found it, and wondered why they had never done it before!

Another company I did some work for was in the business of moving parcels around the state, the country, and internationally for their customers. They wanted to upgrade the software they used to assist in optimizing planning for parcel movements, and for tracking them until they arrived safely.

One software vendor had a package that on the surface seemed to meet the requirements. The heart of their model looked something like the following.

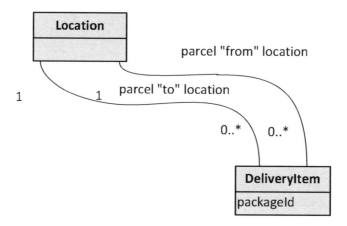

Figure 37: Delivery logistics for simple/atomic items

Each delivery item was a discrete package, and it had a "from" location and a "to" location.

The shipping company wasn't just moving discrete, atomic parcels around, though. It was also constantly putting smaller packages together into larger bundles, then into containers, and then later, progressively pulling them apart. At a regional sorting center all of the individual items for Western Australia might be assembled into one larger parcel, and another parcel made up for all the items heading towards the Northern Territory. When these larger parcels arrived at the state's central hub, these might then be aggregated into aircraft containers. After arrival, the aircraft containers were unpacked, and all the items for a regional town would be put together and sent off. And so on, until the discreet individual items arrived at their final destination.

This was all pretty reasonable. Each individual item had an identifier, a source, and a destination. For example, the source might be 1 Main Street in Perth, Western Australia, and the destination might be 2 High Street in Melbourne, Victoria. Each aggregation of parcels into larger packages also had an identifier, a source (e.g. Perth Airport) and a destination (e.g. Melbourne Airport). To cater for this, all that the model required was a self-referencing relationship to record parcels-in-parcels.

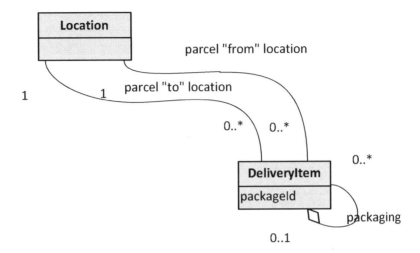

Figure 38: Delivery logistics for complex/composite items

Each delivery item was tracked, whether it was a discrete atomic parcel or a larger container. By knowing where a container was located at a point in time, and by knowing what was inside it, you could imply the location of all its contents.

Unfortunately, the software system being proposed only understood the concept of individual parcels, and had no way to track a "parcel" that was made up of smaller items. I asked for a copy of their logical data model to try and get a feel for how hard it might be to incorporate a self-referencing aggregation association on a parcel. As it happened, they could not produce one, but they did produce a cumbersome and un-necessarily large physical model which, when pasted together, was huge. I spread it out over a board room table, and crawled on hands and knees, following relationships. I soon found the delivery item entity, and lo and behold, the self-referencing relationship already existed.

Good news? You might have hoped so. After all, the data structure catered to just what was needed. The crest-fallen database guru then admitted he had seen this relationship as created by the original designer, but because there was no logical model and no documentation, he had decided it had no useful purpose and used the column for something else! To reinstate this intended feature was going to take quite a bit of time (and money), and the sale of the software package was lost.

What details might I find in a conceptual model?

I have been speaking of conceptual data models and logical data models, so perhaps we'd better get the terms sorted out. There is, however, some divergence of opinion on their definitions. For example, some suggest that a conceptual data model should not include attributes, while others are comfortable with at least some major attributes being defined, especially if they are seen to help clarify the meaning of the conceptual entity. For now, I will ask you to put that controversy aside and accept that a conceptual model might identify some important attributes.

I was once on the sidelines of another debate that highlights how varied views can be. The topic of the debate is portrayed in the following diagram.

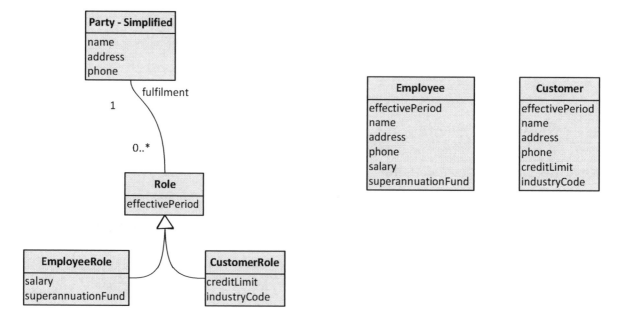

Figure 39: The conceptual versus logical dilemma

On the left-hand side of the diagram we have a (simplified) Party entity, its associated Role entity, plus two subclasses for specialization to handle the Employee Role and the Customer Role. This approximates a fairly classical Party/Role model.

On the right-hand side, we have two entities, one for Employee and one for Customer. This more closely represents the model we might expect when, for whatever reason, the Party/Role model is *not* followed. One could argue that as long as any party fulfills only one role, the data recorded is effectively the same.

You might have expected that the debate was over the merits or otherwise of the Party/Role pattern. In fact, the debate centered on which of the two approaches was "conceptual" and which was a "logical" representation of an implementation.

One argument was that the Party/Role model on the left-hand side was conceptual. It was seen as a theoretical, academic view that might be how the business sees "parties of interest" and the roles they play, but that the right-hand Employee + Customer model was a pragmatic, realistic logical view of what would be implemented.

The counter argument was that the Employee + Customer view represented real-world business concepts, but that a flexible and normalized implementation would be based on the logical Party/Role model. Who on earth was right?!

Given that a Party can be a person *or* an organization, the basic Party/Role pattern allows either type of Party to play any Role. This means a Customer could be a person or an organization. That's probably realistic in many cases. It also means that a person can be an Employee (that's fine), but the model would also allow an organization to be an Employee. Maybe if we loosen the typical definition of an "employee" to allow a company supplying contract labor to be an employee, the latter scenario is possible. Maybe.

Now back to the debate. I have encountered a number of organizations in which employees are unlikely to ever be customers. In one, their customers were only going to be large corporations, and their employees were always people. For this organization, the right-hand Employee + Customer model might reflect both their conceptual *and* their logical/physical implementation view.

Now we swing to the other extreme. A telecommunications company that followed the TM Forum's industry standard model saw the Party/Role model as representing their conceptual model, and saw it also as their logical model, upon which they based a custom systems development.

In the middle was one organization I worked with that saw the Party/Role model as correctly representing their enterprise conceptual view, but due to the realities of the packages they had installed, the physical implementation was more along the lines of the right-hand model.

So having looked at a few examples, it may seem we are no closer to resolving the definition of a conceptual model versus the definition of a logical model. My suggestion is a pragmatic meeting of the ways. As far as how much detail goes into a conceptual model, I recommend modeling of major attributes where their inclusion assists in communication and clarification, whether or not they "should" be there, according to some theory. As far as labeling a high-level model as either conceptual or logical, I am suggesting that if an experienced modeler can see at least one way the concepts could possibly be implemented, the differences may become less of an issue. If that sounds a bit like heresy, all I would ask is that you hang in there with me for a bit longer.

Can conceptual models make a difference?

A work colleague told an entertaining story about a workshop he facilitated that went something like this. The client was a government body responsible for running the train network. At the start of the workshop, my friend said, "You are probably going to think this is a dumb question, but what is a train?" One person at the workshop agreed it was a pretty dumb question, but Geoff asked that he humor him and provide a definition, to which the person responded that a train was made up of rolling stock – carriages and an engine.

Another attendee corrected the first person, saying that the definition provided was really a description of an asset, but an example of a train would be the 8:06 from Dandenong.

To which a third replied that the 8:06 from Dandenong would be the definition for a schedule item but *today's* 8:06 from Dandenong would be a train.

A fourth person corrected them all by stating that a train was a marketing concept, and a well-known example would be the Orient Express between Paris and Istanbul, or the Ghan, here in Australia.

Similar stories could be told from other industries. I worked with an airline, and there was difficultly in defining a "flight". Another common difficulty is in defining a customer. And you probably could add your own amusing anecdotes to the mix. But how important is it to have precise, unambiguous definitions of core concepts? The answer is that it can be vital. Another story highlights this.

I have already referred to a government agency responsible for registration of land ownership. The name of the department included the word "land". Its documents referred to "land", for example the transfer-of-land contract. If I were to draw a data model from first principles, starting from a blank whiteboard, it might be quite reasonable for me to start with an entity called "Land".

This department had a problem with its records. In fact, the problem originated well before the introduction of computerized records of land ownership. There was something that just wasn't working well for them. They had even set up a special group to solve the problem, but after a long time, the group disbanded with no real progress having been made. I had no knowledge of this history, and entered the enterprise with little more than a kitbag of generic data modeling patterns, and the recognition that I would have to be willing to ask the dumb questions if I was to get my head around another problem I was asked to work on.

At one point, I tentatively suggested that, to me (the novice) it looked like they were more in the business of registering "rights" as they sometimes, but not always, related to parcels of land, rather than in registration of the land itself and its properties. A very smart and very senior member of the client team got quite excited, saying something about me having solved the problem. Pretty interesting, since I had no idea what this other problem was that I was meant to have solved!

It turned out that my application of generic patterns, and questioning as to how they might fit (if at all), had led me down a path that gave a new perspective to this senior public servant. He gets the credit for seeing beyond what I was proposing and applying it to the business. All I did was bring a different set of patterns to the table, and he saw the potential of using these concepts to solve their long-standing problems with structuring of information records.

But the story didn't end there. The focus had shifted from physical parcels of land to rights (rights of owners, rights of tenants, rights of passage across an easement, rights for mineral exploration companies to dig up "your" backyard, etc.), but my colleague was able to also see the historical source of the wrong conceptual thinking. With a smile, he said we could blame the English. (Please, his comment was stated in a very light-hearted manner, because Australia's legal system is based on England's, and no offense was intended to those of English heritage.)

Apparently, in the English villages of another era, when one person wanted to buy another's farm, he would assemble the village elders to witness the transaction. There were no written records, but confirmation of ownership by the elders was deemed sufficient. The quaint process started with the buyer producing the appropriate number of gold coins, and the seller then grabbing a handful of soil. In front of the elders, the buyer would place his coins in the open hand of the seller, and the seller would pull up a piece of grass with soil attached and place the piece of "land" in the buyer's open hand, hence completing a "transfer of land" transaction. At this point, the buyer would wave one hand over the soil he held in the other hand, symbolically shooing the previous owner from his "land". As my colleague pointed out, it was really a transfer of rights, not soil.

We can laugh at that story, but the reality is that the wrong concepts had caused decades of pain. In this case, the required understanding came by considering alternative ways of thinking that some base patterns offered.

Linking high level models and implementation models

Sound conceptual models may help the organization to reconsider the way it sees itself, and this can be worthwhile. But can conceptual models help us with the implementation of IT systems?

One consultant I worked with believed there was no need to have any links between a conceptual model and implementation. He resisted any attempt by others to do so, arguing that such activity would only distract the conceptual thinkers from their work. His conceptual models had one-to-one associations all over the place that did not reflect reality, but he didn't care, because it was "only conceptual". Similarly, he didn't care if there was confusion between entities that represented types versus instances – to him, such considerations were mere implementation details. Nor did he want to provide useful descriptions for his conceptual entities (the description for the Action Type entity was "*A type of action*"), and he fought against requests to include real-world examples in his textual description of entities. Perhaps, not surprisingly, he frequently refused to provide any attributes that might throw some light on the intent of his entities.

That may be an extreme of "conceptual" thinking with little or no practical value. In contrast, it has been a pleasure to work with those who take on board some conceptual thinking and see how it can change their enterprise for the better. They *want* to apply the concepts to their real-world implementations.

One such organization was a not-for-profit welfare group. An enterprise-wide model was prepared in 15 days, working with their key people. One of the changes that came out of the modeling exercise related to record-keeping of their assets. For example, a house that was used as a refuge for women at risk of domestic violence appeared (1) in the general ledger system as an asset, (2) in a booking system to manage demand and availability, and (3) in a maintenance system that assisted in the scheduling of regular maintenance, from mowing lawns every few weeks through annual changing of batteries on smoke alarms. Then there were multiple systems related to other assets, such as cars. Having the enterprise model present concepts based on one entity for Asset triggered the rationalization and synchronization of IT systems that tracked assets. The conceptual model shaped implementation outcomes.

It's not rocket science, and of course, the opportunity to seek gains in efficiency *could* have come from sources other than the enterprise modeling exercise. But in this instance, it was the enterprise-wide thinking that highlighted areas of commonality that in turn resulted in rationalization of implemented systems.

There was another good-news story coming out of the enterprise model. The real-world background was a team of delightful and generous social workers, many of whom had specialized in fields such as working with the homeless, the unemployed, victims of abuse, those with drug and alcohol dependencies, and several more ills that are an unfortunate reality in our society. Because of years of specialization, a number of silos had grown up. When the organization called them together to participate in seeking to identify the common elements that could be represented in the enterprise model, I sensed that some of these wonderful people were doubtful that they would find much in common, but we progressed using a slogan of, *"Leverage off what is common and respect what is distinct."*

We could have created models for each silo – one for aged care, one for trauma victims, and so on, and we did rough out some models to extract the special requirements of each group. But then we consolidated the models and aligned them to proven patterns. One small slice through the models follows (with attributes suppressed for brevity).

We start with a few snippets from the specific model for recording applications for residency in aged care facilities, and for recording their subsequent successful placement.

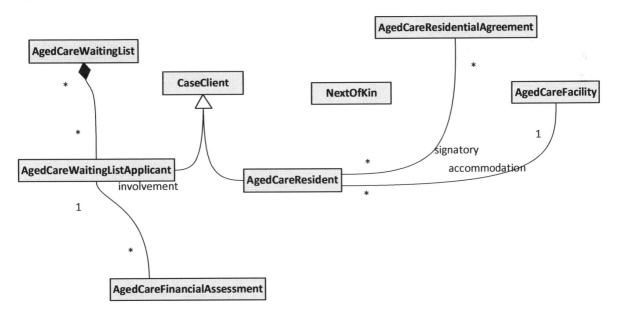

Figure 40: Specific domain model

Aged Care Waiting List Applicants are required to have an Aged Care Financial Assessment as part of the process, and are subsequently placed on the appropriate Aged Care Waiting List. When they move from being applicants to becoming Aged Care Residents of an Aged Care Facility, they sign an Aged Care Residential Agreement to ensure clear understanding of the mutual rights and responsibilities. Whether a person is an Aged Care Waiting List Applicant or an Aged Care Resident, they are looked after by an assigned case worker, and hence both can be seen as specializations of the Case Client class.

That's pretty specific. And there were similar targeted models for each of the other streams of social care. You do not see it in this fine slice, but even at the early stages of each model, proven assembly patterns were used. For example, a Case Client is a specialization of the Role pattern, and the Aged Care Facility is a specialization of the Asset pattern. This meant that when the models from these multiple sources were consolidated, it was a much simpler task.

The consolidated model had many aspects; just one of them related to general "case management". A subset of the case management model is on the facing page.

Rather than going through each class in the model, the key thing I would like to highlight is the inheritance from assembly pattern superclasses. Case Client, Case Worker, and Case Agency are all subclasses of Role, and the Case itself is a subclass of Agreement.

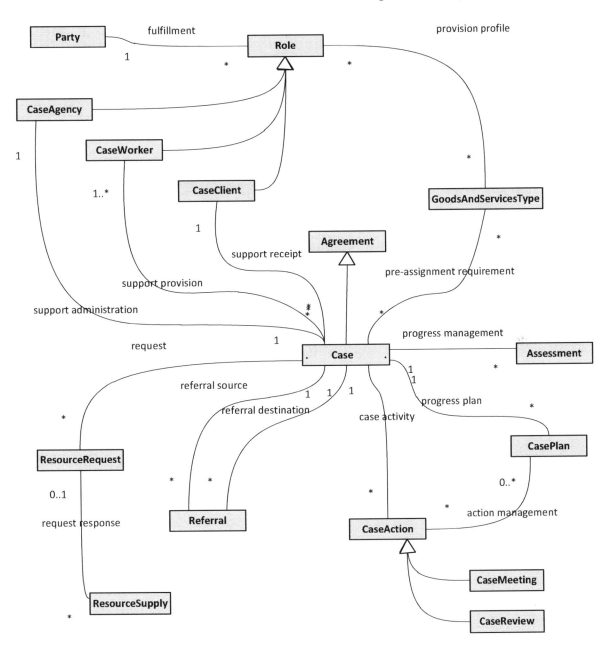

Figure 41: Generalized domain model

If we now go back to the specific model for aged care, and include inheritance from superclasses representing common assembly patterns, we can start to see how they all fit together.

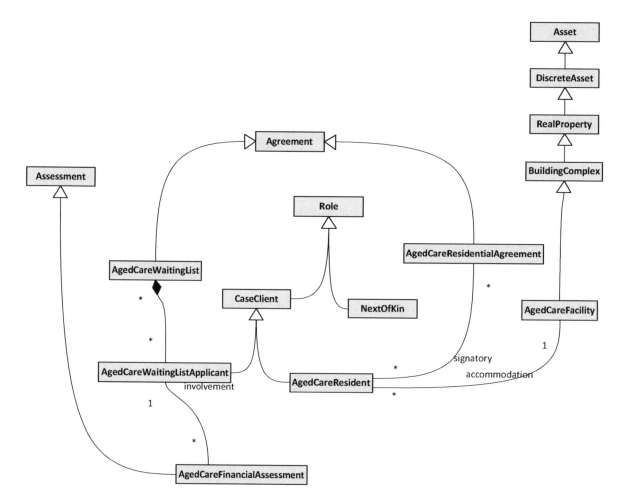

Figure 42: Applying the generalization to specialized domains

One of the hierarchies is a bit deep (Asset), but there on the Aged Care model are the patterns we've grown to love – Agreement, Role, and Asset. We can start to see how the higher level concepts represented by these common patterns provide an integration framework for the detail we need for implementation.

This was important, but even more important was the revelation to these passionate case workers that they really could, *"Leverage off what is common and respect what is distinct"*. They could all be seen as "case workers" who managed "cases" that required "case plans", and so on. As reflected in the slogan above, these generalizations were most certainly not down-playing the aspects of their work that were truly unique. Rather, they were a reflection of how the supporting IT systems, and more importantly, work practices, could potentially be rethought to "leverage off what was common." There was improved IT efficiency, but significantly, there was also increased ease in providing support for those unfortunate people who were challenged on multiple fronts. A great outcome.

Name the patterns

One of the powerful aspects of the patterns movement is the ability to communicate complex ideas in a word or two. As the familiarity with published patterns grows, one data modeler can say to another, "Why don't we use the Characteristic pattern?", or "I think the Party/Role pattern might add value here", and the richness and detail of these patterns is mutually understood.

In data models, sometimes the only indication that patterns have been applied is the language used to name the classes. To aid communication, you might want to explicitly call out your use of patterns. Further, as any pattern can have variations, you may also want to record the alternatives you considered, what you see as their relative merits, and the reasoning behind the choices you made. It may well be that you made the best choice given today's constraints, but in the future, another modeler may benefit from understanding how you arrived at the design decision.

It's not arrogance to question

If you prefer the name "Client" and the organization you're working for prefers the term "Customer", and if you insist on getting your own way, you run the risk of being seen as a bit pushy. But if you respectfully challenge the assumptions behind a business, my experience suggests that they will, at worst, see you as being a bit naïve in challenging the obvious ("Doesn't everyone know what a 'train' is?"), and at best you may promote new ways of thinking.

I have recounted stories where there has been immediate and open acceptance of new ideas. I have also come across cases where the light has dawned a little more slowly. When we, as modelers, play with concepts that challenge the status quo, we must be patient. Maybe they will "see the truth" in time. And maybe time will prove us to be wrong! Either way, I encourage you to use the ideas that arise from looking at an enterprise through the eyes of proven patterns as catalysts for discussion, not grounds for warfare.

As recounted earlier, at one client site, I introduced a few new ideas. Interestingly, the business eagerly embraced the ideas behind the patterns, but a few of the IT developers were not so sure. Five years later, I happened to bump into one of the programmers from the site and asked how things were going. She smiled and said that two of the development team initially blamed me and my models for making their life more difficult. That was in their first implementation. She said they now loved the model, as subsequent releases required little or no extension because the pattern was inherently flexible. A bit more effort the first time yielded rewards later.

Another success story was a site where the enterprise model reflected the vision of senior management, but was more than required initially. Five years after the "implementable conceptual model" (really an enterprise logical model) was first assembled, the developers still had not needed to do any major rework of the model. It was still relevant, and was still providing all they needed.

It's nice when it works out that well, but it doesn't always, hence the need to seek constructive feedback on your models. What worked well? What didn't? We cover more on this in the next chapter, but suffice it to say we need to, on the one hand, be brave and see if we can challenge the entrenched views of an enterprise, while on the other hand, be gracious and realize it may be us who are wrong.

Consolidating the chapter for you

SUMMARY:

- There are differences in purpose and style between conceptual, logical, and physical models, but each is important.
- The conceptual, logical, and physical models should not be independent of each other – one should be able to be mapped to another. The ideas captured in a conceptual model should be considered when creating a logical model, which in turn should shape the physical models.
- Conversely, the patterns identified when creating a logical model should be considered as potentially reshaping the thinking at the conceptual model level. The very act of the business seeing itself in a creative new way can have a huge and positive impact on the business.
- When you consciously use a pattern, name it, and record why you chose it.

APPLYING THIS TO YOUR SITUATION:

- Investigate the possible benefits of challenging and aligning corporate concepts with data model patterns. I know it sounds like IT telling the business how they should work, but we're on the same team and we can learn from each other. Sometimes a totally different perspective can break a deadlock.
- As a quality assurance exercise, cross-check the conceptual, logical, and physical models to see if you can establish clear traceability between them.

Iterate along the model's breadth and depth

We've spoken about how the agile practitioners warn of the dangers of BDUF – Big Design Up Front – it can cost a lot to develop, and it might never be used. Perhaps worse than having an over-architected design and not having it used, is to have it used but discover it has major flaws, or maybe was a good fit at the time but does not reflect your needs when you eventually get to launch the system.

Rather than debating the absolute extremes of heavy-duty architecture before you start versus absolutely no architecture but optimism that it will be discovered over time, there is another option. Put simply, just like code can be developed iteratively, you can develop your data architecture iteratively. However, I recommend that you don't start with a blank palette. Instead, you can start by selecting proven assembly patterns plus common integration patterns, modifying or extending them as required.

IDENTIFYING THE BIG PICTURE

If we take a casual glance at some agile literature, we might be forgiven for thinking that agile developers start coding with no idea of scope. You might think their aim is to just get some functionality out of the door for evaluation, and the extra bits will be added in future iterations. This view may be reinforced by the clear message that for anything but a trivial problem domain, you are unlikely to be able to capture all the requirements until you've produced some working code that users can play with. "What's the scope? I'll tell you when we've finished."

Upon closer inspection, you will find that broad requirements *are* expected, for example in collections of user stories. These may be grouped and prioritized to provide a high-level perspective. An overall scope of requirements *is* encouraged; agile practitioners just don't want to spend months or years of effort elaborating each requirement in excruciating detail before starting.

In the modeling world, there are similar themes. Some bottom-up modeling approaches seem to focus on discovering lots of details and assembling the larger picture from the detail. Such approaches are often rich in capturing today's understanding, but without a conscious effort, these approaches may be less effective in articulating future directions. They also tend to take time... lots of it!

In contrast, those who practice what I might call top-down modeling can be quite nimble in assembling a perspective of the overall scope. And yes, they will need their views challenged by inspecting detailed scenarios. But at least you get a start-up framework assembled quickly. Of course, there are still some traps to be avoided.

STARTING WELL, ENDING POORLY

We might start well on the top-down approach by getting the scope and context defined via a more traditional conceptual model. But if we refuse to engage with our agile colleagues until we have fully drilled down from this conceptual framework into absolute detail in an enterprise-wide logical data model, and then completed the resultant physical models, we may still miss the mark. First, we may be too slow to respond to their timeframes. And second, they may be quite right in telling us we can't identify all the details until they have made some progress in applying the initial thinking.

If we went for the BDUF approach to data architecture, we might identify all the subject areas for our enterprise using a conceptual model, and then for each identified concept, drill down right into physical design. The check-box to ensure we had completed everything might look something like this:

	Account	Agreement	Document	Event	(etc.)
Conceptual	☑	☑	☑	☑	☑
Logical	☑	☑	☑	☑	☑
Physical	☑	☑	☑	☑	☑

Table 15: Coverage matrix – big design up front

A DIFFERENT APPROACH - MILE-WIDE, INCH-DEEP

The previous chapter looked at how the assembly patterns from a logical model might achieve at least two things:

1. Through interaction with the business, patterns may refine the way the business sees itself. If the company already has an enterprise-level conceptual model, the two (the conceptual model plus the pattern-based logical model) can facilitate the modelers entering into a healthy dialogue, resulting in each model being sharpened by the other. If there is no pre-existing conceptual model, a high level logical model based on assembly-patterns might well prove to be a robust and "sufficient" base to mobilize for an agile project.
2. Provide a scoping perspective on subject areas.

If we want to develop the model iteratively, and get value for our efforts as we go, one way is to <u>start</u> by assembling a very thin layer that addresses just the high-level perspectives of the model. It's no coincidence that the subject areas look the same as the in the previous table. Ideally, the interaction between a logical model based solidly on proven assembly patterns, and the way the business expresses its core concepts should be similar, even if not identical.

	Account	Agreement	Document	Event	(etc.)
High-level logical subject areas	☑	☑	☑	☑	☑
Standard logical assembly patterns					
Refined logical assembly patterns					

Table 16: Coverage matrix – mile-wide, inch deep

For several of the assignments I have been involved in, the first pass is nothing more than some scratchy hand-drawn diagrams on a whiteboard. For any of the subject areas, there is very little depth – just enough to engage the participants so that they understand the broad concepts, and so they realize there is more detail coming. To give you a feel for the size of the effort in this first pass, I often achieve the establishment of an initial framework within hours or days - nothing more.

For one of my clients, all they wanted was a consistent framework for understanding the data of their enterprise. Copies of the whiteboard diagrams were taken, and these were the only deliverables required from my consultancy. They had gained the desired new perspective of their organization, and they now saw the way forward for a strategic initiative. They spent very little, but felt that they got good value. We parted after a few days, both happy with the outcome.

For another client, the first-cut enterprise model was likewise roughed out in a few days. It then took about two weeks to flesh out the details and document the baseline framework. A couple of subsequent iterations were required to polish a few aspects, but the model, as produced in the second iteration, was already sufficient to start delivering tangible value to three projects.

One passing comment on the dynamics of workshops to capture the essence of an enterprise. I always suggest that the participants represent the best and brightest of the enterprise, and I also explicitly request that those people sometimes classified as "trouble-makers" not be excluded just because they hold strong views and are not shy about telling management how the company should be run. I often find that diverse opinions can be a real catalyst for healthy debate, of course with the goal of always asking that opinions be expressed in a manner that demonstrates a respectful attitude towards others.

My experience suggests that if these rather vocal individuals are included, a better vision for the company may emerge. Equally important is that they can come away with the realization that they have been heard and that their views have helped shape the direction of the enterprise. Likewise, they will have been exposed to reasons why decisions by management are sometimes not as questionable as they may otherwise appear. In addition, all participants can be encouraged to have a level of ownership. It can be hard work facilitating a group of outspoken individuals with differences of opinion, but I do encourage getting these parties around the table to work towards the articulation of a common view of the enterprise.

T-MODEL FOR DEPTH

For some clients, the very high level model is the final deliverable. Others wish to use the mile-wide/inch-deep model as a framework for looking at specific pain points. I call the resultant model a "T-model" (not to be confused with an early Ford car with the same name). The mile-wide/inch-deep framework forms the top of the letter "T", and the drill-down is the stem.

One of my clients wanted nothing more than a set of hand-drawn models for the framework. Then they wanted to move quickly to resolve a specific problem, and saw no urgent need to have a well-documented framework model. After the initial iteration, we immediately dove into logical model details for the specified domain, and achieved the required understanding. The checklist of completeness looked a bit more like the following, but with the understanding that the top level framework layer was *very* thin, and the client was happy with that.

	Account	Agreement	Document	Party/Role	(etc.)
High-level logical subject areas	☑	☑	☑	☑	☑
Standard logical assembly patterns		☑			
Refined logical assembly patterns					

Table 17: Coverage matrix – initial T-model

In this particular case, with the pressure off, I was then engaged to come back and take the model through another couple of iterations. I was also asked to conduct some deep-dive modeling for another domain, in parallel.

DOESN'T HAVE TO BE FULL-WIDTH, NOR FULL DEPTH

A picture starts to emerge from these and other case studies. As a general guideline, I have found it helpful to develop an initial enterprise-wide perspective quickly, based on proven assembly and integration patterns, whenever possible. From there, you might perform further iterations to quality assure and flesh out just the framework model – instead of mile-wide/inch-deep, it's still a mile wide, but it's a little deeper than one inch. Alternatively, you might choose to treat the light-weight framework model as sufficient to start modeling in more detail on one or more domains of interest. – the "T-model" approach.

It's pretty flexible, but there's even more flexibility to be had.

The first-cut mile-wide/inch-deep model doesn't have to cover all domains. In fact, it's unlikely you will identify them all in one quick pass. If you're using proven assembly patterns and bolting them together according to integration patterns, then all is not lost. You can pick up more detail on the next iteration, with a reasonable chance that the newly discovered bits and pieces will fit in without too much disruption.

Similarly, there is flexibility on how deep a deep-dive might go. At one site, a fairly standard logical model was required to set the strategy for a customer relationship management initiative. That was sufficient. But at the same site, a more detailed model was required to shape the subsequent physical model for a custom order capture application. Two domains were extended from the framework model, but to two different levels of detail. Their model checklist looked a bit like the one below.

	Account	Agreement	Document	Party/Role	(etc.)
High-level logical subject areas	☑	☑	☑	☑	☑
Standard logical assembly patterns		☑		☑	
Refined logical assembly patterns		☑			

Table 18: Coverage matrix – progressive/iterative T-models

I strive to be flexible and to adapt to the client's needs, but sometimes this can bring challenges. An example springs to mind. I was scheduled to facilitate a workshop relating to some aspects of a workflow management domain. The meeting started with the client's representatives informing me that a new pressing need had arisen, and would I mind if we totally abandoned all the plans we had for investigating workflow, and instead, jump in totally unprepared, to grapple with a different issue? We actually had a lot of fun, and collectively were able to identify a few candidate strategic directions. But it is risky, and good outcomes are not guaranteed!

Just to make things a bit more challenging with this client, we had initially envisaged applying the T-model approach, namely to start with a mile-wide/inch-deep framework, then to drill down into detail once the framework was roughed out. However, with a few pressing problems, they asked if we could start by addressing those through a more bottom-up approach, even though they did not have a framework articulated. Is this possible? Is it advisable?

Let's take an example. Harking back to the scenario where we wanted a system to manage agreements relating to the transfer of ownership of properties, mortgages, and the like, we might start creating the fine details of the model for agreements. At first glance, one might envisage the model evolution commences something like the checklist on the facing page.

	Account	Resource	Agreement	Party/Role	Location
High-level logical subject areas					
Standard logical assembly patterns					
Detailed logical model			☑		

Table 19: Coverage matrix – detail without context

From a traditional architect's perspective, this looks a bit risky, as you don't start with the consistent framework of an overarching model. On the other hand, agile practitioners might argue that it's more risky to try to establish the overarching architecture when you don't know what's really required! Here's where the pattern-based approach can reduce the risks perceived by both groups:

1. Where possible, base the detailed modeling on proven assembly patterns. For our agreement-based scenario, this would put a tick in the Standard Logical Assembly Pattern box under the Agreement domain in the table above.
2. Using integration patterns, as well as your own analysis, identify the touch points where the domain you are focusing on interacts with other domains. In this case, that might be the Resource domain for the land assets referenced in the agreement, and the Party/Role domain for the people who are signing the contracts.

The checklist for your evolving model now looks a bit more like a light-weight T-model, but it was driven from the bottom-up.

	Account	Resource	Agreement	Party/Role	Location
High-level logical subject areas		☑	☑	☑	
Standard logical assembly patterns			☑		
Refined logical assembly patterns			☑		

Table 20: Coverage matrix – detail plus context

Please note that the integration patterns may suggest that the Party/Role domain is likely to have touch points into the Location domain to record Party addresses. Or in this scenario, it is even more fundamental to record the location of the parcels of land being referenced. So it looks like we should tick the Location subject area as well. But to prevent scope creep, you may choose to model only the immediate touch points of your selected domain, rather than extending the scope to include the touch points of your touch points. If you trust the integration patterns behind these domains, you may feel it is a manageable risk to leave these extensions to another iteration.

One other caveat... While you might identify the touch points (Resource, Party/Role) of your central domain (Agreement), you do not have to model the touch point domains in excruciating detail. Use proven assembly patterns for these, perform a cursory check to see that they will support the core model, capture that thinking, and then move on. Leave more complete modeling for when that domain is at the center of your focus.

Iterate on concepts via the implementation feedback loop

Concepts must
be implementable

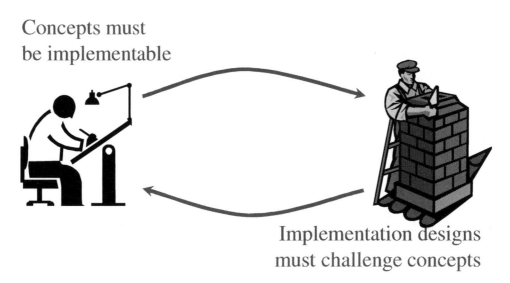

Implementation designs
must challenge concepts

I have some good tradesmen friends who are the envy of many office types. It doesn't seem to matter what the challenge is, they can fix things. Broken cars and broken plumbing, right through to building an entirely new house, nothing seems to faze them. They are pragmatic, practical builder types.

They once told me about one job they were on where one of their responsibilities was to fit a toilet in a new bathroom. The problem was that if they fitted the toilet pan where the architect had drawn it to be placed, there would not be enough room to open the bathroom door. They mentioned it to the architect, but he basically said he couldn't have made such a silly mistake and ordered them to put it where he had indicated.

They tried reasoning again and again, but he was only getting more angry and insistent. So they installed it where he had mandated, and climbed out the bathroom window, as they now could not get out the door – just as they had warned the architect. Not long after, a shamefaced architect rang and asked them to return and fix the problem, as neither he nor anyone else could get into the bathroom!

My friends can tackle everything from conceptual architecture and design (they draw their own house plans) right through implementation of their ideas. But not all tradespeople can do architectural design, and not all architects can implement their ideas. Having tradesmen who don't have a gift for design is OK, but having architects whose designs can't be implemented is a real problem; and in the building trade, it happens more often than you might imagine. Likewise, a data architect who does not stick around to make sure that their design can be implemented runs the risk of not learning from possible mistakes.

One of the things I love about Len Silverston and Paul Agnew's work in Volume 3 of the *Data Model Resource Book*[73] is the way they demonstrate that while high level models may not usually be directly suited for use as an implementation database design, they have a clear path to physical implementation through their lower-level associated patterns. Agile practitioners hold the view that working software is of greater value than comprehensive documentation. It's not that they don't see any value in documentation, but rather that they see the proof-of-the-pudding being in delivered code.

Similarly, I suggest we should not disregard the importance of conceptual modeling. Rather, I suggest that conceptual models that contribute to useful implementation designs are something of great value.

There is a risk that the above statement may be misunderstood. I am *not* saying that a conceptual model must have the detail and rigor required for direct implementation. I think one could argue that it would cease to be a conceptual model if it had that level of precision. I am also not saying that there must be one and only one way of implementing a conceptual model. The books by the patterns authors clearly demonstrate a multiplicity of implementations for a given high-level pattern. What I *am*

---

[73] (Silverston & Agnew, 2009: 7-14)

saying is that when I am asked to quality-assure someone's conceptual model, I feel much more comfortable if I can see at least *one* way it *could* be implemented.

So my first statement of belief is that it is desirable that a conceptual model demonstrate an ability to be implemented. The exercise of grappling with real-life samples and their implementation can often challenge the conceptual view of the world.

My second belief is that it is unfortunate when consultants deliver a model intended to shape an implementation but do not hang around long enough to see the consequences of their design. I realize it is not always possible to be engaged for long enough, but again and again, I have realized that some of my own well-intentioned designs had room for improvement that only became evident during implementation or subsequent use.

I know it is not always possible, but I think agile projects can benefit from the involvement of architects, and architects can benefit from involvement in agile projects. An article on the web site for agile developers makes a less than subtle point, though. They argue that there is no place for *traditional* architects on agile projects. What they want are *agile* architects. In their *"Pathfinder rather than Architect"* paper, they suggest that on an agile team:

> *"... an architect should ... have a fine-grained vision for what the details of the* <u>*implementation*</u> *should be – putting in place expectations for* <u>*patterns*</u> *and tools supporting those patterns ..."* [Emphasis mine] [74]

Iterate to improve

I have just spoken about the desirability of having architects stay around long enough to learn from their mistakes. It is a good thing if they learn and take their insights into their next project. It is even better if they learn and are able to bring those insights back into the project where a better way was first discovered. A fundamental aspect of agile development is an openness to change, and a willingness to incorporate change in the next iteration.

There is also a concept called "technical debt". Each time you deliver a bit of software with, for example, aspects of poor architecture, you may deliver now, but inherit debt (problems) that will have to be paid back later. Unless you consciously plan to repay that debt, it can mount up to the point that it is all consuming – you are spending so

---

[74] http://codebetter.com/scottbellware/2006/09/10/pathfinder-rather-than-archtect/

much time trying to keep unmaintainable code maintained that you can't make any progress.

As is often the case, there can be extremes. One extreme is to fear the accumulation of technical debt so much that you will not make a start until everything is perfect; which means you will never make a start. The other extreme is to have total disregard for short-cuts made, and a refusal to ever consider refactoring of the work already completed. Just keep patching the patches and hope nothing breaks, which is equally unsatisfactory.

The balance is somewhere between these extremes. Make a start based on your best knowledge, using patterns where appropriate. However, when you get feedback that suggests you might have done better, be open to constructive criticism and willing to recommend changes to what has already been done. If the changes are relatively minor, the refactoring approach may serve you well. But sometimes a more major rework is necessary.

A project I have been involved in as a data architect had made great progress, following a somewhat loose "agile" approach. Then a request came for inclusion of temporal aspects into the database, so that it could hold not only the current values for any record, but also versioned snapshots over time. It might sound like a small change, but if you read the work by Snodgrass on temporal and bi-temporal databases[75], you start to realize that it is not as simple as adding a date column to each table. The bottom line is that sometimes a more fundamental change may require more than adopting the new direction in the next iteration. Nonetheless, it may be required.

Strive for incremental improvements in not only added functionality, but also in the refactoring of existing software investments; be willing to make the big changes if really necessary.

---

[75] ("*Developing Time-Oriented Database Application in SQL*", by Richard Snodgrass)

Consolidating the chapter for you

SUMMARY:

- You don't have to have an enterprise logical model fully articulated in excruciating detail before you can start getting benefit from it.
- An effective starting point for an enterprise data model can be to assemble a mile-wide/inch-deep framework quickly, using assembly component patterns to seed the thinking.
- In the spirit of agile/iterative development, this framework model can be fleshed out in greater detail on a project-by-project basis. This is done selectively:
    - Components that are essential to project progress get greater attention.
    - The touch points where the project's world interacts with other elements of the framework can be subject to a little investigation and elaboration.
    - And the rest gets left for another day!
- Unfortunately, delivering a perfect model the first time (whatever "perfect" might mean) is an unrealistic expectation. It is more reasonable to accept that change will occur, especially when people try to actually implement our brilliant data modeling ideas!
- Expect that part of each iteration will be the refinement of earlier modeling work.

APPLYING THIS TO YOUR SITUATION:

- In the spirit of our agile colleagues, embrace change – including feedback from the developers that we could have done better!
- Another lesson from our agile friends is to budget for refactoring. Rather than seeing rework as indicative of failure, build a culture that budgets for progressive improvement and rewards those who seek to keep learning.

It's not an 80/20 silver bullet

It's great when you can find off-the-shelf patterns that are just what you need, independent of whether the requirement is for a running-start model for an agile project or just to keep the boss happy. But you may not always find the patterns you need. Sometimes your palette of patterns comes pretty close, requiring just a minor tweak or a specialized extension and you're ready to go. That's exactly what happened when I needed some emergency contact rule extensions to the baseline Party/Role pattern, as described in the earlier 'Variation via custom extension' section.

Sometimes the news is a bit worse. You don't seem to be able to find anything even remotely close, but you can see a way to build an entirely new assembly pattern from your kit-bag of favorite elementary patterns.

And then there are the times when you despair of finding anything reusable and fear you have to build from scratch. So how will the lack of patterns affect your total time for delivery? The following diagram provides a framework for answering that question.

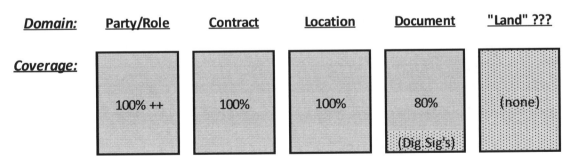

Figure 43: The 80/20 rule mirage

The background for the diagram is the property ownership system we have already looked at a number of times, but this time we are analyzing the effort involved in filling in the gaps when off-the-shelf patterns fall short. The fit for the Party/Role domain was 100%, or maybe we might say even more than 100% - the combined patterns from Dave Hay, Len Silverston, Martin Fowler, Arlow and Neustadt, and others provided more than enough for us. It's similar for the Contract (or Agreement) domain, and the Open Geospatial Consortium (OGC) may provide the foundation for our Location domain model.

So far, so good. Now we hit the Document domain, and Dave Hay's models on documents[76] go a long way towards what we need. But this is not some hypothetical scenario, it's a real world project where, for electronic conveyancing, we need absolutely bullet-proof digital signatures that will stand up in a court of law. If I am buying your home for hundreds of thousands of dollars, and you electronically sign a binding document transferring ownership to me, I want to know that this funny thing called a digital signature on some funny XML document really represents you. I've just given you a sizable amount of my money, and I want the comfort of knowing you really will end up transferring ownership of what previously was your home to me.

It took a relatively short time to assemble a framework for the core of the Document model. It took years of committee meetings and lawyers checking legislation to make significant progress on digital signatures.

In this case, it wasn't so much getting the model right that was the challenge; it was the "business" world around it. For the "Land" domain, getting the model right had also been a big challenge. Perhaps not surprisingly, we had trouble finding a Land model. You may recall that the breakthrough came when we realized that the more generic Resource/Asset pattern actually helped us focus the model on the registration of "rights", rather than "land".

What's the take-away message? That the old 80/20 rule just doesn't apply. Let's say you assemble 80% of the model relatively quickly, and you hope that it's taken 20% of the total time. If that were the case, the remaining 20% of the model should take 80% of the time – four times longer than what it's taken so far. So if it took one month to put together the easy 80%, then another four months should see you finished. In practice, it may take only days or weeks to put together a useful framework to at least kick off a series of iterations for refinement of 80% of the scope. But it may take many months, or even years, to get to the heart of the problem areas.

---

[76] (Hay, 1996: 205-234; Hay, 2011-a: 255-271)

It's much slower to develop a model from the very beginning than to reuse and maybe adapt someone else's pattern. And if the model you are developing is something you want to be flexible for future reuse, it's even harder. That's not good news, but the next section suggests there may be ways we can learn from our agile friends and deliver value iteratively.

Letting "agile" teach us a trick or two

There is most definitely a role for data architects to contribute to agile projects, and to be effective, we need to be more agile, ourselves. That's what this book is about, especially when patterns can give us speed-to-market with robust and extensible models.

But this section is not about *us* contributing to *their* agile world – that topic is investigated more thoroughly in the last part of this book, when we pull together the themes of this book. The focus here is the opposite of seeing how we can help them. It's about how we, the data architects of this world, can benefit by learning a few tips and techniques from the agile practitioners.

We live in a fast-paced world. We are under pressure to deliver data architectures in an efficient manner. Sometimes the catalyst is that our work is required to support an agile project, but not always. Maybe a model is required for an IT strategy initiative, or to shape the construction of an enterprise data warehouse. Totally independent of whether our consumer is an agile project or not, we should see what we can learn from the principles and practices of our agile friends.

THE AGILE MANIFESTO AS A FRAMEWORK FOR DATA ARCHITECTURE ITERATION

The authors of the Agile Manifesto state that they:

> *"... have come to value:*
>
> - *Individuals and interactions over process and tools*
> - *Working software over comprehensive documentation*
> - *Customer collaboration over contract negotiation*
> - *Responding to change over following a plan.*
>
> *That is, while there is value in the items on the right, [they] value the items on the left more."* [77]

---

[77] http://agilemanifesto.org, December 2011

From my own experience, I think data architects can use the Agile Manifesto as a framework for iterative development of data models. I do not want my suggestion to be taken as a new methodology, nor as a legalistic checklist. It is just a collection of ideas that might make sense in some circumstances.

Individuals and interactions: A good friend of mine frequently used the phrase that we should "ride the truck". Instead of sitting in the office and talking to people about their work, he encouraged data architects to get out and see what life was really like for the front-line workers. I clearly recall the day Bill instructed me to wear old clothes to work the following day. We were grappling with data quality issues relating to the computer records of telephone exchange records, and he wanted to literally, physically crawl around an exchange and see the challenges they faced. For a data architect struggling to develop a model without patterns, the analogy to "riding the truck" can be getting out of the office and going and collecting some real-life data samples.

Working software: Sometimes, complex data models can be difficult to evaluate. While I am not suggesting that data architects need to develop some Java or .NET code, I am suggesting that, for example, the throwing together of a sandpit proof-of-concept database may prove to be invaluable. The sample data can include bottom-up samples as collected above to reflect the as-is state. It can also include some top-down thinking on emerging requirements - I know this goes against YAGNI principles, but I also hold the view that a balanced consideration of the future may pay dividends.

Customer collaboration: Having thrown together a proof-of-concept database, it's not rocket science to play back your discoveries to the stakeholders, toss around some alternatives you generated along the way, and consider how what you've built might integrate with other domains. This leads to the next item...

Responding to change: The construction of a proof-of-concept database is likely to address some issues and to raise others. Our agile friends encourage us to welcome change rather than resist it. New topics on the table might mean having to go back to the first step and "ride the truck" again, refine the sandpit database, check it out, and discover even more changes. That's what iteration is all about.

Of course, if you discovered the perfect model before you started, or if you developed a perfect model the first time, there will be no need for iterations - I just haven't achieved perfection yet. A "right-first-time" model may be achievable for simpler domains, but is an unrealistic expectation for more complex scenarios. Let's learn from agile practices and set the expectations of our consumers to a series of refinements.

A CASE STUDY IN USING THE AGILE PRINCIPLES FOR DATA ARCHITECTURE

The Agile Manifesto presents four core values. The related statement of "Principles behind the Agile Manifesto"[78] articulates twelve principles that guide agile practices. These obviously relate to agile projects – that's the patch they play in. But can they also guide the development of data architecture patterns? I believe so.

I have had the pleasure of playing the role of data architect on a project that needed to radically extend a published pattern. While the project was not run formally as an agile project, I believe it followed many of the principles. I realize there is a danger in claiming to be "agile", but in fact using that pretext to break all the rules, including those of common sense. In their book *Balancing Agility and Discipline*[79], the story is told about Bob Martin questioning a supposed adherent to the XP agile methodology. Bob asked how this "adherent" was finding various aspects of XP, and each question resulted in a reply, "We don't do that." Finally Bob asked what aspects the person was actually using, and got the reply, "We don't document anything!" As the authors point out, that's not use of agile – it's misuse.

I believe that a critical review of our informal use of agile principles would suggest data architects can benefit from the use, not misuse, of agile principles in the development of their artifacts. In the real-world story below, the core architecture artifact was a data model. The twelve principles behind the Agile Manifesto are woven in to provide a cross-reference and to highlight their value in the development of a data architecture.

The context for the project was the need to capture and maintain product and service definitions. A fundamental pattern to do this was available, as were a number of commercial off-the-shelf (COTS) tools to manage the product and service catalogue. However, none of the tools available at the time offered the functionality that was required. Essential data was being captured in spreadsheets while waiting for the required tools. They say necessity is the mother of invention - the spreadsheet solution was problematic, to say the least, and an improved temporary solution was suggested. (You can probably already guess at the permanence of the temporary solution!)

As a data architect, I was relocated from my central office and placed alongside the people who needed to populate the proposed tool. [Principle #4. *"Business people and developers must work together daily throughout the project."*].

---

[78] http://agilemanifesto.org/principles.html

[79] (Boehm & Turner, 2009: 6)

The industry pattern for the data model was taken as the baseline. It was known to be more of a logical framework than a directly implementable model, but it gave us a running start, so why not use it? It reflected the collective wisdom of the best thinkers in the industry. The elegant and flexible nature of the framework has proven again and again to have saved us effort. [Principle #10. "*Simplicity--the art of maximizing the amount of work not done--is essential.*"].

We needed a developer to kick things off. The first one to arrive insisted on formally defined specifications, in absolute detail, before work would commence. No flexibility. No self-discovery. A replacement was quickly found. This time I approached a highly competent individual who, in the 1970s, had introduced me to the wonders of databases. (Not relational, but databases nonetheless.) He was one of those amazing people who was very capable of doing "senior" stuff, but who was also brilliant as a hands-on developer and didn't want to be promoted into management, away from all the fun. All I had to do was to brief him on the problem and leave him to deliver. Just as we trusted Terry to look after the technical architecture of the code, the organization was liberating in the amount of authority they had delegated to me for development of the data architecture. [Principle #5. "*Build projects around motivated individuals. Give them the environment and support they need, and trust them to get the job done.*"].

We didn't have anything like a formal project plan, but it was not essential. The data architecture was largely a cut-and-paste of the industry model. Terry got a working prototype assembled in no time flat, and handed it over for evaluation. Of course, refinements were subsequently required, but the users had something to work with from very early on, and refinement followed in quick succession. [Principle #1. "*Our highest priority is to satisfy the customer through early and continuous delivery of valuable software.*", and Principle #7. "*Working software is the primary measure of progress.*"].

The required changes were sometimes just at the coding level, but sometimes they also required tuning of the data architecture. Again and again, we turned the problems into solutions in very little time, and therefore at very little cost. I will admit that it was embarrassing the number of times I would labor over a data model extension for hours or days, and then take it to Terry for estimation on the build effort, only to have him say it would take less time to build the solution than to write up a formal estimate. [Principle #3. "*Deliver working software frequently, from a couple of weeks to a couple of months, with a preference to the shorter timescale.*"].

One of the data model elements I was particularly pleased with related to the dynamic assembly of a spreadsheet-like matrix for attribute-based pricing. Logically, it was a multi-dimensional spreadsheet with multiple values for every "cell". A few challenges for me, and a lot of fun. My design was implemented, but let's say that it had "room for improvement". It can be tough on the ego when the lead programmer tells the data architect that the data model needs changing, but we're a team (and anyway, he was right), so my design was due for refactoring. [Principle #9. "*Continuous attention to technical excellence and good design enhances agility.*"].

It's not just clever developers who challenge my data architecture. It seems that anyone is entitled to highlight my mistakes! I had another bit of the model that held Boolean expressions as structured data. The users of the system could capture business rules in a formal domain-specific language, and the consumers of the central reference data could treat it as machine-executable rules. Again, I was reasonably pleased with this part of the model, but one of the bright youngsters from the team of users worked with me to make the system *more* usable. More damage to my ego! [Principle #11. "*The best architectures, requirements, and designs emerge from self-organizing teams.*"].

In the early days, we had a small team and we were all located in the same corner of the office. It was really easy to toss around ideas and rate their relative merits. [Principle #6. "*The most efficient and effective method of conveying information to and within a development team is face-to-face conversation.*"]. Later, the number of users grew, and several were located in a different country. The team dynamics changed. We were receiving requests for refinement to the data architecture from people I had not even met, and some of whom I would *never* meet. There is no doubt in my mind that co-location is preferable, but that may not always be possible. Two strategies we applied were (1) bringing off-shore people to the central team for a period of assimilation, and (2) establishment of first-point-of-contact personnel to manage interactions in an ever-growing team. These people became what the agile practitioners might label as the CRACK (Collaborative, Representative, Authorized, Committed, and Knowledgeable) representatives for the larger team.

Perhaps human nature resists change, but if we data architects are to truly deliver value to others, we must adopt the attitudes about change encapsulated in agile thinking. [Principle #2. "*Welcome changing requirements, even late in development. Agile processes harness change for the customer's competitive advantage.*"].

Some changes are relatively minor, and can be accommodated via refactoring in the next iteration, but some changes are more fundamental. It is a wonderful feeling when a requested change can be easily accommodated. We might even be tempted to boast about how our data architecture is future-proof. Then along comes someone with a request that bursts our bubble. It cannot be simply adopted – it may mean a significant change to our fundamental architecture. This really tests our willingness to welcome change. But if we are going to faithfully serve our organization, we must not be precious about our data architecture. It can be tough on our self-image, but it may be essential to consider radical change. For the agile practitioner, that can include reviewing the agile methodology itself. [Principle #12. *"At regular intervals, the team reflects on how to become more effective, then tunes and adjusts its behavior accordingly."*]. For us, it can mean having the willingness to consider taking on changes to the data architecture, even the more radical ones.

I hope you have gained the impression that I have really enjoyed working with a bunch of wonderful people who collectively have achieved great things. If you don't enjoy your work, or if you push so hard you get burned out, that's no fun. We laugh together, we work together, we dream together. And we try to keep a good work/life balance. I still smile at the time when Terry rang in and reported he wouldn't be in that day as he had been prescribed some "hydro-therapy". One team member was concerned that Terry was not well and that his doctor had prescribed some remedial actions. I smiled and informed the person not to worry – it was a lovely sunny day, the tides were right, and Terry, who had been putting in some really solid hours, was probably going fishing! [Principle #8. *"Agile processes promote sustainable development. The sponsors, developers, and users should be able to maintain a constant pace indefinitely."*].

Consolidating the chapter for you

SUMMARY:
- You won't always be able to find ready-to-go patterns to meet your needs. The cost of ground-up development of the few missing bits can far exceed the total cost of bolting together all of the other published patterns. (While that may seem like bad news, imagine how much worse it would be if we had to develop the entire model from the ground up!)
- When we have to build our own data model components, we may be able to adopt or adapt some of the agile thinking to the way we work (interact with those who use the data, do some proof-of-concept development, negotiate with our stakeholders if our discoveries of "truth" might mean a rethink, and welcome change, instead of seeing it as the enemy).

APPLYING THIS TO YOUR SITUATION:
- Identify the areas within the overall model where you may have to create your own model components.
- Where the need exists for constructing your own components, see if you can consciously apply agile principles in the way you go about filling in the gaps.

An honorable way to make life harder for yourself

Graeme Simsion and Graham Witt's book, *Data Modeling Essentials*, dedicates a chapter to modeling business rules[80]. Malcolm Chisolm has an entire book on *How to Build a Business Rules Engine*[81]. Ron Ross (sometimes known as the "father of business rules") and others in the Business Rules Group (Dave Hay, John Zachman, etc.) have devoted many years of their lives to the topic, and continue to do so. It has been an area of passionate interest to me, also, and was the subject of a minor thesis I completed some years ago. ("*The Benefits of Object Technology for the Direct Execution of Computational Business Rules*", RMIT university. Melbourne, Australia, October 2001). The Object Management Group (OMG) facilitates the specification and enhancement of a language for business rules, the Semantics of Business Vocabulary and Business Rules (SBVR).

There are many different types of business rules. Some say rules should be embedded in IT systems with sufficient precision to allow direct interpretation and execution, while other say that rules should be expressed in the natural language of business people, but do not necessarily need to be executable by a computer. Some suggest rules are purely used to define facts ("a customer can place orders for products"), some that rules constrain the updating of data in computer systems, and some that rules specify how to compute new values from other, existing values. Some people hold that business rules

---

[80] (Simsion & Witt, 2005: 351-388)

[81] (Chisolm, 2003)

must be declarative, stating facts but not defining the processes that come into play, while others accept procedural rules ("do this first, then do that ...") as also being legitimate types of business rules.

It's probably fair to say that business rules are a huge topic in their own right. Thankfully, I suggest we can get value on the data modeling and agility front by gaining familiarity with the few areas that are described in this chapter and the following one. Once you see the benefits from a few domains, you may be better equipped to spot similar opportunities elsewhere.

Let's open up the topic with a brief look at a hypothetical example. Let's say a parcel courier business currently has a flat rate of $10 per kilogram as a baseline. To keep things simple, let's say this base rate is held in a "global variable" somewhere, but is changed reasonably frequently to reflect competition, fuel costs, and the like. The users of the developing system want to be able to easily change the base rate at will, without involving programmers. That seems pretty reasonable.

On top of the base rate, there may be a surcharge for the extra difficulties encountered in handling heavy goods. Whereas the base rate is highly variable, the company claims the surcharge is stable and hasn't changed for years. The agile programmers decide they can capture these business rules in code. The pseudo code might look something like:

- If Weight <= 20 kg, then Surcharge = 0%
- If Weight > 20 kg and Weight <= 50 kg, then Surcharge = 20%
- If Weight > 50 kg and Weight <= 1,000 kg, then Surcharge = 50%
- If Weight > 1,000 kg and Weight <= 5,000 kg, then Surcharge = 80%

From your perspective as a data modeler, the great feature of having the rules in code is it's not your responsibility! The agile programmers have to capture the logic. It's zero work for you initially, and even if the surcharge rates do change, it's still not your problem. But what happens if the person the developers spoke to was wrong about the stability of the surcharge rates? In some environments, it may take days or even weeks to promote the changes, not because they're hard, but because the governance mechanisms for testing and putting code into production can make "instant" changes impossible.

Another approach involves you, the data modeler. You can create a table that holds the rules, and the programmers simply look it up to determine which surcharge to use. The table holding rules-in-data to match the bullet points above might look something like the following.

Criterion:	Result:
Maximum Weight	Surcharge
20 kg	0%
50 kg	20%
1,000 kg	50%
5,000 kg	80%

Table 21: Simple rules-in-data example

Now, if the surcharges change, or even if the breakpoints at which they apply change, it's pretty easy for the business users to change the "rules-in-data", and it doesn't require any code changes by the programmers. It's a little more work for the data modeler up front, and the programmer has to initially code the look-up, but after that (in an ideal world), both the data modeler and the programmer have done their job.

The bottom line is that if you leave the rules to the developers to put in code, your life is easier, but the total outcome may be less than ideal, especially if the rule changes are frequent. So maybe you should help the agile team by seeing if you can lighten their load (yes, at your expense) and put some rules in data.

The above example is pretty straight forward, but life isn't always that easy. Sometimes not only the *contents* of the rules tables change, but the data *structures* of the rules tables themselves also keep changing. One solution is to make the data structures highly configurable, but this increased level of abstraction can result in significant increases in programming complexity. It's not always a simple task to capture rules in data, even if it is desirable.

Fixed-structure decision tables

The concept of decision tables has been around for decades. Business people can understand and maintain the rules, and computers can make run-time decisions based on their contents.

The classical decision table has a distinctive shape, but there are many variations. For example, Ron Ross has extended the concepts and applied them to his practices for the capture and maintenance of business rules.

The parcel surcharge example above has maximum weight as a "condition" (e.g. "weight is more than 20 kg, but not more than 50 kg") and applicable surcharge as an "action", or "outcome" as Ron Ross calls it (e.g. "apply a surcharge of 20%"). This simple structure can be seen as a form of decision table.

The action/outcome/result (call it what you like) can be a True/False result or a discrete value, such as "20%". We will look at some more interesting and progressively challenging forms of decision tables.

First, let's look again at the parcel rules scenario. For the sake of the exercise, let's assume that surcharge varies by weight *and* by whether or not the goods are dangerous (e.g. toxic chemicals or explosives). Let's also assume that a new result is needed, namely an indicator for whether insurance is required or not, where parcels that are heavy <u>and</u> dangerous must be insured, but light <u>or</u> safe things do not need insurance. A subset of the pseudo code might look a little like the following:

- If Weight <= 20 kg and if Dangerous Goods Indicator = "False", then Surcharge = 0% and Insurance Required = "No"

(through to)

- If Weight > 1,000 kg and Weight <=5,000 kg and if Dangerous Goods Indicator = "True", then Surcharge = 90% and Insurance Required = "Yes"

The matching rules-in-data table might be as follows:

Criteria:		Results:	
Maximum Weight	**Is Dangerous?**	**Surcharge**	**Needs Insurance?**
20 kg	No	0%	No
20 kg	Yes	10%	No
50 kg	No	20%	No
50 kg	Yes	30%	No
1,000 kg	No	50%	No
1,000 kg	Yes	60%	Yes
5,000 kg	No	80%	No
5,000 kg	Yes	90%	Yes

Table 22: Simplified "Decision-table" example

This table is a little more complex, but still quite easy to for the data modeler to define, the business user to maintain, and the developer to program. But it gets more challenging.

Adaptive decision tables

Several times over the years, I have encountered the need for separate rules tables that really were variations on a central theme. One time, it was for wool bales from a grower, where different lots of like bales were classified by certain criteria, and prices and available quantities offered to the market. For example, one farmer might classify his offerings by average fiber thickness, fiber length, and fiber strength. Taking the first line in the sample table below, Farmer Jones might offer 23 tons of wool at $3.45 per kg for wool with an average thickness of 21 micron, an average length of 93 mm, and average strength of 163 MPa[82].

Farmer Jones' Criteria:			Results:	
Thickness (micron)	Length (mm)	Strength (MPa)	Quantity (tons)	Price ($/kg)
21.0	93	163	23	$3.45
20.5	123	150	7	$4.56
19.0	82	140	3	$5.67

Table 23: "Decision table" driven by metadata – example #1

Another farmer might record fiber thickness as above, along with the breakpoint and color, but not length or strength.

Farmer Brown's Criteria:			Results:	
Thickness (micron)	Breakpoint	Color	Quantity (tons)	Price ($/kg)
21.0	Middle	White	17	$3.21
25	Middle	Black	2	$2.10

Table 24: "Decision table" driven by metadata – example #2

---

[82] The symbol MPa represents mega Pascal, a metric unit used in this context to measure tensile strength.

Not only might each farmer classify the wool they want to offer according to different criteria, each buyer might express what they want to buy using different criteria. To have separate physical rules tables for every combination of criteria was impractical. We needed something more flexible.

A similar challenge was faced more recently in a telecommunications company that needed to capture variable criteria for their products, and capture variable results, as well. Two sample tables demonstrate the requirement. The first is for a mobile phone handset product where the price and a mapping to an old product system's codes vary depending on make and color.

Mobile Phone Criteria:		Results:	
Make	**Color**	**Legacy Product Code**	**Price**
Acme	Black	ABC-123	$123
Acme	Silver	ABC-456	$150
Excelsior	Black	XYZ-987	$111
Excelsior	White	XYZ-654	$222

Table 25: "Decision table" driven by metadata – example #3

The second sample is for another telecommunications product, but this time for Internet access, where price varies according to selected technology, speed, and monthly download cap. (I haven't put in units of measure such as megabytes or gigabytes, because any figures I pick will become dated too quickly. In the telecommunications industry, speeds that are unthinkable today may well be mundane and boring by tomorrow!)

Internet Access Criteria:			Result:
Technology	Speed	Download Cap	Price
Cable	100	10	$20
Cable	100	20	$25
Cable	200	10	$30
Cable	200	20	$35
Satellite	50	10	$50
Satellite	50	20	$60
(etc.)			

Table 26: "Decision table" driven by metadata – example #4

A few observations if we want a flexible, generic solution:

- Each decision table can have one or many criteria, and each of these may be for a different "dimension" e.g. Thickness, or Color for wool, or Speed, Technology, and so on for a mobile phone.
- Each decision table can have one or many results, and each of these may be for a different result type; e.g. Price, Parcel Surcharge, some legacy system's Product Code, or whatever.
- Each decision table may be associated with different "things" (a wool farmer's clip, a telecommunications mobile phone product, a telecommunications Internet product ...)
- Although not shown in the samples above, the population may be sparse, i.e., not all possible combinations of criteria values may have matching results, at least at a point in time.

There are plenty of variations as to how you, the data modeler, might capture this decision table data in a way that will facilitate the agile developers offering a user-interface to the business people, and an execution engine for their own code. But the following model might prove to be a helpful framework for you if you need to consider this type of problem.

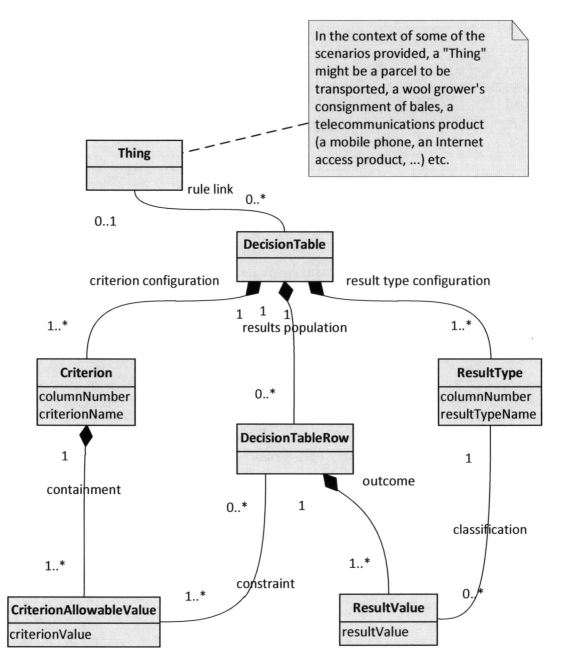

In the context of some of the scenarios provided, a "Thing" might be a parcel to be transported, a wool grower's consignment of bales, a telecommunications product (a mobile phone, an Internet access product, ...) etc.

Figure 44: A model for a metadata-driven "Decision table"

We look again at the Mobile Phone table of rules and apply it to this framework:

- The "Thing" object might be the Mobile Phone row in a Product Definition table. This identifies the "thing" to which the rules in the decision table are to be applied.

- The Decision Table object is the root object representing the entire table of rules. It does little more than provide a central placeholder for its real contents, the associated Criteria, the Result Types, and the Decision Table Rows.
- There would be two Criterion objects for this decision table, one being Make and the other being Color, with the associated Criterion Allowable Values objects being "Acme" and "Excelsior" for the "Make" Criterion, and "Black", "Silver" and "White" for the "Color" Criterion.
- There would be two Result Type objects for this decision table, one being Legacy Product Code, and the other being Price.
- The above data sets can be used to configure a decision table, with its column headings and the allowable values for its criteria. In the Mobile Phone sample, the real rules are contained in four Decision Table Rows, with their associated Result Values (e.g. a Price of $111 for the third row).

This pattern has proven to be a flexible foundation for a number of applications requiring decision table structures. It does require a bit more programming though, than a static decision table such as the introductory Parcel Weight and Surcharge table, where all the columns are fixed and statically defined. So if the criteria and the result types are stable, the additional complexity of this pattern is best avoided.

Consolidating the chapter for you

SUMMARY:
- Business rules can be captured in many ways; e.g. in data structures, in program code, and in structured data (also known as "rules-in-data").
- Where the rules are not stable, rules-in-data can result in IT system stability (it's only the data that changes) plus give the business users a mechanism to manage "their" rules.
- Greater flexibility can be achieved (at a cost) by making even the data structures for rules-in-data driven by configurable metadata structures.

APPLYING THIS TO YOUR SITUATION:
- It's easier to make the capture and maintenance of rules someone else's problem, but the business may thank you if *you* take that responsibility where the changeability of the rules warrants a rules-in-data approach. Consciously and explicitly look at business rules and work with others to evaluate options.

Derivation of computed values

Decision tables are a common way for business rules to be expressed in data. The results are a discrete set of specific values. In the first Parcel Weight and Surcharge decision table presented in the previous chapter, there were exactly 4 surcharge values possible (if a surcharge of zero is included), and in the Parcel Weight, Danger and Surcharge table there were exactly eight values. But what happens if the rule for surcharge determination is that Surcharge equals Delivery Kilometers times Recovery Rate, where Recovery Rate changes each month and is based on average fuel costs. If the current Recovery Rate is $0.25 you might try and set up a table to hold the Surcharges.

Criterion:	Result:
Delivery Kilometers	**Surcharge**
1	$0.25
2	$0.50
3	$0.75
(etc.)	...

Table 27: Simple "derivation" example

You can probably see the problems. If trips can be up to 1,000 km, you will need 1,000 rows in this table. Then somebody decides to record delivery kilometers to one decimal place (0.1 km = $0.025, 0.2 km = $0.05, 0.3 km = $0.075, and so on) – for 10,000 rows! Heaven help us if the accountants also decide to express recovery rates to a decimal of a cent, and for up to 3,000 kilometers - now we need 300,000 rows. And that's just for one month. If we keep a history of surcharges by month, the problem just keeps growing.

Alternatively, we can have _one_ line of code that computes the Surcharge result given the two variables of Recovery Rate and Delivery Kilometers. The whole idea of having rules-in-data instead of rules-in-code for this computation scenario starts to look absurd. The decision table approaches articulated in the previous chapter are great when the criteria and their allowable values are well defined, but decision tables are typically a poor fit when computation formulae are involved. If a formula is itself static (e.g. net price = gross price less discount), then having it in program code is fine.

Having said that, if the _formulae_ change frequently, you might want to consider capturing the formulae themselves in structured data (**not** the results!), and having the program code execute by dynamically interpreting the structured rules.

The lines between data modelers and programmers start to get pretty blurred at this point. If we go far enough (or maybe that should be "if we go too far") we can end up developing a new programming language just for one special group of users. For more information on this topic, you may wish to reference discussions on Domain Specific Languages (DSLs), or "little languages", as they were known at one point in time.

Why, oh why, are we even talking about such things? Because sometimes a little bit of creativity in a data model can capture execution rules in a way that can be easily maintained by business users rather than programmers. It's all about agile data architects proactively contributing to agility among developers. Let's have a quick look at one fun example from real life that might help inspire you to be open to helping our agile developer colleagues in a creative manner.

We have already touched on the case study for a company that manufactured made-to-measure shower screens, mirrored wardrobe doors, etc. Their core need was to define computations in user-maintainable formulae that were sufficiently precise to drive execution of code to generate cutting sizes for components.

Let's look at a hypothetical but realistic order for a Model Number 20 shower screen – a fairly standard 3-panel shower screen (one fixed panel, 2 sliding panels). The salesperson taking the order measures the opening size at the customer's premises. The width at the top (WT) of the gap is 865 mm, the width at the base (WB) is 860 mm (indicating the walls are out-of-square by 5 mm), and the height (H) is 1850 mm. These in-field measurements are now needed as input variables for the computation of the factory floor cutting sizes of the made-to-order shower screen, as shown in the following diagram.

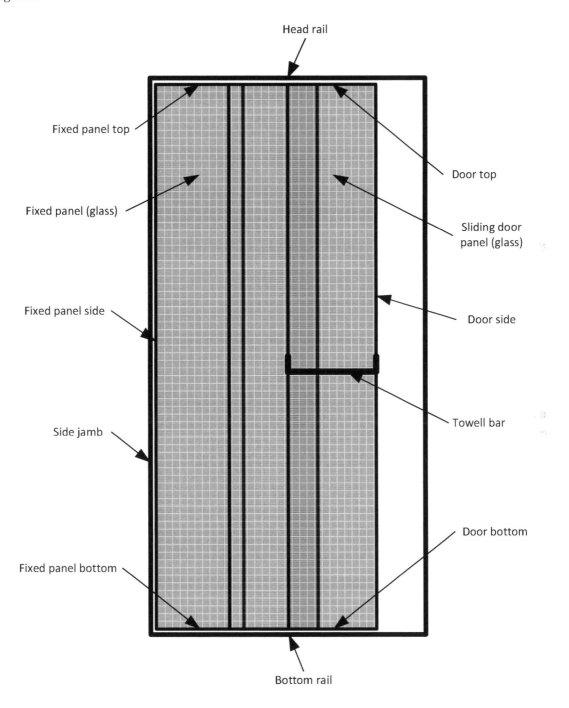

Figure 45: Shower screen schematic

The aluminum strip length calculations for a Model Number 20 are described in the table below, along with the results for this hypothetical order. Formula variables represent either the measurement variables (WT of 865 mm, WB of 860 mm, and H of 1850 mm) or the abbreviations for the components themselves. For example, in the formula 'BR = WB − 7', BR is the variable for the Bottom Rail component, and WB is the variable for the Width-at-Base measurement (measured on site to be 860 mm). The dimensions are expressed in mm.

Measurement Name	Abbrev.	Formula	Result
Head Rail	HR	HR = WT	865
Bottom Rail	BR	BR = WB - 7	853
Side Jamb	SJ	SJ = H - 35	1815
Door Top & Bottom	DT&B	DT&B = (WT + 30) / 3	298
Door Side	DS	DS = H - 60	1790
Fixed Panel Top & Bottom	FPT&B	FPT&B = DT&B	298
Fixed Panel Side	FPS	FPS = H	1850
Towel Bar	TB	TB = DT&B - 60	238

Table 28: Derivation – aluminum components

The glass panel length and width calculations are described in the next table, below.

Measurement Name	Abbrev.	Formula	Result
Sliding Door Panel - Height	SDPH	SDPH = DS - 20	1770
Sliding Door Panel - Width	SDPW	SDPW = DT&B - 20	278
Fixed Panel - Height	FPH	FPH = H - 20	1830
Fixed Panel - Width	FPW	FPW = DT&B - 20	278

Table 29: Derivation – glass components

Based on these calculations, the work to cut and assemble the item could then proceed for the hypothetical order.

The company produced five major product ranges, namely shower screens, security doors, insect screens, mirrored wardrobe doors, and mirrored walls. Across this range, there were approximately 50 models in total, but the range was continually growing.

There were hundreds of job sheets prepared per day. Staff found the computations tedious and made mistakes. Mistakes translated into a number of cost areas. Mainly, there was material waste. A wrongly cut part that was too long could be recovered relatively easily. If it was too short, it might not be reusable, or at least not for some time. More significantly, if errors were not detected on the factory floor and all the components were sent to the customer's site for fitting, the fitter would be unable to complete the job.

A request was made for a custom computer system to reduce computational errors. The intent was for the order's on-site measurements to be entered as part of each order's details, and the system would compute cutting sizes and generate accurate cutting instructions.

Of course, the developed code could have had hard-coded computations. However, a requirement was that the computer solution would support product expansion without the need for ongoing programmer involvement. A new product line should be able to be defined (or an existing one re-defined), along with its formulae, without changing program code.

A data model was developed, containing a number of entities that you may have expected, such as Customer, Order, and Product Type. There were also some entities that captured the cutting size computations in data in a manner that could be interpreted by executable code. Let's look at:

1. A simplified data model.
2. Some sample data that one might expect a (skilled and trained) business user could enter and maintain themselves.
3. Pseudo code fragments that might interpret the computation rules-in-data.

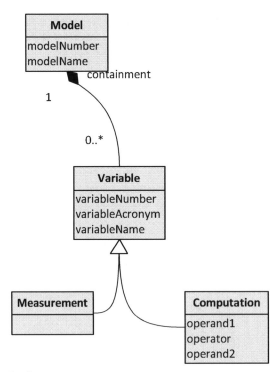

Figure 46: Computation rules-in-data

Each model (e.g. Model 20 – the standard 3-panel shower screen) needs to have a number of variables defined and managed. Some of the variables needed for computation include on-site measurement (e.g. one customer's width-at-top of 865 mm). Other variables are computed and will subsequently provide the factory floor cutting sizes for components. The components themselves are not shown in this model; the focus here is not on how to model shower screen companies, but how to model the entities involved in computation rules that are to be stored in data.

A set of sample data is provided on the facing page to demonstrate how a (simplified) table based on the data model might capture the rules for the Model 20 shower screen.

A few comments:

- For the sake of brevity, the model names and variable names have been excluded from the sample.
- The Variable Type column has been created to handle the consolidation of the two subclasses (Measurement and Computation) into the superclass (Variable).
- At run time, the values of the first three variables would be supplied from the customer order's on-site measurements.
- The operands can be constants enclosed in quotation marks (e.g. "7" to represent 7 mm) or references to other variables.

- The 4th variable is an example of a simple assignment of a value (Head Rail = Width-At-Top), as compared to the 5th variable, which is an example of an arithmetic computation (Bottom Rail = Width-At-Bottom − 7)
- The 7th variable (WT+30) is an interim computation. It is not used directly to determine a cutting size, but is an input into the next computation. Collectively, these two reflect a business rule that the Door-Top-&-Bottom is computed as being equal to (Width-At-Top + 30) / 3. Note that this DT&B result of a compound computation is then itself used as a variable later.

Model Num.	Variable Number	Variable Type	Acronym	Operand 1	Operator	Operand 2
20	1	Measure	WT			
20	2	Measure	WB			
20	3	Measure	H			
20	4	Compute	HR	WT		
20	5	Compute	BR	WB	minus	"7"
20	6	Compute	SJ	H	minus	"35"
20	7	Compute	WT+30	WT	plus	"30"
20	8	Compute	DT&B	WT+30	divided by	"3"
20	9	Compute	DS	H	minus	"60"
20	10	Compute	FPT&B	DT&B		
20	11	Compute	FPS	H		
20	12	Compute	TB	DT&B	minus	"60"
20	13	Compute	SDPH	DS	minus	"20"
20	14	Compute	SDPW	DT&B	minus	"20"
20	15	Compute	FPH	H	minus	"20"
20	16	Compute	FPW	DT&B	minus	"20"

Table 30: Derivation – algorithms

Given a fairly simple user interface, business users can create new models and define the computation rules using a table something like the sample above. Now all we need is some computer code that can take the rules-in-data and execute them to determine calculated cutting sizes. As a pseudo code approximation of the actual code used, an in-memory array is loaded from the rules table above, and a "for-next" loop iterates through the populated values. The pseudo code for each array item might be:

- If the Variable Type = "Measure", prompt the user to enter the site-measurement.
- If the Variable Type = "Compute" and if the Operator and Operand2 are both empty, simply assign the value from the variable referenced in Operand1 to this item's Acronym.
- If the Variable Type = "Compute" and if the Operator and Operand2 are not empty
    - o Assign the value from the variable referenced in Operand1 to a programming variable called "X".
    - o Assign the value from the variable referenced in Operand2 to a programming variable called "Y", or if Operand 2 is a constant enclosed in quotation marks, assign the constant to "Y".
    - o If the Operator = "plus", set Acronym = X + Y.
    - o If the Operator = "minus", set Acronym = X - Y.
    - o If the Operator = "divided by", set Acronym = X / Y.
    - o If the Operator = "multiplied by", set Acronym = X * Y.

My code could be improved, but it's just there to illustrate the point. The actual development for a working proof-of-concept for this client, including solution design, database build, user interface development, population of the rules tables with sample data, and development of the interpretation engine (as per the pseudo code above) took only a couple of days. Yes, the data structure is a bit more abstract, and the logic of the code is likewise dependent on an understanding of the rules-in-data, but it really wasn't that hard to do. There was a lot less code than trying to hard-code the computations for 50 or more models. And the business users could maintain the "code" for their computations.

Hybrid solutions

Ron Ross, the "father of business rules", has done some great work on several fronts, including the structures, maintenance, and usage of decision tables. But as we've seen with the shower screen example above, decision tables may not be the best mechanism to capture and manage computational business rules.

COMBINING DECISION TABLES AND CONSTRAINT LOGIC PROGRAMMING

Earlier, we discussed a system that was proposed to facilitate the management of the supply and demand of Australian wool, and looked at how the criteria used to describe lots of wool (fiber length, thickness, strength, …) were captured using a form of decision table. However, most decision tables have parts for defining the criteria, and parts for defining the outcome (or "actions") to be taken. In the samples provided in the previous chapter, we portrayed data such as price and quantity available as an "outcome". In practice, the quantity available from a farmer and the minimum asking price were constraints, or criteria of getting a sale. Similarly, the wool buyer provided criteria such as desired fiber thickness, color, and required purchase quantity and maximum price.

So if quantity and price are criteria, not results, what are the results from this system? The desired outcome is to match supply with demand in a way that achieves the best outcome for all parties, and that optimizes the logistics of transportation. Determination of these results required some very heavy-duty constraint logic / optimization programming – certainly not the domain of decision tables, even though the input parameters looked something like a set of decision tables. This problem domain is just an example of how some variations of rules-in-data patterns can be applied to deliver agility. Before this hybrid solution was considered, the project manager feared that the remaining 8 months of development time would be insufficient. Due to a number of design strategies, of which one was adopting a rules-in-data approach combined with constraint logic programming, the actual development time was reduced to 4 months.

COMBINING DECISION TABLES AND WORKFLOW

Sometimes the rules relate to triggering actions. This concept is at the heart of traditional decision table thinking. When the decision making is simple but the resulting events are complex, i.e., involving many steps, many resources, and pools of resources, complex scheduling, notification of slippage against expectations, escalation, and so on, you may be better off forgetting all about decision tables and deploying a workflow management set of tools.

Again, though, you may still come across situations where you can combine rules-in-data approaches with other tool sets for a great outcome.

Our first example relates to the loyalty scheme application that was briefly introduced earlier in this book. The determination of rewards was driven by a rules-in-data approach. However, when loyalty rewards were computed and allocated, a whole set of processes kicked off. If the rewards were in the form of gifts, delivery processes were initiated. Or the reward could be a holiday for two, and the recipient of the award had to be contacted to propose dates. Or maybe the reward was financial, and transactions had to be triggered in the accounting system.

The actions were fairly deterministic and simple. Rather than integrating the decision table mechanism with a full-blown workforce management tool, a simple notification mechanism was added to the core decision table functionality.

In another situation, a large telecommunications corporation had a great diversity of products, with a matching variety of service level agreements. The proposal was to include a rules-in-data approach to capture the service level agreement expectations. For example, a decision table structure could record expected service restoration times depending on criteria such as distance from major cities, criticality of the service, and grade of the customer. Similarly, the quality of the data service might also depend on distance from major cities, but also on the technology deployed in delivering bandwidth.

Not only could the *expectations* be captured in decision table structures, but also the *consequences* of failure to meet those expectations. (If the restoration of the service goes beyond expectations by up to two hours, then one consequence is applied; if the restoration is late by more than two hours, then another consequence applies, and so on.)

Defining the consequences is easily accommodated in decision tables. Triggering workforce actions when things go wrong is more difficult, and in this case is probably better left to a workflow management package.

A case study in business rule agility

A fundamental aspect of agile development is iterative learning. You see some needs, you design a solution, and give it a try. You get some feedback, you refine the solution, and try again.

With the involvement of an experienced data architect and a collection of proven data model patterns, there is an increased likelihood that the rework of the data architecture between each iteration is minimized. For example, for the first iteration, a subset of a stable pattern is deployed. As further needs emerge, the greater functionality of the full pattern can be progressively added, ideally without major refactoring.

At one client site, a need arose for some very simple Boolean expressions to be captured in data. All that was required was to capture expressions such as "This applies if Make = Cisco". We could have hard-coded Make as a foreign key to a reference table of device manufacturers (Cisco, Juniper, D-Link, etc.), but another condition might be "... if

Location = International"; and yet another might be "... if Size = Small". So we implemented the Boolean condition as two columns:

1. Identification of the Criterion dimension (Make, Location, Size, ...)
2. Identification of the match value (Cisco, International, ...)

This was fine for a while. Then the users wanted to have composite conditions such as "... if Make = Cisco _**and**_ if Location = International". The data structure needed a small tweak to accommodate sets of conditions joined by an implied "AND" operator.

The next requirement was to have the option for an "OR" operator, but never combined with "AND" operators in the same condition. All that was needed was to add an "And/Or Indicator" column to the data structure defining the set.

Then they wanted "AND" and "OR" operators combined, with brackets. Now we have nested complex Booleans - yet another data structure.

How did this scenario work out in practice? In the past, I had encountered requirements for full, nested Boolean conditions to be captured as structured data. The conditions could, of course, have been captured as text strings, but the application required the expressions to be executable, and therefore they had to have enforced referential integrity to the reference sets of data. The data model pattern isn't too difficult, but the extra flexibility does make the capture of very simple rules a little bit more tedious. I wanted to implement the full solution from the outset, but this was resisted. So we moved step-by-step, progressively implementing parts of the full pattern and taking the business users on the journey. The next iteration provided a natural language interface to allow the business people to define the rules in text, yet store the rules as structured data. Everyone was happy.

The key message is that I encourage the data architects on agile projects to look ahead to the directions the application might go, ensure familiarity with relevant patterns, and see if each iteration's short-term objectives can be met in a manner that can easily be expanded according to possible refinements.

A few comments

As they say, there is good news and bad news – first the bad news. Modeling to accommodate the flexibility for end users to capture and maintain business rules, and for IT systems to execute them at run time, is hard work. Not all modelers or developers are comfortable with, or have the ability to work with, the greater levels of abstraction. Make sure you count the cost of doing it versus the cost of not doing it.

The good news is that a well architected rules-in-data solution can deliver enormous benefit. And it can be a lot of fun for the modeler who enjoys a bit of a challenge!

One more consideration... Incorporating rules-in-data can be a major shift in position. It may turn out to be the simple addition of a little feature on the side, or it may require a significant re-architecting of the solution, including impacts on downstream consumers of data. In the two cases I have encountered, the change was major. But in both cases, the returns were enormous. Again, compare the cost of taking this approach and the cost of not! You may decide a later change of strategy is not something that can be handled easily by refactoring.

Consolidating the chapter for you

SUMMARY:

- Many see business rules as being limited to applying <u>constraints</u>. Another whole family of rules relates to the capture and execution of algorithms for the <u>derivation</u> of computed values. This requirement may be less common than constraint-based rules, but nonetheless its effective management can be critical when the problem arises.
- There are other computer science areas related to rules that may contribute to an effective solution. Not all problems are best handled by the data modeler! Specialist areas can include management of optimization rules, and workflow rules.
- Sometimes the implications of a rules-in-data approach are profound, and cannot reasonably be left to be accommodated by future refactoring.

APPLYING THIS TO YOUR SITUATION:

- Consider formally classifying the types of business rules to be managed, and seriously evaluating the merits of a rules-in-data approach.
- If you are really interested in this topic, you may want to pursue literature on what used to be called "little languages", but are now more widely known as "domain specific languages".

TO DREAM THE IMPOSSIBLE DREAM ...

We're needed (aren't we?)

It's nice to think we are the most important part of the enterprise, if not the world - I love enthusiasm and passion. It's a pity it needs to be toned down with a dose of reality, but how important are we really?

You can read plenty of arguments *for* the value of a data architect's contributions. Because most of the arguments are written *by* data architects, one can understand the rest of the world being a bit cynical. Of course, if our contribution fails, people will feel the pain, and then we *will* feel like we are at the center of the universe – everyone will be blaming us.

I remember one project where I was told that the good news was that if I succeeded, the whole company would know about it. And the bad news? If I failed, the whole company would know about it! So being visible when the data architecture fails might not be good news. It's a bit like a car - the carburetor might feel it's the most important component because hey, if it ceases to work, the car stops. But if carburetors keep letting the team down, some engineers are bound to find another way to get the fuel and oxygen into the engine. And they have.

Likewise, if we data modelers/data architects are going to be valued in the future, we will have to become more "agile" while still delivering quality consulting. And part of this refactoring of ourselves is going to involve rolling up our sleeves and engaging with the agile developers of this new world order.

On his web site, Scott Ambler states:

> *"Data has been an important aspect of every single business application which I have ever built. Then again, so have business rules, user interfaces, networks, and a slew of other issues. My experience is that left to their own devices software developers will usually struggle to get the data stuff right, and will often make questionable decisions from an enterprise data point of view."* [83]

I believe Scott is clearly stating that there is a role for data architects, and I wholeheartedly agree. I also agree with his caution expressed elsewhere on his site that while there is work for "data" people to do, they will have to change some of their ways.

Contributing to the agile world

Back to basics... Why do we architects even exist? (And while this book is focusing on the role of data architects, many of our goals are common with our fellow enterprise architects, who look after things like technology, application integration, and "the business"). There are whole text books on areas in which we can, and arguably should, make contributions, but a selection of items follows.

THE BIG PICTURE (FOR TODAY)

There is a danger that agile projects might solve the specific problems of their beneficiaries, only to find that the enterprise, as a whole, is getting deeper into trouble while trying to achieve cross-silo integration.

I remember consulting to an airline as a data architect. One project team was working on a human resources system that included, among other responsibilities, keeping a basic skills register on all employees – "Alex can type 50 words a minute and has a driver's license; Brooke is qualified to perform first aid and can speak Japanese; ..." In another corner, a project team was working on a flight crew roster system. One aspect was keeping an up-to-date record of accredited competencies, including the ability to fly certain aircraft, speak certain languages, and administer first aid.

There was an obvious overlap, and common data was shared. The sad thing was that this opportunity for reuse was spotted over a cup of coffee by members from the two teams, not by the data architects! Oops.

---

[83] http://www.agiledata.org

THE LONG-TERM VIEW (FOR TOMORROW)

One catch-cry of agile is YAGNI – "You ain't gonna need it". They argue we should build for today's known needs, rather than building stuff that might never get used. That's a good point, but the balancing factor is if the enterprise knows of emerging needs that aren't yet visible to the agile team, a compromise might be worthwhile. One outcome might be that future functionality is still rejected, but at least it should be a considered, reasoned decision.

BETTER ABSTRACTIONS AND/OR GENERALIZATIONS

A number of years ago, Alistair Cockburn reported some interesting observations[84]. In his *"Open letter to object technology newcomers"*, he recalls how he interacted with some data modelers and some OO designers/modelers, both working on the same business problem. His observation was that the data modelers got closer to the final design quicker than the OO people.

Along a similar vein, a developers' web site comments on the role of an agile architect (i.e., an architect who has adapted to the world of agile development):

"Abstraction is a sixth sense. Not everyone has it, not everyone is good at it, and not everyone is interested or aware of it."[85]

A good data architect lives and breathes abstractions, and potentially has much to contribute to an agile project.

"Strict modeling of the real world leads to a system that reflects today's realities but not necessarily tomorrow's. The abstractions that emerge during design are key to making a design flexible."[86]

"... using simpler and more generic models, we will find they stand the test of time better, are cheaper to implement and maintain, and often cater to changes in the business not known about initially."[87]

---

[84] http://alistair.cockburn.us/An+open+letter+to+object+technology+newcomers

[85] http://codebetter.com/scottbellware/2006/09/10/pathfinder-rather-than-archtect

[86] (Gamma, Helm, Johnson & Vlissides, 1994: 11)

[87] (Hay, 1996: xvii)

GOOD CORPORATE CITIZENSHIP

There is no doubt in my mind that the essence of agile approaches is to deliver real value to the project's stakeholders. In that sense, in many ways, agile developers are better "corporate citizens" than those who act as handbrakes to progress. But ...

Sometimes, the inward focus of an agile project means the participants miss an opportunity to change their game a little for the greater good of the whole. I realize that even raising such a possibility might seem like heresy to some, but I recommend that architects proactively look for scenarios where a little give and take may reap significant benefits for the organization. You might not spot any, or you might spot them but the decision makers chose to keep a level of separation, which might actually be a good strategy, in some cases. All I am suggesting is let's keep this as an option.

AVOIDANCE OF THE DEATH-TRAPS

Some problems can be tackled when or if they arise, and refactoring can often accommodate the resultant change, but not always. We data architects don't want to be guilty of costly and unnecessary over engineering. But we also don't want to be guilty of not detecting what Barry Boehm and Richard Turner call "architectural breakers" – defects that cost lots to fix, but could have been avoided with a little architectural attention at the outset.

CONSOLIDATION OF FEEDBACK

Many project teams, be they agile or otherwise, are happy when they have delivered a working system. But if the lessons of experience are to benefit the next set of solutions, it is important for architects to embrace the new perspectives and incorporate them into the updated baseline.

GOVERNANCE?

Many react negatively to the whole idea of governance. For some, it conjures up images of authority figures who are there to make life difficult. I cannot help but agree that some enforced standards reflect old-school thinking and need to be updated, if not abandoned. So rather than encourage a big-stick mentality, I prefer to position architects as enablers. Yes, you may encounter cowboys who have no regard for the welfare of their colleagues in the larger enterprise world, so a big stick may, unfortunately, be necessary; but let's not start there.

The story goes that an animal trainer had a reputation for achieving great things by communication rather than force. Some animal lovers were keen to see him at work, and were invited to see the entire process by observing his training of a previously unhandled donkey. On the appointed day, they gathered in anticipation, wanting to see how this famous person used communication rather than brutality.

The trainer walked up to the donkey, and said, "Hey, donkey!" No response. He repeated this twice more, and still the donkey completely ignored him. So the trainer went to the fence and picked up a stick, walked back to the donkey, and gave him a sound smack between the ears.

The animal lovers were understandably horrified, exclaiming that they had been led to believe his secret to working with the animals was communication. To which the trainer replied, "The communication starts *after* I get his attention."

Given a choice between a carrot and a stick (enablement or enforcement), let's aim for using a carrot. However, I sometimes joke that a really big carrot works wonders. If it fails to gently coax others, it can act as a replacement stick – just to get people's attention, of course.

BOILERPLATE ARCHITECTURES

Last but not least, I'll paint a sunny-day scenario. An agile project realizes it could really benefit from having an experienced data modeler design their persistence layer. They approach the corporate data architecture group, and an architect pulls an existing model off the shelf and says, "I think this might be just what you are looking for".

Wouldn't it be nice? It may not happen as often as we would like, but it does happen.

Style and timing of engagement

Let's get one option out of the way immediately. If we only engage with the agile projects *after* they've finished, by becoming the governance body that tells them they've failed to comply with enterprise standards, it's actually we that have failed, not them. We need to engage much earlier.

ARCHITECTURE ROLES BEFORE THE PROJECT STARTS

Agile projects don't just start. Somebody wants a solution to a problem, and somebody is willing to pay to get the solution developed. One core aspect of an agile project is that neither the intended architecture, nor even the set of requirements, are pinned down in excruciating and unchangeable detail. However, some broad requirements will have been identified, even if not formally documented, and some assumptions are likely to have been made about architecture. Some agile practitioners may object and say that no prejudged architectural decisions are to be made before project launch.

You might build a kennel for your dog without getting council approved planning permits (I would like to think you don't need them), but you probably have some architectural design in mind before you cut the first timber. It may not be written on paper, but one would hope that it exists at least in your thinking. Similarly, some database administrators may point to a physical database implementation and exclaim there is no logical data model that preceded the physical implementation. Graeme Simsion, in the preface to the third edition of *Data Modeling Essentials*, challenges this view by stating:

> "... *data modeling is not optional; no database was ever built without at least an implicit model, just as no house was ever built without a plan.*" [88]

And I suggest that even if the architecture behind an agile project is likewise implicit, it still exists. One role of a data architect, therefore, can be to encourage an explicit articulation of the underlying data architecture, and bring his or her skills to bear on options.

Some of the roles a data architect might play during the formative stages of an agile project, in addition to those listed in the "Contributing to the agile world" section above, could include:

- Commenting on feasibility.
- Consideration of whether or not an agile approach is the most appropriate. (Even asking the question may be considered heresy by some, but I do recommend the book, *Balancing Agility and Discipline* by Boehm and Turner.)[89]
- Identification of integration issues, including identification of gaps/overlaps with complementary projects and systems.
- Shaping, or reshaping, the project for possible project and/or enterprise benefits.
- Identification of non-compliance with corporate standards, and hopefully provision of proactive suggestions to overcome possible clashes.

And last but not least, the data architect ideally will be in a position to offer a start-up data model for an agile project by delivering an enterprise data model as a framework. And if such an artifact does not exist, well, that's what much of the preceding chapters of this book are all about – developing a quality model in a limited period of time. In addition to the class model/data model diagrams, other benefits can include definition of

---

[88] (Simsion & Witt, 2005: 25)

[89] (Boehm & Turner, 2009)

terms that have been thrashed out and resolved, even such as clarification as to what a product or a customer really is.

One agile project I was invited to consult to was extremely grateful for the fast-start models I was able to share. Great for them, and quite frankly, nice for me to feel welcome. We're there to offer directions that might give them an outcome that's good for them and good for the enterprise.

ARCHITECTURE ENGAGEMENT DURING THE PROJECT

Once the project is underway, is the data architect still required? My view is that, at a minimum, the data architect should continue to be engaged in the same roles listed in "Contributing to the agile world", above (providing an overview for today and tomorrow, delivering better abstractions, reducing the risk of encountering architectural show-stoppers, etc.). The difference is, rather than *shaping* the project, the focus is on *keeping it aligned* with the vision. Perhaps just as important is being open to the lessons learned from the agile team acting as the catalyst for at least fleshing out or perhaps even changing the enterprise view! One core aspect of an agile project is an openness to change. Each change has the potential to move the project off-target, and/or to enrich the corporate view. You need to stay engaged.

When changes occur, as they will, you may need to escalate issues to make sure the agile team gets all the support they need. You may need to develop extensions to the data architecture, and, I hope it goes without saying, this work must be performed by you in an agile way!

You may also consider active involvement in shaping the test scenarios. It is possible that some aspects of testing might not have even been considered if it were not for your presence.

I think there is fairly widespread agreement that data architects may be usefully engaged in agile projects. What is perhaps more debatable, is the level and intensity of their involvement. Some hold the view that you can't wear the title "agile architect" unless you actually cut code - not just playing on the edges, but taking responsibility for the most important bits of the solution. For what it's worth, I suggest that the term "architect" can be very broad, and I can't see most <u>data</u> architects cutting Java code. But I have seen experienced data architects getting down-and-dirty by shaping, for example, a bit of particularly tricky SQL.

Should they? My personal view is that while it might not be a realistic demand that all data architects have that ability, if they do have the required skill set, and if 30 minutes of their time gets the project back on track, why not? We should be flexible (or should I say, agile).

In contrast to the view that you can't be an agile architect unless you code, the Agile Architect site (www.agilearchitect.org) is, I think, more realistic in suggesting that *some* architects spend time getting their hands dirty, and others spend most of their time drawing 'big picture' views of an enterprise's whole IT portfolio. It's not just about individual ability and preference, either. While an enterprise might want to get all of its architects onto agile projects, it is more likely that they simply don't have the resources. They may have to either assign them in an oversight role, monitoring progress and reviewing deliverables, or alternatively, assign one of the agile team members to act as an architect, and give that newly created "architect" a direct hotline back to the enterprise team.

At the most distant level, the architecture group can express their expectations in a similar way to the requirements of the intended users of the emerging system. They can articulate functional and non-functional requirements, integration concerns, or whatever. I suggest that this is the absolute minimum involvement required, but if possible, I would encourage a greater level of involvement. The architect doesn't have to be available on site full time, but I think direct involvement is better than tossing the requirements over the wall and hoping the recipients understand and comply.

If we want to feel loved ...

In the early days of flight, many questioned if an aircraft could fly faster than the speed of sound. Many pilots tried and failed. Rather than trying to develop new planes, some tried to force the old-style aircraft to achieve something they really were not designed for. They would be taken as high as they could go, and then turned straight down in a vertical dive with the engine gunned to maximum revs. Sadly, a number of these attempts resulted in the old planes shaking apart or losing control, and lives were lost. The real solution wasn't to make the old-design aircraft go faster, but to find new designs.

Another story. Up until 1954, nobody had run a mile in under 4 minutes. The first person to break the barrier was Britain's Roger Bannister, who said,

> *"There was ... a belief that it couldn't be done, but I think it was more of a psychological barrier than a physical barrier."*

The lessons from these two stories? First, you might find it hard to make data modeling go faster if you stick with old ways. I suggest that the use of data model patterns is one component of the new, agile way. Second, if you don't believe you can produce quality models faster, you might not try. But if you're willing to try the patterns approach, you may be pleasantly surprised to discover you can deliver quality models at a speed more appropriate to agile development projects.

You still might not get the model exactly "right" the first time, but in the agile world, there is not an expectation of achieving first-time perfection. Instead, you may get a speedy return on investment and a data architecture that is more likely to prove to be robust, in the longer term.

THEY DON'T WANT OLD-SCHOOL ARCHITECTS

There are clear messages coming from the agile camp. The Code Better website says:

> *"The question always seems to pop up: 'What's an architect to do on an agile project?' It's not even an honest question. There is an inherent prejudice embedded in the very language used in this question. A more precise wording would be something like, 'What's a traditional architect to do on an agile team.' The answer should be obvious – the role of the traditional architect has little place on an agile team."*[90]

Another article on the web has an article whose title confronts us by stating the often encountered view that agile practitioners don't want us. Well, that is unless we change our ways from the style of an architect who:

> *"... contemplates their navel for months on end, or sits atop an ivory tower dictating policy, standards, monolithic specifications, and the 'one right way' to all."*[91]

DO WE NEED DETAILED TECHNICAL SKILLS?

You may have encountered debates as to the level of hands-on technical skills that are required of architects. Some architects have done time as developers, some have not; and even for those with a hands-on background, some of the skills may be current, and some are museum pieces. Long ago I ceased to include certain programming skills on my CV – ever heard of Neat/3, RPG2, Manage, Focus or MANTIS for CICS on IBM mainframes?

---

[90] http://codebetter.com/scottbellware/2006/09/10/pathfinder-rather-than-archtect/

[91] http://leanandkanban.wordpress.com

For what it's worth, I feel that some of my technical experiences (well, at least the more recent ones) help me in my role as a data architect; having said that, though, I have encountered architects who have had little in the way of technical experience, and yet make solid, valuable contributions. So in the debate on the value of technical skills, who is right?

I would suggest the answer probably varies according to the type of architecture role being filled. I do not play seriously in the *business* architecture space, nor in the domain of *technology* architecture, so my views are based on arms-length perceptions. However, I think it's reasonable to suggest that the level of current technology skill required for a technology architect exceeds that of a business architect! The title probably says it all.

But how much hands-on developer skills are required for a *data* architect? Again I may seem like I am ducking and weaving to avoid a direct answer by saying, "It depends". At one client site, I am up to my armpits in direct involvement with the developers, yet my manager is not. He is more than capable of getting down-and-dirty. In fact, he was my mentor back in the 1990s in some technical areas, so I have absolutely no doubt he *could* get directly involved in an agile project in a way that would bring significant value to the project.

However, I suggest there are at least two reasons why this may not happen for him. First, there is such demand for his time that I cannot conceive of him being "released" to have the fun of getting back into front-line development. And second, it is arguable that such a role may not maximize the contribution he is capable of making.

Some architects have a strong aptitude and passion for detailed technical work, others for the grand plans, and yet others could happily play a role at either extreme or anywhere in between. And some roles absolutely demand detailed technical skills. I think the key is to recognize when such skills are needed, and to play to the strengths of each individual in the team. It would be unkind to assign an architect to a role that he or she cannot reasonably deliver on, and conversely it may be unfulfilling to assign a person to a role they can fulfill but in which they have no passion.

Now here's the crunch. The stereotypical agile project is about software development. And while data architects may engage in different roles and stages of an agile project, I suggest that their contribution will be greater if they can at least comfortably interact with developers on the team.

SO WHAT'S REQUIRED OF US TO CHANGE?

To adapt to the new world of "agile" we must change.

We need to use whatever approaches assist us in the delivery of jump-start models for agile projects. This entire book suggests that an important part of the equation is familiarity with the ever-growing library of data model patterns, be it in the form of pattern books, industry patterns, or patterns you have refined in your own work place.

We also need to be willing to get alongside the agile practitioners and be humble enough to learn from them. Yes, we do have skills to bring to the table, but so do they.

We also have to do more than just provide lip-service to supporting agile development. A woman can't be half-pregnant; she might be half-term in her pregnancy, but she is still fully pregnant. Similarly, we may be part-way in learning, but let's be committed. A web site with a bit of cynicism has altered the Agile Manifesto to reflect the half-hearted attempts of some corporations to adopt agile. A slightly modified version states:

"We have heard about new ways of developing software by paying consultants and reading [consultant] reports. Through this we have been told to value:

- *Individuals and interactions over processes and tools*

and we have mandatory processes and tools to control how those individuals (we prefer to call them 'resources') interact.

- *Working software over comprehensive documentation*

as long as that software is comprehensively documented.

- *Customer collaboration over contract negotiation*

within the boundaries of strict contracts, of course, and subject to rigorous change control.

- *Responding to change over following a plan*

provided a detailed plan is in place to respond to the change, and it is followed precisely.

That is, while the items on the left sound nice in theory, we're an enterprise company, and there's no way we're letting go of the items on the right." [92] [Apologies for the name in the web site that may cause offense.]

---

[92] http://www.halfarsedagilemanifesto.org/

Many data architects are solidly grounded in relational databases and entity-relationship models. Like it or not, to be positioned to offer our skills to the agile world, we need to have more than a passing acquaintance with the object-oriented world. And if you're not, the object-oriented bridge-building chapter, "Chapter 17: Object-orientation - A Data Modeler's Primer", will hopefully make you much more comfortable. But before we get to that, let's consolidate the learning so far by a worked case study.

Consolidating the chapter for you

SUMMARY:

- Data modelers are important, even in agile projects. (Can I assume that most of those reading this book won't need convincing?)
- Data architects should ideally be engaged before an agile project starts, and continue throughout its life.
- To maximize the contribution of data architects in agile projects, the data architects are increasingly likely to need to not just understand object-oriented notation (and not pretend it's really just another data modeling notation), but also understand the fundamental perspective of object-orientation, and its way of working.

APPLYING THIS TO YOUR SITUATION:

- If your data modelers wish to maximize their contribution to agile projects, challenge things in your enterprise such as chargeback models, reporting lines, etc., and see if things need to change to facilitate their involvement.
- Encourage your data architects/modelers to gain a real working knowledge of object-orientation.

We have covered quite a number of topics in this book. Now, to pull them together, let's look at the end-to-end life-cycle of one scenario. It is firmly based on real-world experiences with one client. However, I have woven in a few bits and pieces from other experiences to create a richer, composite perspective.

I have tried to write the story in a laid-back way. I enjoy my work, I love interacting with people, I am motivated by technical challenges, and I feel rewarded when the whole team (business people and techies, alike) all have fun together while delivering real value. This topic is important, but I hope that you, too, enjoy this somewhat cheeky romp through what was a really enjoyable project.

The business scenario is founded on a real-world company I dealt with some time ago, but which in this book I have named Acme Home Installations. The company manufactures products such as made-to-order shower screens and security doors. We've looked at variations on this theme a number of times already. We discussed the debate as to when a design might be considered over-engineered. We also looked at different levels of granularity of models. And finally we looked at business rules mechanisms to support the requirement to capture algorithms used to compute factory floor cutting sizes. That's a very brief recap of some of the facets of the problem we've already touched on. Now let's get into the case study.

Getting ready to start

If you're a roving consultant, you're going to be thrown into all sorts of industries. Today it's banking (bother, that's not my strength - there's a reason my wife does all the accounts). Tomorrow it's a retail organization, and the day after it's a manufacturer. There are at least two good reasons to do a bit of research on a company before you arrive. One is out of respect for their time – why waste the one hour with the CEO by asking, "Now what do you do?" The other reason is less noble – it lessens the number of times you make a fool of yourself by asking dumb questions. (I did say lessens, not eliminates.)

So for Acme Home Installations, I've looked at their web site, read a glossy brochure, and know that they make and install shower screens. And I've read the briefing letter that says they are having problems due to cutting the raw materials to the wrong length, and they want to increase the dependability of their factory floor processes.

I make some guesses and decide I might need familiarity with patterns such as Party/Role (for their customers and their third-party installers), Product (for defining their range of 50 lines), Resource (for keeping track of their raw material inventory), and Task (to manage a quality process regime that will improve the accuracy of their cutting floor operations). I'm already pretty familiar with all those patterns, so I'm ready to go.

Scoping the project, or "How big is the enterprise?"

Now I meet some of the management team. It seems that they have one urgent problem, namely the cost and wastage related to cutting floor errors. It's bad enough to have good material cut too short and thrown into the scrap metal bin. It's worse when the error isn't detected until the installer tries to install an oversize shower screen into a gap in the client's bathroom where it just won't fit.

Being a good data architect, I tell them that the classical approach is to get an enterprise conceptual model developed first so we can see where their problem fits into the bigger picture, and it will only take a few months. They get angry, and tell me they don't want any academic rubbish, and if I can't deliver what they need they'll get someone who can.

Actually, that previous paragraph was inserted just to stir the possum a little.[93] I didn't and wouldn't start a conversation that way. Instead, I want to hear from the business what is important to them. I do have some going-in assumptions to get the ball rolling, but I keep them to myself. And I expect those assumptions to be challenged and changed. One of the assumptions relates to where on the "enterprise continuum" they fit. For systems integration purposes, an enterprise can be as large as the supply chain

---

[93] "Stir the possum" is an Aussie phrase, meaning to stir up a bit of a debate. Our possums (a bit like squirrels?) are usually delightful, docile, cute and furry little things you'd like to cuddle. But disturb one when he or she wants a sleep and wants to be left alone, and you may regret stirring them up from their slumber.

of which their company is but one member, or as small as one division or section within the corporation. As a default position, I had assumed the enterprise was the whole company, but the focus of this group was on the factory floor. I had my context.

Starting a context model with the first assembly pattern

In this book, we built up a picture of three levels of patterns; elementary patterns as the basic building blocks, assembly patterns, which provide bite-sized chunks the business can understand, and integration patterns, that pull all the pieces together. In practice, while I often have an integration pattern in the back of my mind, I often start with grabbing an assembly pattern or two that seem to fit.

I start by assuming we can use the Product Type pattern. There are plenty of variations on this theme to choose from, especially when combined with (or part of) more generic Classification patterns – Dave Hay and Len Silverston have plenty to reference, plus I have a few variations of my own. We look at some examples of Acme's product types – simple 3-panel shower screens, screens with returns over the bath end, screens with different finishes (bronze or gold aluminum with flat or brushed surfaces, glass that is plain, smoked or colored, and so on). And they've got mirrored wardrobe doors, security doors, and more.

Two messages emerge. First, they do not make "standard" fittings – their market is *just* the made-to-measure segment. Second, their product line, materials, and finishes keep expanding. They are gearing up for security screens for windows, and talking about custom-made skylights. Fortunately, the flexibility in the standard patterns will serve us well for such extensions.

We're underway! And it's only taken a few minutes.

Some choices appear

Next, they talk about their raw material stocks, from sheets of glass and lengths of aluminum, to screws and tubes of silicon. That's simple. We use one of the many Inventory patterns available. Just as a side note, after working with these patterns for a while, you'll find you've adopted much of the thinking of such authors - you don't need to carry around a truckload of books. Yes, there are times when you hit something a bit out of the ordinary and you use their works as reference material, but much of the time, just mentioning the name of an author when talking about a pattern with other experienced modelers is sufficient to keep you on the same page.

I've now got a Product Type pattern to represent the finished goods Acme sells, and I have an Inventory pattern to represent the raw materials. If I wanted to, I could also recognize the creation of assemblies, such as a shower door assembly. Going back to a diagram from "Chapter 6: Use Patterns Beyond Their Intended Purpose", we could have a model something like the following:

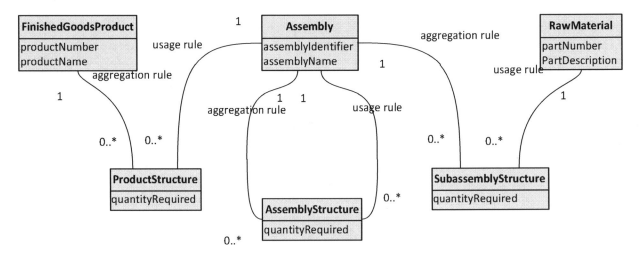

Figure 47: Simplified bill-of-materials pattern

Or, from the same chapter, we could generalize the model and end up with something more like:

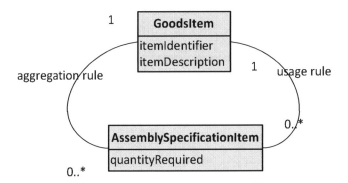

Figure 48: Generalized bill-of-materials pattern

Since Acme has said that they are interested in just the quantities of raw materials in the final end product, not in the assemblies, I might make a compromise and have the following:

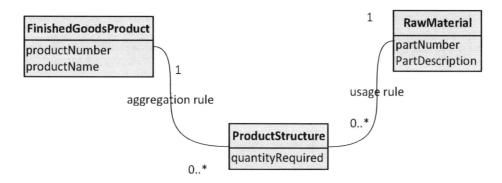

Figure 49: Shower screen bill-of-materials

So which way do I go? One part of me says to go for the more generalized model. It's more flexible, and if Acme wants to introduce recording of assemblies later, the data model doesn't change. Conversely, it's a little more difficult for the business to understand. So right or wrong, with the intention of developing a working prototype in a few days, I go for the simpler model in Figure 49 above. A key consideration, though, is that I have a clear understanding of how to move from this more specific model to a more generalized model when or if I want to.

Another assembly pattern

Next we play with the Party/Role model. Yes, they have people and organizations playing different roles – they obviously have customers and employees. They also subcontract the installation to companies and to individuals.

On the one hand, they think that they are only really interested in two of these groups – customers and installers. On the other hand, they agree that the ability to hold names and addresses of all these parties in one consistent "address book" manner has some appeal. The use of the Party/Role model is debated.

They like the idea of a Party. That way it doesn't matter whether the contract installer is an individual or a company that provides installers. The people and the contract companies are all just parties.

They also like the fact that relationships between parties can be easily recorded. The most obvious one is for contract companies and all the contractors on their books.

And when we dig a bit deeper, they recognize there are other roles of interest. When they take an order, if it's for a house that has a tenant, they want to record the tenant as one role (for arranging access times) and the owner as another (for paying the bill).

They also want to differentiate between the different roles of their full time employees, including the factory floor fabricators and the sales team members.

The standard Party/Role pattern gets added to the mix.

A wrong assumption by me: Rules instead of Process

Acme has quality problems on the cutting floor. As part of my "homework" in preparing for the assignment, I made a few assumptions on how things might shape up. There is a whole heap of literature on improving quality through having well recognized and managed business processes. I thought this might help, and hoped that a Task pattern that edged into workflow management might assist.

I was wrong. The problem isn't with processes.

The first weak link in the chain relates to capturing on-site measurements. Different types of products require different measurements to be taken at the customer's premises. For a simple 3-door shower screen, width at the bottom of the opening, width at the top, and intended screen height are required. If it's the model with a return over the end of a bath, we need to measure the width of the bath and its height off the floor. A system for defining measurement requirements by model number was requested.

The second weak link was in the actual computation of cutting sizes for each and every made-to-measure component. This problem, and the chosen solution, are described in more detail in the "Derivation of computed values" section in "Chapter 14: Going Further with Rules in Data!"

The bottom line is that I chose to replace the assumed use of a Task pattern (extended for workflow management) with a very simple custom rules engine. I didn't need to manage the process; I needed to control the computations.

An agile iteration begins

At this point, the developer takes over. In a matter of days, a working prototype is produced and delivered for evaluation. It is very well received. The development initiative can then commence.

Integration Patterns

Meanwhile, I am able to pull together the logical data model for the initiative. I could have started the project by doing a more conventional conceptual model, but that was strongly rejected by the client. Instead, I am able to pictorially portray the major assembly patterns as pseudo-conceptual entities. This framework is based on an integration pattern.

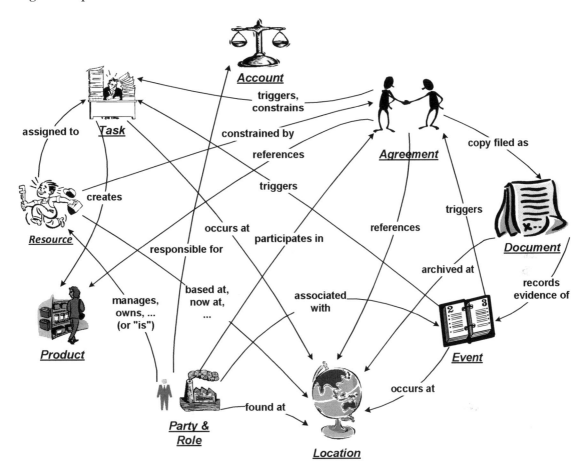

Figure 50: Integration pattern / shower screen scenario

The business people at the client site are able to interact with this portrayal, and provide feedback. But now I want to move from a pictorial perspective to something a bit more technical. Although the icons may look to be soft, fuzzy concepts with no substance, they are actually light-weight representations of solid, implementable patterns.

It is really not a large task to take the above framework and start the population of an enterprise class model. The following diagram is indicative of what might be captured in the overall context diagram – a bit squashed and some detail left out, but if it was on a larger piece of paper, it could have been a little more realistic. Hopefully, it gives you a taste of what can be produced quite easily.

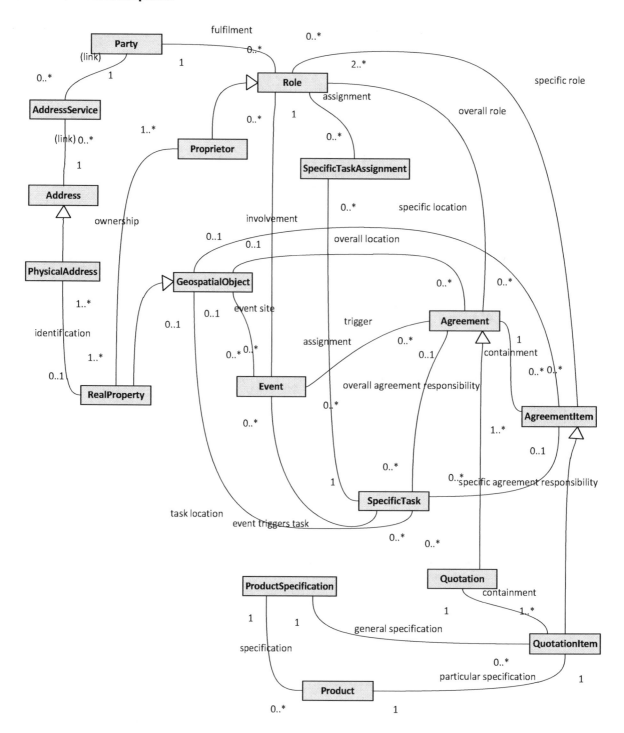

Figure 51: Logical context diagram / shower screen scenario

Again, as noted just a few paragraphs above, each icon in the graphical representation, and/or each high-level class on this model, represents the much richer details in published assembly patterns. The Agreement domain is portrayed below as an example.

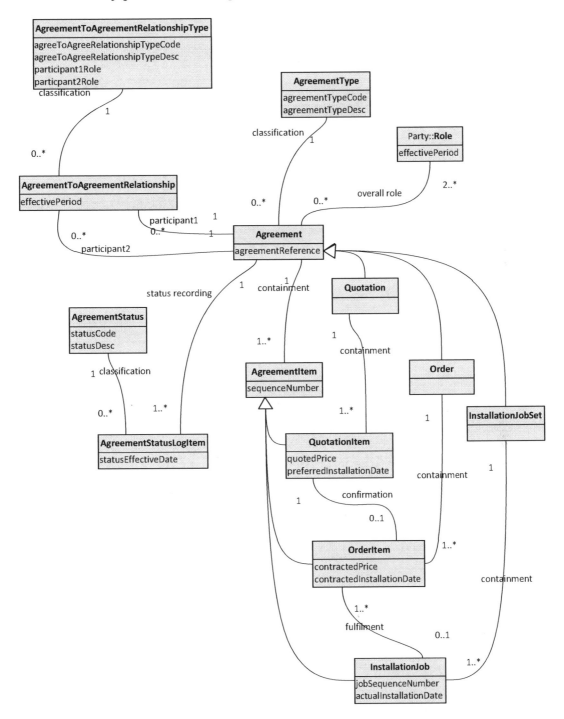

Figure 52: Logical domain (Agreement) model / shower screen scenario

Finally, each class and its attributes are described in a document. This documentation, along with articulation of the company profile, modeling alternatives considered, and guidelines on understanding the notation, takes only a few weeks to produce. And as development continues iteratively, it's not hard to refine.

Back to reality?

This scenario is based on an aggregation of actual experiences, but it is for a relatively trivial problem domain. Can such an approach work for larger corporations with more challenging problems. The answer is a resounding but qualified, "Yes". I have repeated a similar process a number of times, with encouraging results.

But there is one qualification. As noted in "Chapter 12: When Patterns Don't Exist", there are times when you cannot find the pattern you are looking for, or you find one but it doesn't quite fit. Let's say that you can locate 80 percent of what you are after; it might only take a few weeks to assemble that much of a high-level but well architected framework, but the missing bits can take months (or worse). Bad news? Yes. But I am still grateful to Len Silverston, Dave Hay, and others that they have made the first 80 percent such fun.

Consolidating the chapter for you

SUMMARY:

This chapter is a case study, rather than one that seeks to present material on a particular topic. As such, there are no specific topics to be summarized.

*** PLEASE READ - APPLYING THIS TO YOUR SITUATION:

Each of the previous chapters has had questions for your consideration. Some of them may be the catalyst for bringing change to your organization. It is good for a book to bring new knowledge and perspective. It is even better if a book is the trigger for lasting and beneficial change in your workplace.

So the final bit of "homework" you may wish to consider is to take the sequence of events from the case study, *and* your answers to the questions from the preceding chapters, and see if you can assemble a plan of action to apply the messages from this book to your situation.

It is my sincere hope you look back on this exercise as one of the many little things in your life that made that life richer.

Now, before you put the book down, one more thing... Please consider the challenges of the next section and see if you can go away with two life-changing take-away ideas from this book – the application of the ideas in this book to your world, and the learning of new skills that may stand you in good stead!

I wish you well.

John.

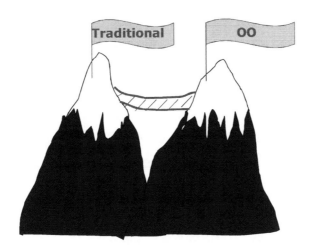

At a technology level, you may have encountered people describing an "impedance mismatch" between object orientation and relational databases. It's a fancy way to describe the fact that trying to fit the shape of an object-oriented (OO) programmer's world into the shapes of relational tables is sometimes just plain hard work. The two world views just don't automatically line up.

It's not just hard work fitting OO shapes into the relational world, it can also be quite hard for an experienced "data" practitioner to get his or her head around the OO concepts. Throw the two groups into one agile team, and these two world views can find themselves at odds. We have spoken throughout the book about possible tensions between an architectural view and an agile view, but this is another dimension of potential tension. It's about the possible clash between traditional, relational thinking, and object-orientation.

I suggest there may be at least a few good reasons why we should build a bridge between these sometimes opposing camps. First, as mentioned earlier, the skills that traditional data modelers have honed over the years have the potential to deliver value to the models that OO programmers work with, but only if we can communicate with them. Second, we can and should be willing to learn from them, too. And last, like it or not, if we are going to be valued in the new world order, we may find we have to work with the OO types. And a warning: it's not enough to be able to just read a UML class diagram – you will need to understand the ideas behind the thinking of the OO developers.

We can sit back and complain about them not understanding us, or *we* can make the effort to understand them. And having done so, we may be pleasantly surprised to discover they're actually really nice people and that while we do have some fundamental differences, we also have much in common. Dave Hay[94] provides a means of taking the UML language constructs from the OO world back to the data modelers' world. While that will be appropriate for some, this chapter is the reverse, intending to help data modelers move across the chasm to the OO world.

There's some bad news (and some good news, too). First the bad news... It can be daunting for someone raised in the relational world to be hit with terms such as polymorphism, information hiding (why on earth would anyone want to hide data?!), behavior, methods, multiple inheritance, and so on.

The good news is that many of the relational concepts we know and love can help us build a bridge to the object-oriented way of thinking. The other piece of good news is that if you are already comfortable with the OO world (and not just their UML class modeling notation), you may decide that you do not need to read further on this topic!

---

[94] (Hay, 2011-b)

The style of this chapter is intended to help a person with a relational background make the transition to OO thinking. We deliberately start with tables and columns, and bit of procedural code, and move little by little to the adoption of a few core OO ideas. The analogies may not be 100% precise, from an OO purist's point of view, but if they're helpful in building a bridge from the relational world view to that of object orientation, I suggest this more casual and friendly approach still has merit.

Encapsulation, or "They've hidden my data"

Let's assume we've got a relational table for employees[95], and it's got columns such as Employee No for the employee's number, and Employee Name for their name. We've also got a Date-Of-Birth column, and we want to be able to compute their "age". Using UML notation, where the "age" column name is preceded by a slash ("/") to indicate it is derivable, we might represent this "table" as follows, where the name of the table is in the first internal rectangle, and the list of columns is in the second internal rectangle:

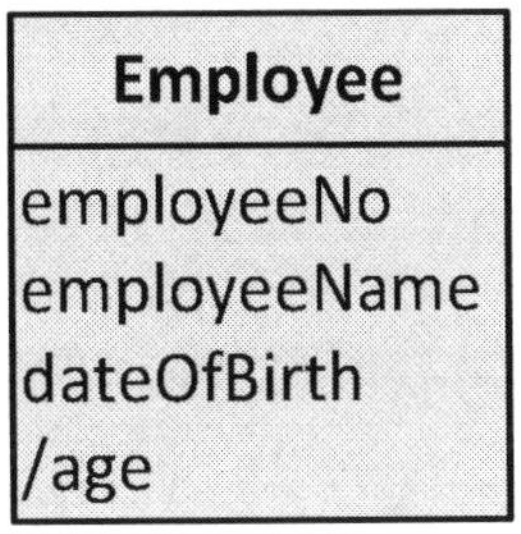

Employee
employeeNo
employeeName
dateOfBirth
/age

Figure 53: UML – derivable attribute

Instead of calling the representation of Employee information a table or an entity, let's call it a <u>class</u>. And instead of speaking of its columns, we'll call them <u>attributes</u>. That's two OO words we've learned already!

---

[95] In this chapter, I have "broken" the pattern for Party/Role when I represent the Employee class. It is arguable that attributes such as the employee's name and date of birth should belong to the Party class, with the Employee class being a subclass of a Role class. I would not fight such an argument. My only (poor) defense is that it suited me to keep the hypothetical model a little bit simpler. My apologies to all.

Maybe you've encountered subroutine libraries from the mainframe days? Or maybe stored procedures in a relational database? Either way, you've probably come across little bits of code that manipulate data, so let's assume we have a subroutine called "getAge", that computes an employee's age. We could represent it as follows, where the subroutines are presented in the third internal rectangle (the first entry representing the "getAge" subroutine):

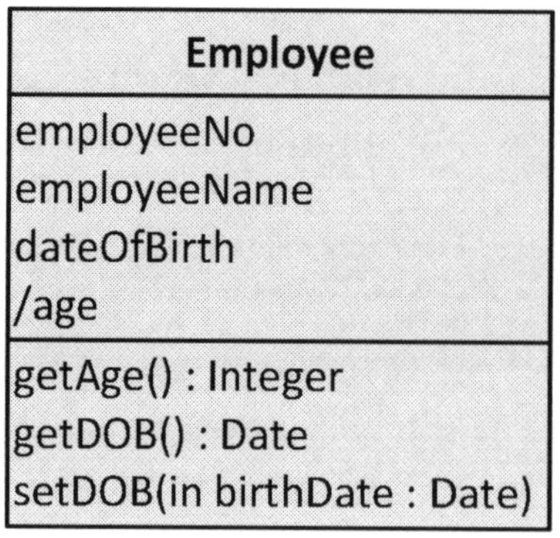

Employee
employeeNo employeeName dateOfBirth /age
getAge() : Integer getDOB() : Date setDOB(in birthDate : Date)

Figure 54: UML – operations

The getAge "subroutine" *operates* on the data and does something for us, namely returning the employee's age. Using OO-speak, we call it the getAge <u>operation</u>. That seems like a reasonably logical term. If we want to look a bit deeper and see how it does the work for us (i.e., we want to look at the actual code), we call it a <u>method</u>. An example follows of what we might find if we lift the covers on the getAge operation and look at the code in its method, using some pretty crude pseudo-code that doesn't take into account leap years or even whether the day-and-month of the birth date are before or after today's day-and-month. Nevertheless, you'll get the idea.

<u>getAge()</u> method:

Birth_Year = the "year" bit from employee's Date Of Birth

This_Year = the "year" bit from today's date

Return (as an Integer) = This_Year minus Birth_Year

We could also have an even simpler bit of code to return the employee's Date-Of-Birth. It might look something like:

<u>getDOB()</u> method:

Return (as a Date) = employee's Date Of Birth

Why on earth would you want to write such code when you can get the data you want straight from the attribute? That's a good question. Without going into too much detail, it's a bit like some site standards for relational databases that say you should never access a raw table, but get to the data via relational views.

In such a relational view of an underlying table, you might be presented with some raw data plus some "columns" that are derived. For example, you could do a select from the Employee table, then compute and return an "Age" column, even though it doesn't really exist. If this causes performance problems, you might change the table and create a physical "Age" column that is updated in a batch run at midnight each evening. The external appearance of the view would not change.

In a similar manner, the getAge and getDOB methods return data, but from the outside you cannot tell if "age" is actually stored or if it's computed on the fly. The data is said to be "encapsulated", or "hidden" behind the methods. Another OO term introduced!

One more introductory topic - let's have a brief look at parameters. The two methods we've looked at return data, but don't require any input parameters. The setAge method is different – it takes a parameter and updates the employee's data.

> **setDOB(birthdate)** method:
>
> Set employee's Date Of Birth = input parameter "birthdate"
>
> Return nothing! (or maybe a message saying "OK")

In summary, classes are somewhat like entities – they both have attributes. But they also have a fundamental difference in that classes have bits of code stuck to them. These code fragments are identified by their labels, known as "operations", and the actual code segments are known as methods. Oh, and by the way, we use a different name for the individual instances. Instead of "rows" in a relational table, we have "objects" in a class. For now, let's say they are reasonable approximations of each other.

Object IDs, or "Who stole my keys?"

To uniquely identify each row in a relational table, such as an Employee table, there may be a variety of options. Examples might include:

- Employee Surname plus given name. That would work fine until you employ the second John Smith.
- A code generated by an external authority. In Australia, that might be a national tax file number, until you realize that might be illegal – the law in some countries says you cannot use a tax file number for other than taxation purposes.

- An internally generated number or code that is assigned by the personnel department, probably called an Employee Number. It may be printed on the security badge, and could be used as part of single-sign-on identification. That sounds like a pretty good choice.
- A "surrogate key"; i.e., a system-generated number that may not even be visible to other than IT systems.

At this point, we could enter into a long debate about the relative merits of surrogate keys, but suffice it to say that the OO world uses this concept. Every object has its own unique <u>Object Id</u>. That relatively simple and consistent mechanism provides what we would call the primary key for each object.

Now it gets interesting... If all classes have a surrogate "Object ID" as their primary key, one could argue that we don't need to show it on a model. It's always there, so why take up space displaying it! And class diagrams don't, in fact, offer a mechanism for defining the primary key, let alone displaying it - it just happens on your behalf. If you feel really uncomfortable, I sympathize with you. But please try and understand there really is a unique identifier, even if we can't see it.

So in the Vehicle class below, we might hope that a vehicle's registration number is a good primary key, only to find not all vehicles are registered, and even if they are, they are not guaranteed to be unique across all states. The simple solution is to let the OO world do the work for us. We have a Vehicle class with no (obvious) unique identifier, but it's got an Object ID that we cannot see.

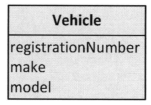

Figure 55: UML – unique object ID?

That might be bad enough, but what about foreign keys? In the relational world, you expect that behind one relationship between a pair of entities there will be a foreign key in one that references the primary key in another. In the OO world, you can have <u>associations</u> (their name for relationships) between classes. You would hope that the similarity continues, namely that a foreign key in one class will be defined to reference the primary key in another class. But since it's good enough for the OO world to assume a primary key that's hidden from view, the same minimalistic approach to foreign keys can be taken. They might exist, but they are implied by the definition of the association. Let's look at one example.

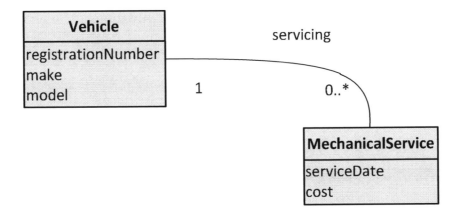

Figure 56: UML – associations and "foreign keys"?

We have already (reluctantly) conceded that Vehicle has an Object ID as a surrogate key, even though we can't see it. A one-to-many association exists that says each Vehicle can be related to zero or more Mechanical Service instances (e.g. the vehicle had its 30,000 mile service on February 2nd, which cost $500, and another service on May 19th, which cost $800). The Mechanical Service class will need a way to point back to the Vehicle to which it applies. Assuming "navigability" has been declared from Mechanical Service to Vehicle (an OO way of saying you want what is effectively a foreign key, so you can navigate from one object to another), the "foreign key" equivalent will actually exist – we just can't see it. The association tells us we have one, and we don't have to do anything more.

Attributes and Data types on steroids

It may be helpful for data modelers to understand aspects of the OO developer's world such as the coding "methods", but they are unlikely to get personally involved in developing the code. However, understanding some of the new ways of seeing data is of vital importance to a data modeler!

MULTIPLICITY

There are times when we may need to model repeating attributes. For example, let's assume the rules for an Employee's attributes include the following:

- The employee number attribute is mandatory. Using UML multiplicity notation, we might say that each Employee must have a minimum of one employee number, and also a maximum of one employee number, entered as "1..1" – arguably a long-winded way of saying it's mandatory, but in OO land we are allowed to abbreviate this multiplicity as a simple "1".

- The date-of-birth attribute (and its derived "age" attribute) is optional (i.e., it has a minimum multiplicity of zero). An employee can only have one date of birth, so it has a maximum multiplicity of one. This rule is defined using a multiplicity of "0..1".

- The employee name attribute is mandatory (i.e., its minimum multiplicity is one) but its maximum is "*" (many). Maybe we want to record birth names, married names, stage names, and so on.

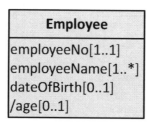

Figure 57: UML – attribute multiplicity (optionality, cardinality)

It is easy to *model* a multiplicity of greater than one for the employee's name, but it is a breach of first normal form to allow a "repeating" group entry. And what's more, it cannot be *implemented* in a relational database!

The interesting thing is that in the world of object-orientation, multiplicities of greater than one are not only permitted in the model, but can also be directly implemented. How might this be achieved? In the above example, the employee name attribute *could* have been implemented as a serialized character string, with each one of many names separated by a suitable character. For example, one American boxer from the past might have his multiple names recorded as one character string such as "Cassius Clay / Muhammad Ali". That's not really how the OO world handles multiplicity, but if it helps you feel comfortable that it could be done, that's good, and for the sake of brevity, we will push on. Suffice it to say that OO models and their implementation can very happily handle what we might see as repeating groups.

DEFINING NEW DATA TYPES

In Australia, our national postal service provider manages a database of addresses. Well, at least postal addresses, but for the sake of this exercise, can we please simplify matters by assuming all addresses of interest are held in this database? The attributes of each address are actually a bit complicated, but again for simplification, let's assume this register has a core class something like the following. And because we're now looking at data types, I've displayed the data types for each of the attributes. For example, the data type of the Postal Code attribute is Integer, and the data type for the Country attribute is String.

Address

nationalAddressIdentifier : Integer
street : String
town : String
state : String
postalCode : Integer
country : String

Figure 58: UML – attribute data types

Let's extend our Employee class by associating it with addresses from this central register so that we can record home and work addresses. Our class diagram might now look something like the one below. Note that the multiplicity on the work address association permits up to two work addresses to be recorded.

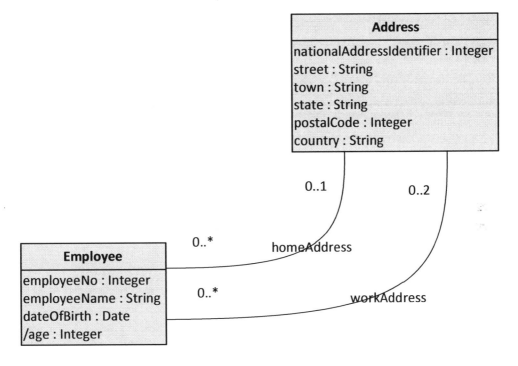

Figure 59: UML – properties as associations

In the OO way of thinking, there is an alternative way of representing essentially the same model. We still have the same Address class, as above, but this time we do not have the "homeAddress" and "workAddress" *associations*. Instead, we have two equivalent *attributes* (that in my somewhat contrived example happen to have the same names as the associations they have replaced), each with a data type of Address.

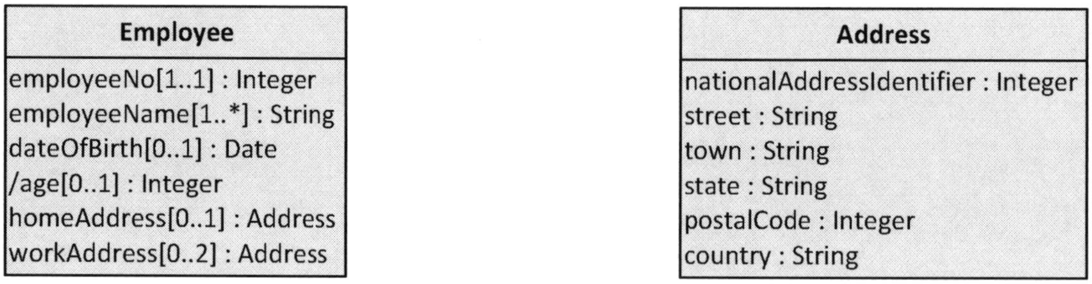

Employee
employeeNo[1..1] : Integer
employeeName[1..*] : String
dateOfBirth[0..1] : Date
/age[0..1] : Integer
homeAddress[0..1] : Address
workAddress[0..2] : Address

Address
nationalAddressIdentifier : Integer
street : String
town : String
state : String
postalCode : Integer
country : String

Figure 60: UML – properties as attributes

From an OO perspective, the two diagrams are presenting effectively equivalent information. Whether addresses are represented via associations or via attributes, they are collectively known as "properties" of the class. (And out of interest, as noted when using associations, one of the attributes has a multiplicity of greater than one!)

DATA TYPES WITH OPERATIONS!

Would we actually want to model Address as a data type? Maybe, maybe not. But we can if we want to. Perhaps an example that might be a bit more comfortable for you is if we assume we have a database with primitive data types such as String, Date, and Integer, but we want a "Period" data type that has a start date and an end date, plus a derivable number of days covered by that period. We can very quickly and easily define this new "Period" class.

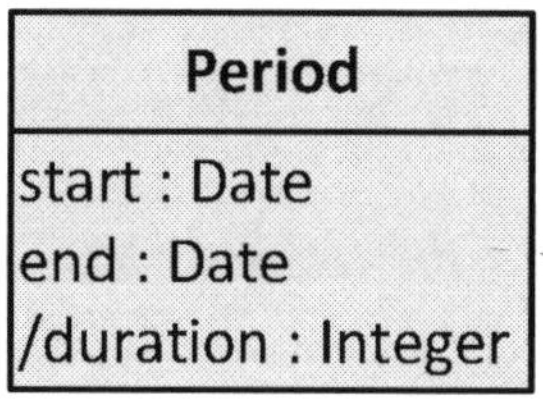

Period
start : Date
end : Date
/duration : Integer

Figure 61: UML – data types with operations

Next we put it to work. Instead of recording an employee's start date and termination date, we will have an attribute called "employmentPeriod", with Period as a data type. Similarly, we want a "projectPeriod" attribute in a Project class. And while we are at it, we define an operation on the Period class to calculate the derived "duration" attribute's value by working out the difference between the start date and the end date.

Employee
employeeNo : Integer
employeeName : String
dateOfBirth : Date
/age : Integer
homeAddress : Address
workAddress : Address
employmentPeriod : Period

Project
projectName : String
projectBudget : Integer
projectPeriod : Period

Period
start : Date
end : Date
/duration : Integer
getDuration() : Integer

Figure 62: UML – rich, user-defined data types

The magic behind all of this is the Period class, which is acting as a data type, but has a useful operation for calculating the period interval between the start and end dates. This means that the other classes that use this data type can also use this function to calculate their duration (the employee's employment duration, or the project's duration). The one bit of code in the "data type" class is reusable.

A bit more on associations

When we looked at object identifiers, we introduced associations between classes, noting that they were somewhat similar to relationships between entities in the traditional data modeler's world. Now we look at a few interesting ways that they are different.

THINGS THAT CONTAIN THINGS

Let's start with a relational perspective, showing the one-to-many relationship between a Project and a Task entity. For simplicity, attributes are suppressed, and because we want to play with the meaning of the relationship, its name is also deliberately excluded.

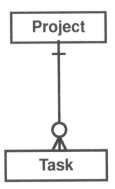

Figure 63: Traditional entities and relationships

The ERD is communicating that any one Project may have zero, one, or more associated Tasks.

Here we present a UML view of the same two entities (but now we call them classes), again with attributes (and operations) suppressed. But this time, we have included a name on the association to communicate that the association represents "containment" i.e., that a Project contains Tasks.

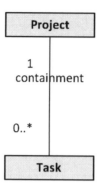

Figure 64: Classes and associations

This is what I will call a "regular" association. It has no special symbols at its end(s). All it is saying is that there is some sort of association between the Project class and the Task class, and that we might get an idea of the meaning behind the association by looking at its name.

Now we look at what the UML notation calls "aggregation" associations. They have an empty diamond at one end to indicate the aggregate, i.e., the thing that is the container. We have repeated the Project-to-Task association, but removed the association name – the "containment" is communicated by the aggregation association. We have also shown a Vehicle class and noted that it is an aggregate, made up of one and only one Engine, plus at least two Wheels.

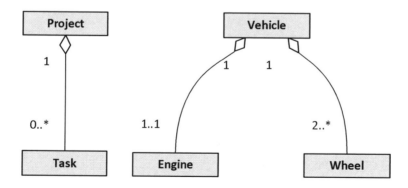

Figure 65: UML – aggregation

The implied message behind an aggregation association is that we can choose to destroy the Vehicle, but keep the Wheels and Engine to fit on another vehicle. Similarly, the diagram for Project and Task implies that a Project is an aggregate object that may be comprised of many Tasks, but that if we choose to close down a project, we might wish to transfer some of its tasks to another project.

Alternatively, we might have a business rule that says that if we close down a Project, we must also get rid of the project's Tasks. Similarly, a rule might state that if we choose to destroy a Vehicle, we will also scrap the Engine and Wheels, rather than reusing them. A "composition" association (with a solid, filled-in diamond at its end) carries this message.

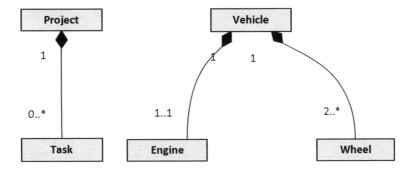

Figure 66: UML – composition

For you relational database types, you might see some parallels with referential integrity rules. The aggregation association allows the "child" to exist without its "parent", effectively setting the foreign key to null, whereas the composition association is more akin to a cascade delete.

Do we need these notation extras? Some would argue that they really are not needed – appropriate naming of regular associations, plus recording of cascade deletion intentions, may be sufficient. Nonetheless, you may encounter them, and it's worthwhile to be comfortable with them. You might also consider using them if they are effective in communicating to your intended audience.

MANY-TO-MANY ASSOCIATIONS

I would like to note one final difference regarding relationships between entities versus associations between classes. In the relational world, we might be able to *model* many-to-many relationships, but we typically *implement* them by creating an intermediate table to resolve the relationship. For example, an Employee might have acquired many Skill Types (e.g. Chris can weld, speak French, and perform first aid). Conversely, each Skill Type might have been acquired by many Employees (e.g. the ability to weld might be a skill acquired by Chris, Dan, and Ed). Using the UML notation, we can portray this as follows.

Figure 67: UML – many-to-many associations with no resolution

It is true that ERD notations as well as UML notation may be able to represent many-to-many associations, but there's a difference. The OO world can implement a many-to-many association! How is this done?

We have already noted that classes can have attributes with a multiplicity greater than one. The example we looked at was an Employee class that permitted more than one work address. If we think of the "foreign keys" of a class (albeit hidden from view in the OO world) as allowing multiple entries, one employee object can reference many skill types, and one skill type can reference many employees. So as objects in memory, it's relatively easy to use sets of pointers to link one object to its many associated other objects. Further, if the objects are stored directly in an object-oriented database management system (as compared to a relational database management system) where pointers are employed, again it's easy to directly record these sorts of relationships.

Of course, if the objects in a many-to-many relationship are mapped to a relational database implementation, classical resolution entities may still be required. This is also true if the association itself requires attributes, as it will then require an explicit association class. For example, for every link between one employee and one skill type, if we want to record the date the employee acquired the skill type and the level of proficiency, we will need an Employee Skill class with these attributes. But if we simply want to be able to directly record the many-to-many associations, in the OO world we can.

Inheritance of data and code

INHERITANCE OF DATA (ATTRIBUTES)

In the data modeling world, you probably have encountered the concept of supertypes and subtypes. Graeme Simsion and Graham Witt's book, *"Data Modeling Essentials"*[96], devotes an entire chapter to the topic. At the heart of the topic is a relatively simple idea. You may have a number of entities in your data model that share several attributes and/or relationships in common. If so, you may wish to pull the attributes and/or relationships out of the detailed entities and put them in a generalized entity – the supertype.

For example, let's assume you have two types of employees – managers and engineers. All employees have an employee number, a name, and a date of birth. In addition to the common attributes, for managers we also record a credit limit (engineers in this company are not provided with a line of credit) and an annual salary amount. Engineers have their primary engineering discipline (chemical engineering, mechanical engineering, etc.) and their hourly rate recorded. Using UML notation, we might define the following.

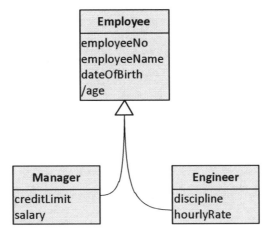

Figure 68: UML – inheritance of data

The Employee class is the superclass, containing the common attributes; Manager and Engineer are subclasses, each with their own special attributes. The similarities are strong between relational modeling supertypes/subtypes, and OO superclasses/subclasses, at least at the data level. One minor area of difference relates

---

[96] (Simsion & Witt, 2005: 111-143)

to implementation. In a relational world, we have a number of choices. For example, the above structure might be implemented as:

- One "Employee" table, with all the columns from the subclasses included.
- Two tables - one for each subclass table, with columns from the superclass table replicated.
- Three tables as per the class diagram, with one-to-one joins linking them.

In the OO world, the implementation is closer to the third option – we end up with every class (i.e., the superclass and all its subclasses) represented.

INHERITANCE OF CODE (OPERATIONS)

Relational entities have attributes, but OO classes have attributes and operations (and the underlying code routines, called methods). So while the relational concepts of supertypes and subtypes only needs to consider data inheritance, classes must grapple with inheritance of data *and* code. We look again at the model for Employees, Managers, and Engineers, this time with some selected operations visible.

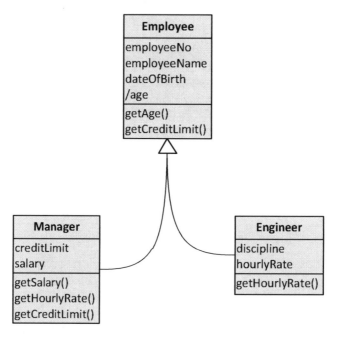

Figure 69: UML – inheritance of code

The Employee class has a "dateOfBirth" attribute, which is inherited by the Manager and Engineer subclasses. The Employee class also has a "getAge" method that computes an employee's age by calculating the number of years between today's date and the employee's date of birth. But let's say you ask a Manager how old he or she is. Because the Manager class doesn't have a Get Age method of its own, it looks to its superclass to see if it can help; and it can. So when a Manager object is asked to execute the getAge method, it looks to the code associated with the Employee class and executes it, instead. Similarly, an engineer's age can be determined by asking the Engineer object to execute getAge, and its superclass method will execute on its behalf.

That's basic inheritance of code, and it's really pretty easy. Now we look at the "getHourlyRate" method. Let's assume that the business rules for determination of a nominal hourly rate for any employee are as follows:

- If the employee is an engineer, simply look up the value in the Engineer's Hourly Rate attribute.
- If the employee is a manager, for the sake of charging out a manager's time, approximate the hourly rate by assuming a weekly rate of one 52nd of the annual salary, and also assume a 40-hour week, i.e., the manager's hourly rate is the Salary attribute's value divided by 2,080 (52 weeks times 40 hours).

The method (code) for the Manager's getHourlyRate method, and for the Engineer's getHourlyRate method, would reflect these rules.

Similarly, the hypothetical example assumes a business rule that all Employees have a credit limit of $500. This logic can be captured in the getCreditLimit method in the Employee class. However, Managers are special, and can have a tailored credit limit, returned via the getCreditLimit method in their class.

At run time, there is no confusion. You ask a Manager what his/her credit limit is, and get the answer from the Manager class. Conversely, when you ask an Engineer what his/her credit limit is, the Engineer class cannot provide the answer, so it executes the more generic getCreditLimit from the Employee superclass.

Multiple inheritance

We've got one more topic to look at on inheritance. Most subclasses have only one superclass. In fact, a number of object-oriented languages only permit one superclass per subclass, but many modeling tools, and some languages, support the idea of multiple inheritance; i.e., a subclass having multiple superclasses. A common example given in textbooks is to have a Land Vehicle class and a Water Vehicle class, and then to have Amphibious Vehicle as a subclass of both land and water vehicles.

If we extend our Employee example, we might identify a new type of employee – a "senior engineer". These people have management responsibilities and also engineering responsibilities. Further, they have some things that are unique to them – the example given below reflects a business requirement that they provide a way of being contacted in an emergency.

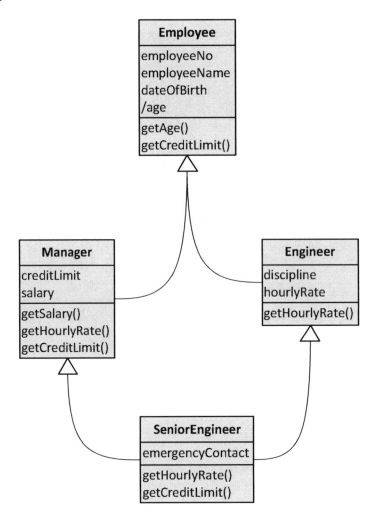

Figure 70: UML – multiple inheritance

By showing the Senior Engineer class as a subclass of Manager, it means that they can be paid a salary and be given a line of credit. By showing them also as a subclass of Engineer, we can record their primary engineering discipline (chemical, civil, …). Now some of the problems of multiple inheritance start to appear.

To begin with, Senior Engineers inherit a salary attribute from Manager, *and* an hourly rate attribute from Engineer. If we asked a Senior Engineer object to execute a "getHourlyRate" method, it may get confused – it can find one in both superclasses. How this is resolved in a given OO language may vary, but for the sake of looking at the concepts, we'll use a specialized "getHourlyRate" method for Senior Engineers that simply, but explicitly, directs that the method of the associated Manager class be used (assuming the business rule is that Senior Engineers are paid as if they are Managers).

Another example of the challenges of multiple inheritance relates to credit limits. Again, we make an assumption for the sake of the scenario that the business rule is that Senior Engineers are given the greater of the amounts determined via the Manager method or the amount determined via the generic Employee method. The code would have to execute both methods and select the larger of the amounts.

The bottom line is that while simple inheritance from one superclass is a powerful tool, multiple inheritance is probably best avoided, if at all possible.

Persistence, or "What do you mean the data isn't stored?"

You might hear OO people speak of persistence of data. To them, this means that data associated with an object might actually be stored somewhere for later use. To people coming from a database background, this may sound like a really dumb discussion. Why on earth *wouldn't* you store data? Isn't that what you do with data?

If an object exists in memory, what happens when the computer is turned off? By default, the information is lost forever! In the OO world, objects include not only business objects, such as one employee and then another, or one project and each of its tasks, but also include objects such as the bits and pieces that make up a graphic user interface. When you open a window, a window object is created, and when you close it, you throw it away. You typically would not store data about the "window" in a database.

In a similar manner, a business object such as an employee will initially be created as a throw-away object in memory. If you want to actually keep it (as we know you typically will), it's very easy (at least conceptually). Assuming you have mapped class structures to database structures, you just tell the system you want to "persist" (i.e., store) the object and it happens. So it's really not hard. The major difference is that by default, the object gets thrown away; however, if you want to keep it, just say so and it will happen.

You can understand how data about a window can be thrown away with no consequences, and you can understand how a business object such as an employee has data you do want to store. But what about, for example, the data in the on-board computer controlling the flight path for a military missile? Once it has reached its destination, even if the data had been stored on an on-board magnetic storage device, at the end of the mission, there isn't much left! I take that just as an example that in some domains, the data world's assumption that data will persist in long-term storage doesn't always apply.

Summary of OO concepts and terms

<u>Note</u>: The following list of terms relates primarily to the artifacts you are likely to encounter in a UML *class* diagram. The UML has many other forms of diagrams that may be beneficial if you are seriously getting into OO modeling (for example, sequence diagrams, use case diagrams, and activity diagrams). For those interested in pursuing OO concepts further, a highly recommended (and delightfully short) book is *"UML Distilled"* by Martin Fowler[97].

Name of OO concept or term	Description of OO concept or term (as seen by data modelers!)
Class	Traditional data modelers speak in terms of entities and their attributes, and relationships between those entities.
	There are strong parallels in the OO world. OO modelers talk in terms of classes (instead of entities) and their *attributes*, and *associations* (instead of relationships) between those classes.
	The most significant difference, however, is that classes include code for accessing and manipulating the data. The code that defines how to access or change the data is known as the *"method"*, and the signature for calling it is known as its *"operation"*.
Object	Traditional relational database practitioners think in terms of sets of data. For example, a relational table may have many rows, but data access and manipulation is based on sets of rows (though the "set" may, in some cases, have only one row).
	In contrast, in the OO world, we are more oriented towards individual objects – hence the name "object-oriented". As a very roughly approximation, if an entity (and possibly its implementation as a relational table) is something like a *class* (but without its *operations/methods*), then one row in a table is something like an object. But I did say it was just an approximation.

---

[97] (Fowler, 2003)

Name of OO concept or term	Description of OO concept or term (as seen by data modelers!)
Attribute	Just as relational entities have attributes, so do *classes*. Some significant differences include: The ability of OO classes to have much richer, user-defined *data types*. The ability to define *multiplicity* greater than one; i.e., something like having a repeating group that, in relational terms, would breach first normal form.
Method	When you work out the "method" you'll use to access or manipulate a bit of data, and attach this code to a *class*, it's called a method!
Operation	The "signature" for a *method* includes items such as its name and parameters. If you like, it's the template shape for how you get things done, and the underlying *method* is the actual code that does the work. Often, in a UML class diagram, you will see the *class* name in the top box, the *attributes* in the next box, and the *operations* in the third box of a class. So you can see what *methods* can be called via their *operation* signatures, but you can't see the actual *method's* code.
Polymorphism	A horrible word and one I hope you don't need to use. But if pushed, in simple terms, it means that if you have two *classes* with the same *method* against them but different code, the system is smart enough to not get the *methods* confused. For example, if you have a "DisplayMe" *method* against an Employee *class*, and also a "DisplayMe" *method* against a Project *class*, and you ask an Employee *object* to display itself, it will behave as you would hope (and not display itself as if it's a Project).
Encapsulation	The idea behind encapsulation, or "information hiding", is that the attributes of a *class* are not directly visible from outside the *class*. You only get to interact with their values via *operations/methods*. For example, an Employee *class* might have a "Get Age" *method*, but you can't tell from the outside whether age is calculated on the fly or stored as data.

Name of OO concept or term	Description of OO concept or term (as seen by data modelers!)
Object ID	For those with a relational background, you may choose to see an object's identifier as a surrogate key. However, in contrast to many relational implementations where the surrogate is unique within one table, in the OO world the Object ID is unique across the whole domain.
Data Type	Attributes in a relational database have a data type. It might be a Date, an Integer, a Boolean, and so on. Some relational database systems offer little more than a handful of pre-packaged data types. In the OO world, you have a similar concept, but the primitive data types (such as Date, Integer, Boolean, etc.) can be supplemented by rich user-defined data types. For what it's worth, the data types are defined as *classes*, just as the business things like Employee or Project are also *classes*. This means that your new data types can have their own *operations/methods* to provide functionality, and also can be made up of *attributes* with data types.
Association	An association between a pair of *classes* approximates a relationship between a pair of entities in the data modeler's world. And just like a relationship records optionality and cardinality, an association records *multiplicity*. For example, a relationship that is "optional / many" would translate to an association that has a multiplicity of "0..*" (where the zero indicates a minimum of zero, and the "*" represents a maximum of "many"). Additionally, the UML notation has special symbols for containment, where an open diamond represents aggregation (the "child" has a life of its own) and composition (if a "parent" is deleted, the child ceases to exist, just like in a relational cascade delete). Further, in the OO world you can specify a many-to-many association without the need for a resolution entity/*class*, and not only model it that way but actually implement it directly, e.g., in an object-oriented database management system such as Gemstone or Versant.

Name of OO concept or term	Description of OO concept or term (as seen by data modelers!)
Multiplicity	Multiplicity records the minimum and maximum numbers, and can be used in all sort of places. The two of primary interest here are multiplicities in *associations* (somewhat aligned to the idea of optionality and cardinality on relationships between entities) and multiplicities against *attributes* (e.g. an attribute of Given Name in a Person *class* might have a multiplicity of "1..3" to indicate a minimum of one given name and a maximum of three).
Property	A collective term for the *attributes* and *associations* of a *class*.
Inheritance	Entities in a data modeler's entity-relationship diagram can have supertypes for generalized entities and subtypes for specialized entities. An OO class model can similarly have superclasses and subclasses. The link between a superclass and a subclass is known as inheritance; i.e., the subclass is said to "inherit" the *attributes* (and *operations*) of its superclass. And then there's multiple inheritance, where a subclass has two (or more) superclasses. But this concept introduces complexity and danger, and is not even supported by some OO platforms.
Persistence	This simply means that the data for an *object* is stored somewhere for later retrieval and reuse. The ability to store data is motherhood and apple pie for relational database people, so it takes a bit of getting used to that you might have *objects* and their data that are used for a short time, but never stored. As a side comment, often the data in an *object* is mapped to a relational database for storage, but there are object databases that exist and that handle persistence of *objects* in a much more natural manner. They just typically don't have the market presence of the mainstream relational database management systems.

Table 31: Object-oriented glossary of terms

Arlow, Jim and Neustadt, Ila. (2004) *Enterprise Patterns and MDA: Building Better Software with Archetype Patterns and UML*. Addison-Wesley, USA.

Boehm, Barry and Turner, Richard. (2009 – 7th printing) *Balancing Agility and Discipline: A guide for the Perplexed*. Addison-Wesley, USA.

Burns, Larry. (2011) *Building the Agile Database: How to Build a Successful Application Using Agile Without Sacrificing Data Management*. Technics Publications, USA.

Chisolm, Malcolm. (2003) *How to Build a Business Rules Engine: Extending Application Functionality through Metadata Engineering*. Morgan Kaufmann Publishers, USA.

Fowler, Martin. (1997) *Analysis Patterns: Reusable Object Models*. Addison-Wesley, USA.

Fowler, Martin. (2003) *UML Distilled Third Edition: A Brief Guide to the Standard Object Modeling Language*. Addison-Wesley, USA.

Gamma, Erich; Helm, Richard; Johnson, Ralph and Vlissides, John. (1994) *Design Patterns: Elements of Reusable Objet-Oriented Software*. Addison-Wesley, USA.

Hay, David. (1996) *Data Model Patterns: Conventions of Thought*. Dorset House Publishing, USA.

Hay, David. (2011-a) *Enterprise Model Patterns: Describing the World*. Technics Publications, USA.

Hay, David. (2011-b) *UML & Data Modeling: A Reconciliation*. Technics Publications, USA.

Hoberman, Steve. (2010) *Is Agile Enterprise Data Modeling an Oxymoron*. Information Management Magazine, Jan/Feb 2010.

Silverston, Len. (2001-a) *The Data Model Resource Book – Revised Edition – Volume 1: A Library of Universal Data Models for All Enterprises*. Wiley Computer Publishing, USA.

Silverston, Len. (2001-b) *The Data Model Resource Book – Revised Edition – Volume 2: A Library of Universal Data Models by Industry Types.* Wiley Computer Publishing, USA.

Silverston, Len and Agnew, Paul. (2009) *The Data Model Resource Book – Volume 3: Universal Patterns for Data Modeling.* Wiley Computer Publishing, USA.

Simsion, Graeme and Witt, Graham. (2001) *Data Modeling Essentials.* The Coriolis Group, USA.

Simsion, Graeme and Witt, Graham. (2005) *Data Modeling Essentials*, Third Edition. Morgan Kaufmann, USA.

Simsion, Graeme. (2007) *Data Modeling Theory and Practice.* Technics Publications, USA.

Term / Acronym	Definition
Assembly patterns	As defined in this book, assembly patterns represent the building blocks that span the business and data modeler worlds. Business people can understand them – assets, documents, people and organizations, and the like. Equally importantly, they are often the subject of published data model patterns that can give the modeler proven, robust, extensible, and implementable designs. See also Elementary patterns, and Integration patterns.
BDUF	Big Design Up Front – an agile developer's critical view of over-investment in design features that slow the project down and may never be used.
Canonical model	A model used as a central reference.
CDM	Conceptual Data Model.
CLEM	A light-hearted acronym to describe a model that is Canonical, Logical, and whose intended scope of usage is as an Enterprise Model.
COTS	Commercial-Off-The-Shelf software.
CRACK	Collaborative, Representative, Authorized, Committed and Knowledgeable user representatives – refer to *Balancing Agility and Discipline: A guide for the Perplexed* by Boehm and Turner.
Elementary patterns	As defined in this book, elementary patterns are the "nuts and bolts" of data modeling. They include ways to resolve many-to-many relationships, and to construct self-referencing hierarchies. They are handy (and even essential) design patterns, but they are too technical to excite most business people. See also Assembly patterns, and Integration patterns.
ERD	Entity Relationship Diagram.

Term / Acronym	Definition
Frameworx	A suite of standards from the TM Forum intended to provide blueprints spanning processes, information, applications, and their integration. It is the Information Framework (also known as the Shared Information/Data model, or SID) that is of particular interest in this book.
Integration patterns	As defined in this book, integration patterns (or "patterns of patterns") provide the framework for linking the assembly patterns in common ways. See also Elementary patterns and Assembly patterns.
LDM	Logical Data Model.
OMG	Object Management Group.
Pattern of patterns	(See "Integration patterns")
PDM	Physical Data Model.
RDBMS	Relational Database Management System.
SBVR	Semantics of Business Vocabulary and Business Rules.
Self-referencing	[See 'Self-referencing'] (Hope you don't mind my sense of humor!)
TM Forum	A global, non-profit association originally targeted at the telecommunications industry but now with a more generic focus.
TOGAF	The Open Group Architecture Framework.
YAGNI	You Ain't Gonna Need It – a phrase coming out of the agile practitioner's camp that warns against implementation of features you *think* you might need.
XMI	XML Metadata Interchange – an OMG standard for sharing metadata.

43847715R00142

Made in the USA
Middletown, DE
20 May 2017